INSIGHT GUIDES

Bangkok

Update Editor: Susan Cunningham
Executive Editor: Scott Rutherford

Editorial Director: Brian Bell

APA PUBLICATIONS

Part of the Langenscheidt Publishing Group

L

Bangkok simply overwhelms, and attempts to condense the place – and the experience and sensations and opportunities – into a guidebook can be a daunting and perplexing experience.

An asset in covering an Asian location is familiarity and knowledge. Apa Publications has been based in Singapore for over a quarter of a century, and during those years, a network of correspondents and writers has assured quality coverage of destinations throughout the region.

Insight Guide: Bangkok is part of the 190-title Insight Guide series, created in 1970 by **Hans Höfer**, founder of Apa Publications. Each book encourages readers to celebrate the essence of a place, rather than try to tailor it to their expectations. The books are edited in the belief that, without insight into a people's character and culture, travel can narrow the mind rather than broaden it.

Thailand's culture is extensive and deeply layered. Any writer trying to share the allure of Thailand takes a risk in recycling clichés. And the clichés – the adjectives, if you will – that have been written over the centuries to describe Thailand would fill a thesaurus. Yet, in fact, Thailand is a place of superlatives, and Bangkok is a place of super superlatives.

The original team producing the first *Insight Guide: Bangkok* a decade ago was anchored by long-time Asian hands and residents of Bangkok. Writer **Steve Van Beek** arrived in Asia in the mid 1960s with the Peace Corps. He then settled in Bangkok, working as a free-lance writer for magazines and authoring a number of books about Thailand and Asia. Van Beek has been a regular contributor to Apa Publications' Insight Guides and Pocket Guides.

Van Beek

M.R. Priyanandana Rangsit attended London University, with emphasis on Asia's ancient period. Her work has appeared in numerous Asian and European publications. The great-granddaughter of King Chulalongkorn, she contributed much of the historical perspective on both Bangkok and Thailand.

Other contributors to the first edition of *Insight Guide: Bangkok* included writer **Robert Halliday**, **Savika Srisawat**, **Siripimporn Phoosomporn**, **Gayle Miller**, and **Sara Lai**.

Rangsit

Bangkok is considerably different than a decade ago, of course, and it eventually came time for the book to be overhauled to reflect the monumental and extensive changes of the city itself. This new edition began with Apa's executive editor in Singapore, **Scott Rutherford**, tracking down new contributors to give the book a fresh and contemporary perspective, for both the city and its people. With a distinctly questionable

Rutherford

degree in philosophy, Rutherford first came to Asia – Japan – on a *National Geographic* photographic assignment in the mid 1980s. He later moved to Tokyo, where he lived for nearly four years before heading south to Singapore.

Rutherford enlisted Bangkok-resident **Susan Cunningham** to undertake a large percentage of the chores in updating this book. Cunningham has worked as a journalist in Washington, D.C., Tokyo, Hong Kong, and now Bangkok, where she lives somewhere amidst the chaos of Bangkok. With degrees in journalism and literature, she likes to write about economics and politics, and beaches and mountains

Cunningham

plenty of the former in Bangkok, none of the latter. Cunningham wrote new essays on history and contemporary issues. She also contributed to *Insight Guide: Thailand*.

Contributing new material to the Features section – and updating the utilitarian but critical Travel Tips – was **Neil Kelly**, who reports from Bangkok for international radio, including for London's BBC.

Upcountry sections were fine-tuned by our correspondents elsewhere in Thailand. **Steve Rosse**, a columnist for *The Nation* who lives on Phuket, updated some of the southern Thailand material, as did **Ken Scott**, who also lives in southern Thailand and contributed to material from that area.

Italian-born **Luca Invernizzi Tettoni** studied archeology before turning to the camera to interpret the world. His photographic work has graced numerous books about the cultures and countries of Southeast Asia. He now

Tettoni

lives in Singapore, where he has a photo agency, Photobank.

Contributing new photography for this edition is **David Bowden**, based in Kuala Lumpur and usually rambling along the back roads of Asia.

Marcus Wilson-Smith has been a frequent photographic contributor to Apa Publications on a number of projects around the world. Once a fashion photographer, London-based Wilson-Smith now specializes in expedition photography in Africa.

Other contributors over the years include **Marcus Brooke, Robert Burrows, Jerry Dillon, Nancy Grace, Frank Green, John Stirling, Aporanee Buatong, Kultida Wongsawatdichart** and **Tony Wheeler**.

Assistance for this and earlier editions came from a number of people and institutions, including the Tourism Authority of Thailand, **Kurt Wachtveitl** of The Oriental Hotel, **Skip Heinecke** of Royal Garden Resorts, **Jerry Hopkins, John Gottberg Anderson, Yvan Van Outrive, Per Bang-Jensen, James Stanton, Henry Aronson, Patrick (Shrimp) Gauvain,** and **Sam Chan** – and an uncountable number of people throughout Bangkok.

CONTENTS

History

Introduction 19

Dawn of Bangkok 27

The Absolute Monarchy 36

The Quest for Democracy 45

Features

Centers of Power 55

Religion 65

The Cultural Arts 73

Ramayana and Ramakien 76

Natural History 84

Markets 88

Food and Cuisine 92

A Calendar of Fruits 94

On the Town 101

Her Fate, or Choice? 108

Hotels 110

Shopping 116

Places

Bangkok Introduction 133

Rattanakosin:
Royal Bangkok 141

Preceding pages: The Golden Mount was once Bangkok's highest point; temple image.

Across the River 150

Bangkok Traffic 152

The Old City and Dusit 155

Waterways 159

Chinatown 164

Modern Bangkok 171

Outside of Bangkok

West of Bangkok 179

Southeast of Bangkok 184

Ayutthaya:
North of Bangkok 186

Northeast of Bangkok 192

Upcountry

Introduction 199

Sukhothai 201

Chiang Mai 204

South to Pattaya 210

Southern Islands 215

Maps

Bangkok 134/135

Central Thailand 136

Thailand 137

Getting Acquainted

The Place 222
Time Zones 222
Climate 222
The Population 222
The People 222

Planning the Trip

What to Bring 224
What to Wear 224
Entry Regulations 224
Health 224
Hygiene 225
Currency 225
Public Holidays 226
Getting There 226
Special Facilities 227
Useful Addresses 227

Practical Tips

Emergencies 228
Weights and Measures 230
Business Hours 230
Tipping 230
Religious Services 231
Media 231
Postal Services 231
Telecoms 232
Tourists Offices 233
Embassies 234

Getting Around

On Arrival 234
Domestic Travel 235
Public Transport 236
Private Transport 237

Where to Stay

Hotels 237
Guesthouses 239

Eating Out

What to Eat 240
Where to Eat 240
Drinking Notes 243

Attractions

Sightseeing Tours 243
Culture 244
Nightlife 245
Festivals and Fairs 246

Shopping

Shopping Hours 249
Export 249
Complaints 249
Shopping Areas 249
What to Buy 249

Sports & Leisure

Participant Sports 251
Spectator Sports 251

Language

Origins and Intonation 252
Thai Names 252
Phonology 253
Useful Phrases 253

Further Reading

General 253
History 254
People 254
Religion 254
Art and Culture 254
Thai Writers 254
Other Insight Guides 254

Art/Photo Credits 255
Index 256

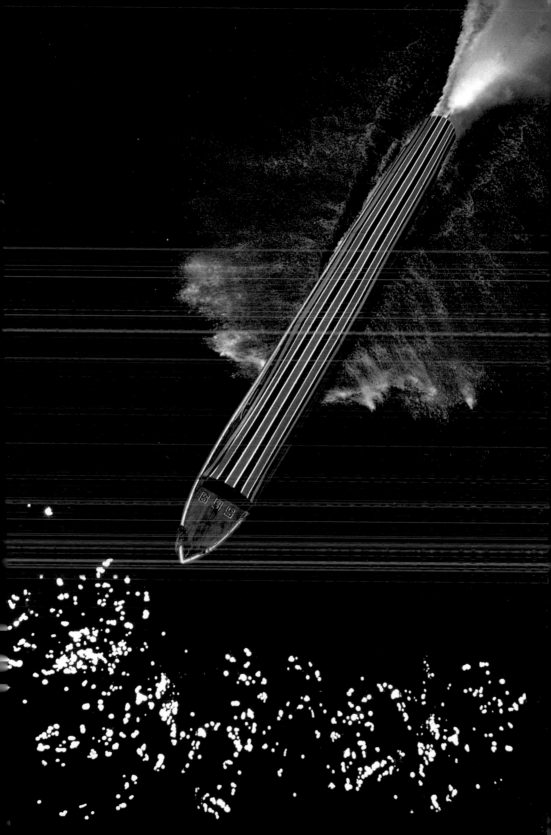

INTRODUCTION

Perhaps it is somewhat obvious, but Bangkok appears to be a place lacking in order and planning. It certainly seems a place where no one has sat down and thought things through to an orderly outcome. If Bangkok does seem to lack order, it is because, in fact, it never has had much order, save for Rattanakosin, the royal core of the city and where the kings built their palaces and temples. The rest of the city simply happened, and as one moves outward from the royal island, which is defined by canals and the Chao Phraya River, the city increasingly turns less and less organized. The constant construction confounds one, suggesting both increasing chaos and promises of future order.

If the city's planning lacks apparent certainty, what is unquestionably certain is that when civic leaders in other Asian cities talk of urban planning, Bangkok is the paradigm that no other city cares to emulate – a city planner's nightmare.

And, indeed, so it is. In a dark way, that is one of Bangkok's appeals. It is, quite simply, a city for the senses and for the intellect.

Yet it is undeniably one of the world's great cities, and travelers inevitably leave Bangkok with a wealth of impressions, opinions and stories to tell. Few regret the time they have spent exploring its historical alleys and contemporary boulevards. Yes, it is polluted and it is noisy and it is traffic-clogged. Yes, it can take hours to travel a few kilometers by motor vehicle. And, yes, the situation – and it matters not of what situation in particular one is discussing – never seems to improve.

Bangkok began as a city of canals and elephant paths. When motor vehicles redefined urban transportation, the old thoroughfares were simply filled in or paved over for the new wheels. Little attempt was made to accommodate the new needs of a motorized society. Construction begat chaos, and a large part of what assaults the eye today started in the late 1950s.

The Thai name for Bangkok (which means City of Wild Plums) is *Krungthep Mahanakhon Amonrattanakosin Mahintharayutthaya Mahadilokphop Nopphosin Ratchathuniburirom Udomrathani- wetmahasa Amonphiman Awatansathit Sakkathatiya Witsanukamprasit*, or translated, "City of Angels, the Great City, the Residence of the Emerald Buddha, the Impregnable City of Ayutthaya of God Indra, the Grand Capital of the World Endowed with Nine Precious Gems, the Happy City Abounding in Enormous Royal Palaces That Resemble the Heavenly Abode Wherein Dwell the Reincarnated Gods, a City Given by Indra and Built by Vishnukarm." Most Thais, however, use the shortened, and simpler, *Krung Thep*, or City of Angels.

Today, about one out of every eight Thais live in Bangkok – from 8 to 11 million people, depending upon the statistical source. The

Preceding pages: lighting of incense at a temple; Rattanakosin and the royal grounds; detail of Wat Phra Kaeo; skyline along Surawong Road. **Left**, typical evening Bangkok ritual.

second-largest city in the country, Chiang Mai, is just one-fortieth to one-fiftieth (urban population estimates are inexact) the size of Bangkok, whose population has grown nearly ten-fold since World War II. The city is Thailand's only metropolitan area, and its only true cultural, economic and political center.

Metropolitan Bangkok was once two separate urban entities: Thonburi on the west side of the Chao Phraya, and Krung Thep (Bangkok) on the eastern side. In the early 1970s, the two were united into a single metropolitan government, and the expanded city was then merged with the two surrounding provinces into one densely-populated province: Bangkok Metropolis. This metropolitan area is slightly over 1,500 square kilometers (600 sq mi) in size.

About 50 kilometers from the Gulf of Thailand, Bangkok is atop the gulf delta of the Chao Phraya River, which flows from the north. Since it is on an alluvial plain, Bangkok is quite flat and without geographical boundaries, save for the river itself. When the early kings established Bangkok as the royal city, several attempts were undertaken to provide some sort of geographical relief to the skyline. The Golden Mount is probably the most notable today, though it is no longer the highest point. If Bangkok continues to slowly sink, as it is now doing, the city's few high points will no doubt escalate in popular appeal.

Bangkok's future is simple: doing something about its infrastructure mess. The telecommunications system is improving, and noticeably. The transportation network is, well, continuing to be a lesson for all. In any case, whether the city planners manage to unknot the traffic or not, and whether the city eventually stabilizes its growth, or else implodes, or explodes, Bangkok will never fail to demand a response.

Right, watery solitude, Lumpini Park.

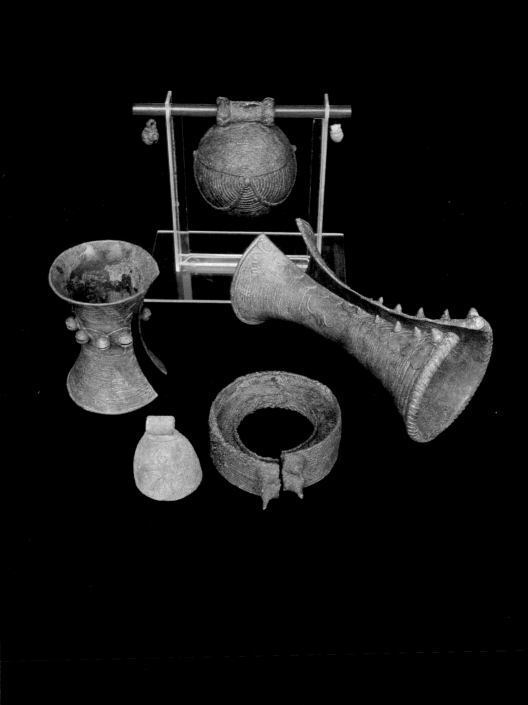

Bangkok is a young city with an old history. Although an important town for hundreds of years, it sat on the sidelines, watching history pass up and down the Chao Phraya River on its way between the ancient capital of Ayutthaya and the world beyond the seas. It was only by an accident of history that Bangkok became what it is today.

The story of Bangkok begins in the far north of Thailand. The soil from which tall buildings now sprout once provided sustenance for rice. At that time, as little as 1,500 years ago, the future capital city lay beneath the ocean's waters. Each monsoon season, the powerful currents of the Chao Phraya River swept southwards, carrying eroded farmland into the sea, each year nudging the shoreline a little further into the Gulf of Thailand.

Eventually, the mudbanks rose above the waterline, the mangrove trees took root and the lungfish moved in. Soon, houses rose on stilts above the tidal mudflats. Their inhabitants used their self-made islands as bases for fishing expeditions into the nearby sea. Each year, the river added more soil until the delta was high enough that farmers could till and plant rice in it. From those fields grew villages, then towns, and finally a city.

Because it originated atop an alluvial plain, Bangkok is a flat city, with no natural point more than a few meters above any other. Floods have always swamped the city during October, when the Chao Phraya River spills over into the streets, turning Bangkok into a veritable Venice. Today, Bangkok is sinking by about 10 centimeters each year and the days when boats plied the avenues may one day return.

Village in the plum-olive trees: Bangkok's history as a town began in the 16th century, when a small-time king commanded that a two-kilometer-long canal be dug across the neck of a 17-kilometer loop of the river to cut the distance between the sea and Ayutthaya. The annual monsoon floods scoured the banks of the canal like sandpaper until the canal widened to become the main course of the river. On its banks rose two towns – trading posts along the river route up to Ayutthaya, 75 kilometers upriver – Thonburi and, across the river, Bangkok.

At the time, Bangkok was little more than a village (*bang*) in an orchard of trees, whose fruit has stumped botanists to the point they cannot decide if they were olives or plums, settling instead for the Thai compromise word *kok* (wild plum-olive). Hence, the

town's name, Bangkok or Village of the Wild Plumb.

During the 17th century, the town was inhabited by a few Chinese merchants and farmers who tended their *kok* trees on low ground. As the area was subject to flooding, it had little commercial value and there was no reason for it to grow. But grow it did, becoming one of Asia's grandest cities, an accident of history. To understand why Bangkok developed as it did, one must look to its past, and to that of Thailand's.

Ban Chiang culture: The origin of the ethnic Thai has been hotly debated for decades. Popular tradition claims that the first people fled to Siam from China to escape the depredations of Kublai Khan's hordes sweeping southward out of Mongolia. The theory would explain Thai empathy with later immigrants.

Other theories suggest they originated in Thailand a millennium or two ago; those Thais found in today's China are said to have emigrated north from Thailand about 1,000 years ago. Whichever conjecture is correct, it is accepted that the Thais' first home in Thailand was in the northern hills. As the centuries passed, they shared the country with ethnic Laotians, who populated the northeast, bringing a similar language and culture. The southern isthmus linking Thailand (from Bangkok south) with the Malay

in the northeast. Systematic excavation revealed painted pottery, jewelry, and bronze and iron tools.

The identity of the Ban Chiang people is a mystery. According to archaeological timetables, the existence of pottery normally suggests a culture already 2,000 years along the road to civilization; Ban Chiang's pottery dates from about 3600 BC. Settlement seems to have lasted until 250 BC, after which the people mysteriously faded from history. While they thrived, they farmed rice, domesticated animals, and developed highly original pottery-decorating skills, with each design unique to that pot alone and not repeated in others. Their red-painted jars, decorated

Peninsula became the home of Moslems.

But long before the Thai people migrated into today's Thailand, the Chao Phraya valley was inhabited by a high civilization.

The first discovery of prehistoric relics was made during World War II, by a Dutch prisoner of war forced to work on the Siam-Burma "Death Railway." He uncovered Stone Age implements at Ban Kao, in the western province of Kanchanaburi, which led to the discovery of paleolithic and neolithic caves, and cemeteries containing a wealth of pottery, tools and other artifacts.

The most important site, however, is the tiny village of Ban Chiang, near Udon Thani,

with fingerprint whorl patterns, were buried in funeral mounds as offerings.

The Ban Chiang culture illustrates the high level of technology achieved by prehistoric people in Southeast Asia.

Indian influence: Archaeological evidence has yet to be unearthed, but ancient texts discuss the presence of people from India around the 3rd century BC. In later centuries, Buddhism and Hinduism – along with Indian ceremonial rites, iconography, law codes, and cosmological and architectural treatises – were adopted *en bloc* by the Southeast Asian ruling elite and modified to suit local requirements and tastes. Sanskrit became the court language, while Pali was the language of the Buddhist canons.

Native chiefs wanting to consolidate power and increase their prestige may have been responsible for this diffusion of culture, calling in *Brahman* (Indians of the priestly caste) to validate their rule.

Arrival of the Thais: As noted earlier, there are several theories to explain the early habitation of Thailand. The most persuasive one says that from perhaps as early as the 10th century, a people living in China's Yunnan province migrated down rivers and streams into the upper valleys of the Southeast Asian river system. There, they branched off. The Shans, also known as *Thai Yai* (Great Thais),

edge of Thai penetration. Then came Chiang Rai, in 1281, and Chiang Mai, in 1296. Long after the main group of Thais moved farther down the peninsula to establish more powerful states, Chiang Mai continued to rule more or less autonomously over the northern region, maintaining a distinctive culture of its own.

Dawn of Sukhothai: The name *Sukhothai* translates into "the dawn of happiness", and if early inscriptions are to be believed, its people enjoyed considerable freedom to pursue their livelihoods. This first independent Thai kingdom is considered the golden era of Thai history, and is often looked back upon with nostalgia as the ideal Thai state. It was

went to Upper Burma; the Ahom Thais established themselves in Assam; another group settled in Laos; yet another occupied the island of Hainan, off the Vietnamese coast.

The greatest number of *Thai Noi* (Little Thais) first settled in the north of modern Thailand, around Chiang Saen and valleys to the south. They formed themselves into principalities, some of which later became independent kingdoms. The first was in 1238, at Sukhothai, at the southernmost

Left, perhaps originally from southern India, terracotta figures found in central Thailand. **Above**, Sukhothai engraving on stone.

a land of plenty, governed by just and paternal kings who ruled over peaceful, contented citizens. Sukhothai represented early Thai tribal society in its purest form.

The most famous king of Sukhothai was Ramkamhaeng. He was the first Thai ruler to leave detailed epigraphical accounts of the Thai state, beginning with his own early life. He earned his title at age 19 on a campaign with his father against a neighboring state, in which he defeated the enemy leader in a Thai form of medieval jousting: hand-to-hand combat on elephant-back.

At the time of Ramkamhaeng's accession, the Sukhothai kingdom was quite small, consisting only of the city and surrounding areas. By the end of his reign, he had increased its size tenfold – from Luang Prabang in the east, through the Central Plains to the southern peninsula. The Mon state in Lower Burma also accepted his control.

Ramkamhaeng was noted as an administrator, legislator and statesman – and sometimes as an amorous king. He is credited with the invention of Thai script, which he achieved by systematizing the Khmer alphabet with Thai words. A stone inscription bearing the date 1292 and employing the new script has been attributed to Ramkamhaeng. In the inscription, he depicted the idyllic conditions of his kingdom: fertile land and plentiful food, free trade, prohibition of slavery and guaranteed inheritance. However, some experts now doubt its authenticity and believe the inscription to be a much later work.

The king was a devout and conscientious Buddhist, of the Theravada school practiced in Sukhothai. There is no doubt that, since the days of Sukhothai, Buddhism has been deeply rooted in the Thai way of life.

The year Pagan fell to the armies of Kublai Khan, in 1287, Ramkamhaeng formed a pact with two northern Thai princes, Mengrai of Chiang Rai and Ngam Muang of Phayo. The three agreed not to transgress, but instead to protect each others' borders against common enemies. The alliance was maintained throughout their lifetimes.

Founding of Chiang Mai: Mengrai completed Thai political ascendancy in the north by annexing the last Mon kingdom of Haripunjaya, in about 1292. He first sent an agent provocateur to sow discord, and when the time was right, his army "plucked the town like a ripe fruit."

Wishing to found a new capital, Mengrai invited his two allies to help him select a site. The location they agreed upon as truly auspicious was one where two white sambars, two white barking deer, and a family of five white mice were seen together. On that spot by the river Ping, Mengrai laid the foundation of Chiang Mai (New Town) in 1296, supplanting his former capital at Chiang Rai and giving him a more centralized location from which to administer the southern portion of his newly-expanded kingdom.

Tradition says Ramkamhaeng drowned in the rapids of the Yom River at Sawan-

khalok. His son, Lo Thai (ruled 1318–1347), preferring religion to war, lost the feudatory states as fast as he had gained them. He was called Dharmaraja, "the Pious King," an epithet his successors also bore. The relationship between Sukhothai and Sri Lanka, the center of orthodox Buddhism, intensified during his rule; Lo Thai recorded that he built many monuments to house sacred relics of the Buddha newly obtained from Sri Lanka.

Lo Thai's son, Li Thai, was as pious as his father. As heir to the throne, he composed a famous treatise on Buddhist cosmology, the *Traibhumikatha,* or Tales of the Three Worlds. When he became king in 1347, he declared a rule according to the Ten Royal Precepts of the Buddha. He pardoned criminals, for example, as he desired to become a Buddha, "to lead all creatures beyond the oceans of sorrow and transmigration."

The prioritizing of religion over military affairs might have permitted the meteoric rise of one of Sukhothai's former vassal states, Ayutthaya. The southern kingdom expanded rapidly, extending its control over the Chao Phraya River valley, until Li Thai was forced to acknowledge its hegemony. Deprived of his independence, the pious king took deeper refuge in religion, eventually assuming the yellow robe.

His family ruled for three more generations, but in 1378, power shifted to Phitsanulok, and Sukhothai's population followed. By 1438, Sukhothai was nearly deserted.

The Sukhothai period saw the Thai people, for the first time, develop a distinctive civilization with their own administrative institutions, art and architecture. Sukhothai Buddha images, characterized by refined facial features, linear fluidity, and harmony of form, are perhaps the most beautiful and the most original of Thai artistic expressions. Many say that the Sukhothai aesthetic is the high point of Thai civilization.

Rise of Ayutthaya: Historically, U-Thong was an independent principality in today's Suphan Buri. Its rulers were members of the prestigious line of Chiang Saen kings. During the reign of Phya U-Thong, a cholera outbreak forced the ruler to evacuate his people to the site of Ayodhya (Ayutthaya), an ancient Indianized settlement named after Rama's legendary kingdom in India.

The location of Phya U-Thong's new capital was blessed with several advantages. Situated on an island at the confluence of the Chao Phraya, Lop Buri and Pasak rivers, not far from the sea and surrounded by fertile rice plains, it was an ideal center of administration and communications. Phya U-Thong officially established the city in 1350, after three years of preparation. Within a few years, the king united the whole of central Siam – including Sukhothai – under his rule, and extended control to the Malay Peninsula and Lower Burma. He and his successors pursued expansionist campaigns against Chiang Mai and the Khmer civilization in Cambodia.

Ironically, although the Thais were re-

of cannon, the first recorded use of this weapon in Siam. Ramesuen's army sacked Angkor three years later, and according to the *Pongsawadan*, the Annals of Ayutthaya, some 90,000 prisoners of war were taken. Given the economics of the time, acquisition of people for labor was more precious than any amount of gold.

Reign of King Trailok: Two centuries of wars between Chiang Mai and Ayutthaya reached a climax during the reign of King Boroma Trailokanath, more popularly known as Trailok (ruled 1448–1488).

Trailok is important for having introduced reforms that shaped the administrative and social structures of Siam, up until the 19th

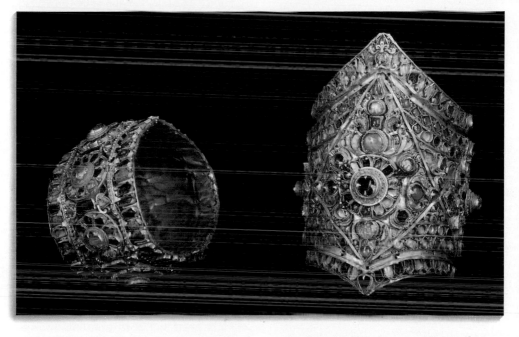

sponsible for the decline and eventual collapse of Angkor, the Ayutthaya kings adopted Khmer cultural influences from the very beginning. No longer the paternal and accessible rulers that the kings of Sukhothai had been, Ayutthaya's sovereigns were absolute monarchs, Lords of Life, whose position was enhanced by trappings of royalty reflective of a Khmer *devaraja* (god-king).

The king's son, Ramesuen, captured Chiang Mai in 1390, reportedly with the use

Above, exquisite royal jewelry recovered from Wat Ratchaburana, and created during the period of Ayutthaya's golden age.

century. He brought Ayutthaya's loosely controlled provinces under centralized rule, and regulated *sakdi na*, an ancient system of land ownership that had stratified society, dictated responsibilities of both overlord and tenants, and determined salary levels of the official hierarchy.

Trailok also defined a system of corvee labor, under which all able-bodied men were required to contribute labor during part of each working year to the state. This system indirectly heightened the status of women, who were responsible for the welfare of their families in the absence of the men.

Trailok's Palace Law of 1450 spelled out

the relative ranks of members of the royal family, prescribed functions of officials, and regulated ceremonies. It also fixed punishments, which included death for "introducing amatory poems" into the palace, or for whispering during a royal audience, and amputation of the foot of anyone kicking a palace door. While these sentences may not often have been carried out to the letter, they certainly exalted the aura of the king and dissuaded malefactors. Even royalty was not spared punishment, although the Palace Law stipulated that no menial hands could touch royal flesh. It was therefore the executioner's task to beat the condemned royalty at the nape of the neck with a sandalwood club.

On the whole, the rules fixed by King Trailok helped to maintain the fluidity of Thai society, which persists today. Ranks of nobility were, and are, earned rather than inherited. Titles of royal descendants are not retained in perpetuity; they degenerate, reaching a common status within five generations.

Portuguese and Burmese: The 16th century was marked by the first arrival of Europeans, and by continual conflict with the Burmese. Alfonso de Albuquerque, of Portugal, conquered Malacca in 1511, and soon thereafter his ships sailed to Siam. King Ramathibodi II (ruled 1491–1529) granted the Portuguese permission to reside and trade within the kingdom, in return for arms and ammunition. Portuguese mercenaries fought alongside the king in campaigns against Chiang Mai and taught the Thais the arts of cannon foundry and musketry.

But this did nothing to stem the rising tide of Burmese aggression. The Burmese invasion of 1549 was doomed to failure. But 20 years later, Ayutthaya fell to Burmese forces. The invading Burmese thoroughly ransacked and plundered the city, and forcibly removed much of Ayutthaya's population to Burma.

Maha Thammaraja, the defeated king's leading deputy, was appointed by the Burmese to rule Siam as a vassal state. His eldest son, Naresuen, was taken to Burma as a guarantee for Maha Thammaraja's good conduct. The boy was repatriated to Siam at the age of 15. Together with his younger brother, Ekatotsarot, Naresuen began to gather armed followers.

Naresuen had gained an insight into Burmese armed strength and strategies during his formative gears. He trained his troops in the art of guerrilla warfare; their hit-and-run tactics earned them the nicknames Wild Tigers and Peeping Cats.

Naresuen's opportunity to restore Siamese independence came following internal chaos in Burma. Naresuen declared Ayutthaya's freedom, in 1584. During the following nine years, the Burmese made several attempts to resubjugate Siam, but Naresuen had taken thorough defensive measures and repulsed all invasions.

Naresuen reconsolidated the Siamese kingdom, then turned the tables on Burma with repeated attacks that contributed to the disintegration of the Burmese empire. The Khmers, who had been whittling away at Siam's eastern boundary during Ayutthaya's period of weakness, were also subdued. Under Naresuen, Ayutthaya prospered and became the thriving metropolis described by 17th-century European visitors.

Door to the East: The reign of Naresuen's brother, Ekatotsarot, between 1605 and 1610, coincided with the arrival of the Dutch in Siam. Ekatotsarot was not interested in pursuing Naresuen's militaristic policies; instead, he sought to develop Ayutthaya's economy. The Dutch opened their first trading station at Ayutthaya, in 1608.

The peace initiated by Naresuen had given rise to a surplus of wealth, which created a demand in Thai society for imported luxury items such as porcelain and silk.

The Dutch established maritime dominance in the Far East when they drove the Portuguese out of Malacca, in 1641. Later, they persuaded the Thais to agree to trade concessions, giving the Dutch virtual economic control in Siam. King Narai (ruled 1656–1688) despised the Dutch and welcomed the English as an ally to counter Holland's growing influence in the region.

The Greek favorite: It was the French who gained greatest favor in Narai's court. Their story is interwoven with that of a Greek adventurer, opportunist and interloper named Constantine Phaulkon.

confidence he slowly and surely cultivated.

As Phaulkon moved firmly into the French camp, so did King Narai. He sent two ambassadors to Louis's court, and the French reciprocated with a visit to Ayutthaya in 1685. Following another exchange of embassies between the courts of Louis and Narai, a French squadron accompanied French and Thai delegations aboard warships to Siam. The small, but disciplined and well-equipped, French force of 500 soldiers was given landing rights by King Narai, under Phaulkon's advice to do exactly thus.

Then the tables began to turn against Phaulkon's influence and his extravagant lifestyle. His unpopularity was fueled not

The son of a Greek innkeeper, he began his career with the East India Company as a cabin boy. He worked his way east with the British, arriving in Siam in 1678. A talented linguist, he learned the Thai language in just two years, and with the help of his English benefactors, he was hired as interpreter within the court. Within five years, Phaulkon had risen through Thai society to the rank of *Phya Vijayendra*. In this powerful position, he had continual access to the king, whose

Left, detail from a Thai manuscript showing a royal parade, 17th century. Above left, King Narai. Above right, Constantine Phaulkon

only by the ominous French military presence, but also by a rumor that Phaulkon had converted King Narai's adopted son to Christianity, intending to secure succession to the throne.

When Narai fell gravely ill in 1688, a nationalistic, anti-French faction took immediate action. The rebels confined the ailing king to his palace. Phaulkon was arrested for treason, and in June was executed outside Lop Buri. Narai died the following month. The French eventually removed their soldiers from Thailand.

The presence of Europeans throughout Narai's reign gave the West most of its early knowledge of Siam. Voluminous literature was generated by Western visitors to Narai's court. Their attempts at cartography left a record of Ayutthaya's appearance, though few maps exist today. Royal palaces and hundreds of temples crowded the area within the walls around the island on which the capital stood. Some Western visitors called it "the most beautiful city in the east."

The kings who succeeded Narai ended his open-door policy. A modest amount of trade was maintained and missionaries were permitted to remain, but Ayutthaya embarked on an isolation that would last 150 years.

Golden Age: The reign of King Boromakot (1733–1758) began with a particularly violent struggle for power, but Boromakot's 25-year term was an unusually peaceful one and became known as Ayutthaya's Golden Age. Poets and artists abounded at his court, enabling literature and the arts to flourish.

The tranquil days proved to be the calm before the storm. Boromakot's son Ekatat ascended to the throne in 1758, after a bitter succession struggle with his brother, and surrounded himself with female company to ensure his pleasure. Meanwhile, the Burmese once again set their sights on Ayutthaya, and in 1767 captured Ayutthaya after a siege of 14 months.

The Burmese killed, looted and set fire to the whole city, thereby expunging four centuries of Thai civilization. The Burmese plundered Ayutthaya's rich temples, melting down all the available gold from Buddha images. Members of the royal family, along with 90,000 captives and the accumulated booty, were removed to Burma.

Despite their overwhelming victory, the Burmese didn't retain control of Siam for long. A young general named Phya Tak Sin gathered a small band of followers during the final Burmese siege of the Thai capital. He recognized the hopelessness of the Siamese situation. He and his comrades broke through the Burmese encirclement and escaped to the southeast coast. There, Phya Tak Sin assembled an army and navy. Seven months after the fall of Ayutthaya, the general and his forces returned to the capital and expelled the Burmese occupiers.

Move to Bangkok: Taksin, as Phya Tak Sin is popularly known, had barely spent a night at Ayutthaya when he decided to transfer the capital. He revealed to his troops that the old

kings had appeared to him in a dream and told him to move.

In fact, strategic considerations were probably more important than supernatural ones in Taksin's decision. A site nearer to the sea would facilitate foreign trade, ensure the procurement of arms, and make defense and withdrawal easier.

During the 17th century, a small fishing village downstream had become an important trade and defense outpost for Ayutthaya. Known as Bangkok, "village of wild olive groves," it contained fortifications built by the French. The settlement straddled both sides of the Chao Phraya River, at a place where a short-cut canal had widened into the main stream. On the west bank, at Thonburi, Taksin officially established his new capital and was proclaimed king.

Taksin ruled until 1782. In the last seven years of his reign, he relied heavily on two trusted generals, the brothers Chao Phya Chakri and Chao Phya Sarasih, who were given absolute command in military campaigns. They liberated Chiang Mai and the rest of northern Thailand from Burmese rule, and brought Cambodia and most of present-day Laos under Thai suzerainty.

It was from the victorious Laotian campaign that Thailand obtained the famed Emerald Buddha. Chao Phya Chakri carried the Buddha from Vientiane to Thonburi in 1779. Carved of solid jadeite, the image was allegedly discovered at Chiang Rai, in 1436, inside a pagoda struck asunder by lightning. The Emerald Buddha is regarded by Thais as the most sacred of all Buddha images, and is believed to guarantee the independence and prosperity of the nation.

When a revolt broke out in 1782, Taksin was forced to abdicate and enter a monastery. A minor official who engineered the revolt offered the throne to Chao Phya Chakri upon his return from a Cambodian campaign. General Chakri assumed the kingship on April 6 – a date still commemorated annually as Chakri Day – and established the still-reigning Chakri dynasty.

Taksin, unstable in mind and regarded by a council of generals as a threat to stability, was executed in a royal manner.

Right, a museum collection of some of the fine and detailed jewelry produced during the creative decades of Ayutthaya.

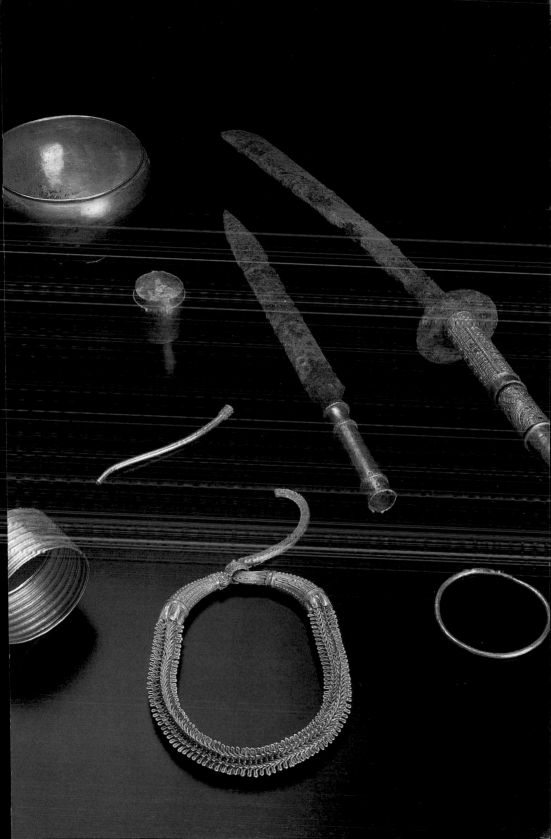

Upon assuming the throne, General Chakri took the name of Ramathibodi. Later known as Rama I, he ruled from 1782 until 1809. His first action as king was to transfer his administrative headquarters from the marshy confines of Thonburi to the more spacious Bangkok, across the river.

Chakri Dynasty: Rama I was an ambitious man eager to reestablish the Thai kingdom as a dominant civilization. He ordered the digging of a canal across a neck of land on the Bangkok side, creating an island and an

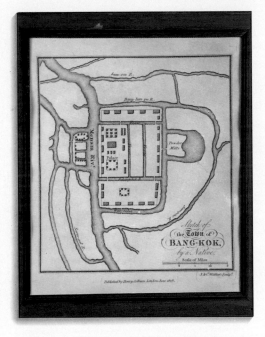

inner city. This canal, Khlong Lawd, runs north from today's Pak Klong Talat market, and served as a boundary, a moat and an artery of communication and commerce.

Rama I envisioned this artificial island as the core of his new capital. Within its rim, he would concentrate the principal components of the Thai nation: religion, monarchy and administration. To underscore his recognition of the power of the country's principal Buddha image, he called this island *Rattanakosin*, or the "Resting Place of the Emerald Buddha."

To dedicate the area solely to statecraft and religion, he formally requested that the

Chinese living there move to an area to the southeast. This new district, Sampeng, soon sprouted thriving shops and busy streets, becoming the commercial heart of the city in what is now known as Chinatown.

On April 6, 1782, at a time and place chosen by geomancers and astrologers, the new monarch proclaimed both the establishment of a new City of Angels and the Chakri dynasty, which continues today.

Rama I modeled Bangkok's defensive system on that of Ayutthaya. Recognizing that Bangkok would need room to expand, he ordered 10,000 Cambodian captives to dig a second canal in a concentric arc some 800 meters (2,640 ft) east of Khlong Lawd.

To gird and guard the city, 5,000 Laotian captives built a high, stout wall along the inner banks of the second canal and the river, lining it with 14 octagonal watchtowers, only two of which remain today.

He next sent his workers north to Ayutthaya to dismantle the ruined city's buildings. The bricks were transported downriver to Bangkok and cemented together to form the wall. By doing so, Rama I ensured that Bangkok would be imbued with the spirit of ancient Ayutthaya.

As the city grew, a third canal was dug a further 800 meters to the east, again in a concentric arc. A network of canals was then dug to connect them.

In the early days, the city had only three dirt roadways, tracks really: Bamrungmuang, an elephant path running east from the city wall; a road circling the outside of the city wall; and a third one inside the wall. (It would be 80 years before Bangkok would have its first paved road. And by the middle of this century, most of the canals had been filled in to make roads.)

Rama I then turned his attention to constructing the royal island's principal buildings. First was a home for the Emerald Buddha, the most sacred image in the realm, and, which up until then, had been resting in a temple in Thonburi. Two years later, in 1784, Wat Phra Kaeo was completed.

In commemoration of the event, a new word was added to the lengthy official title of the capital city (the longest city name in the world nowadays): Krung Thep Phra Maha Nakorn Amorn Rattanakosin... et cetera. The new word altered the title to mean "City of Angels, Abode of the Emerald Buddha..." It was later shortened to Krung Thep, but Bangkok became the accepted name.

Rama I then turned his attention to building a palace for himself.

The Grand Palace was more than a home; it contained buildings for receiving royal visitors and debating matters of state. The last building to be constructed, the Chakri

fragments of historical and religious treatises, few of which had survived the destruction of Ayutthaya in 1767.

Rama I perpetuated another Ayutthaya tradition by appointing his brother as *maha uparaja*, a "second" or deputy king, with powers almost equal to his own. His home, the *Wang Na* or "palace at the back," now houses the National Museum and once extended across the northern half of Sanam Luang. Because the royal regalia had been destroyed with everything else during the

Maha Prasad with its triple crowns, was not erected until late in the 19th century. Until 1946, the Grand Palace was home to Thailand's kings.

The palace grounds also contain Wat Po, the National Museum, one of the nation's two most prestigious universities (Thammasat), the National Theater, and various government offices.

Modern Thailand is indebted to Rama I for his assiduous cultural revival program. He appointed experts to review and assemble

<u>Left</u>, early map of Bangkok highlights its network of waterways. <u>Above</u>, old view of a city *khlong*.

siege of Ayutthaya, Rama I had a new crown and robes commissioned for his coronation. In his old age, he commissioned a golden urn to be prepared for his body, in accordance with ancient court protocol prescribing that the bodies of high-ranking royalty be placed in urns between death and later cremation.

The king was so pleased with the golden urn created by his craftsmen that he placed it in his bedroom to admire it fully. Upon seeing this, one of his wives burst into tears. It was a bad omen, she said. "Nonsense," replied the king, laughing. "If I don't see it from the outside while I'm alive, how do you think I can ever see it?"

Rama II and Rama III: Rama I's successors, Rama II and Rama III, completed the consolidation of the Siamese kingdom and the revival of Ayutthaya's arts and culture.

If Rama I laid the foundations of Bangkok, it was Rama II who instilled it with the spirit of the past. Best remembered as an artist, Rama II (ruled 1809–1824), the second ruler of the Chakri dynasty, was responsible for building and repairing numerous Bangkok monasteries. His most famous construction was Wat Arun, the Temple of Dawn, which was later enlarged to its present height by Rama IV. He is said to have carved the great doors of Wat Suthat, throwing away the chisels so his work could never be replicated.

During his father's reign, Rama II had gained renown as a great poet. His *magnum opus* was the *Inao*, an epic poem adopted from a Javanese legend. His classic version of the *Ramakien*, the Thai interpretation of the Indian classical saga, *Ramayana*, was completed during his reign, with large sections composed by the king himself, as well as by other poets. At his court, Rama II employed *khon* and *lakhon* dance-drama troupes to enact his compositions, just as in the courts of Ayutthaya.

Rama II reopened relations with the West, suspended since the time of Narai, and allowed the Portuguese to open the first Western embassy in Bangkok. Rama III, who ruled from 1824 to 1851, continued to open Siam's doors to foreigners.

The ready availability of Chinese porcelain led him to decorate many temples, including Wat Arun, with ceramic fragments. This vogue did not survive his lifetime, so that today, when visiting any temple with porcelain-decorated gables, travelers can immediately ascribe it to the reign of Rama III.

A pious Buddhist, Rama III was considered to be "austere and reactionary" by some Europeans. But he encouraged American missionaries to introduce Western medicine, such as smallpox vaccinations, to Siam.

Mongkut (Rama IV): With the help of Hollywood, Rama IV (ruled 1851–1868) became the most famous King of Siam. More commonly known as King Mongkut, he was portrayed in *The King and I* as a frivolous, bald-headed despot. But nothing could have been further from the truth. He was the first Thai – and in many instances, first Asian – king to understand Western culture and technology, and his reign has been described as the bridge spanning the new and the old.

The younger brother of Rama III, Mongkut spent 27 years as a Buddhist monk prior to his accession to the throne. This gave him a unique opportunity to roam as a commoner among the populace. He learned to read Buddhist scriptures in the Pali language; missionaries taught him Latin and English, thus enabling him to read European texts. As a monk, Mongkut delved into many subjects: history, geography and the sciences, especially astronomy.

Even as an abbot, he established himself as a reformer, ridding the Buddhist scriptures of their superstitious elements and founding a sect, the Dhammakaiya, which stressed strict adherence to Buddhist tenets. Today, these monks can be recognized by their brown robes. Mongkut realized that traditional Thai values would not save his country from Western encroachment. On the contrary, he believed that modernization would bring Siam in line with the West and reduce hostilities with foreigners.

England was the first European country to benefit from this policy, when an 1855 treaty – not gained entirely without coercion by the British – granted extraterritorial privileges: a duty of only three percent on imports, and permission to import Indian opium duty-free. Other Western nations followed suit with similar treaties. And when Mongkut lifted the state monopoly on rice, that crop rapidly became Siam's leading export.

In 1863, Mongkut built Bangkok's first paved road – Charoen Krung (prosperous city) or, as it was known to foreigners, New Road. This six-kilometer-long street, running from the palace southeast along the river, was lined with shophouses.

He paved other dirt roads, and introduced new technology to encourage commerce.

The foreign community quickly moved into the areas opened by the construction of New Road. They built their homes in the area where the Oriental Hotel now stands, and

himself. For this purpose, he engaged Anna Leonowens as an English teacher. The self-elevated governess greatly exaggerated her role in the Thai court in her autobiographical writings, misrepresenting the king as a cruel autocrat permanently involved in harem intrigues. In fact, her five years in Siam are hardly mentioned in Thai chronicles.

Mongkut's beloved hobby, astronomy, was the indirect cause of his death. From observatories at his favorite palaces, the Summer Palace at Bang Pa-in and the Palace on the Hill, at Petchburi, he successfully calculated and predicted a total eclipse of the sun in 1868. European and Asian skeptics joined him on the southeastern coast of the Gulf of

along Silom and Sathorn roads, both bucholic retreats at that time. Numerous letters to the editor of the *Bangkok Times* in 1900 complain of the writers' inability to take the evening air or ride in their carriages along Windmill Road (Silom) due to the "foul odors" from the gardens that the Chinese farmers nourished with fertilizer.

Mongkut wanted his children to gain the same benefits from the English language as

Left, King Mongkut, Rama IV, and his Queen. **Above left**, King Chulalongkorn, Rama V, and entourage in Heidelberg. **Above right**, a son of King Chulalongkorn.

Thailand to await the event. As the moon blocked the sun's light, both the Europeans and the scoffers among the royal astrologers raised an exclamation of admiration, raising the king's esteem among both parties. But his triumph was short-lived. The king contracted malaria during the trip, and died from it two weeks later.

Chulalongkorn (Rama V): Mongkut's son, Chulalongkorn, was only 15 when he ascended the throne. But he reigned over Siam as Rama V for 42 years – longer than any Thai king until the present King Bhumibol, who surpassed that record in 1988.

The farsighted Chulalongkorn immediately revolutionized his court by ending the ancient custom of prostration, and by allowing officials to sit on chairs during royal audiences. He abolished serfdom in stages, giving owners and serfs time to readjust to the new order, and replaced corvee labor with direct taxation.

His reign was truly a revolution from the throne. When Chulalongkorn assumed power, Siam had no schools, and few roads, railways, hospitals, or well-equipped military forces. To achieve the enormous task of modernization, he brought in foreign advisors and sent his sons and other young men abroad for education. He also founded a palace school for children of the aristocracy,

roads to link it with his palace. Other noble families followed, building elegant mansions. In the same area, he arranged the construction of Wat Benjamabophit, the last major Buddhist temple built in Bangkok.

A watershed year was 1892, when the four government ministries were expanded to 12, a post-and-telegraph office was established, and construction of the first railway was begun. Chulalongkorn's brothers were leading figures in his government, especially Prince Devawongse, the foreign minister, and Prince Damrong, the first interior minister and a historian who has come to be known as the father of Thai history. Chulalongkorn's elder children returned home from their European

following this with other schools and vocational centers. Until then, the only previous schools in Siam had been the monasteries.

During his reign, he abolished the last vestiges of slavery and introduced electric lighting in 1884. He hired Danish engineers to build an electric tram system 10 years before the one in Copenhagen was completed. He encouraged the importation of automobiles about the same time they began appearing on the streets of America.

He changed the face of Bangkok. By 1900, the city was growing rapidly eastward. In the Dusit area, on the northeastern outskirts of the city, he built a palace and constructed

schools in the 1890s, contributing to the modernization of the army and navy.

The first hospital, Siriraj, was opened in 1886 after years of unrelenting opposition – most of the common people preferred herbal remedies to *farang* medicine. Besides, there was a shortage of doctors. Eventually, the obstacles were overcome.

In foreign relations, Chulalongkorn had to compromise and give up parts of his kingdom to protect Siam from foreign colonization. When France conquered Annam in 1883 and Britain annexed Upper Burma in 1886, Siam found itself sandwiched uncomfortably between two rival expansionist powers. Border conflicts and gunboat diplomacy forced Siam to surrender to France its claims to Laos and western Cambodia. Similarly, certain Malay Peninsula territories were ceded to Britain in exchange for renunciation of British extraterritorial rights in Siam. By the end of Chulalongkorn's reign, Siam had given up 120,000 square kilometers of fringe territory. But that seemed a small price to pay for maintaining the peace and independence of Siam.

Chulalongkorn made two European tours during his reign, in 1897 and 1907. These led him to seek more spacious surroundings than those of the Grand Palace, so he built the Dusit Palace on the site of a fruit orchard. It was directly connected to the Grand Palace

by the wide Ratchadamnern Avenue. At Dusit, he held intimate parties and even fancy-dress balls, often cooking the food outside himself.

Chulalongkorn's many reforms bore fruit within his lifetime. The economy of the country flourished, and Thai peasantry – by comparison with their counterparts in French Indochina and British Burma – were very well-off. It is no wonder that Chulalongkorn was posthumously named *Piya Maharaj*, the

Left, Chulalongkorn's widow. Vajiravudh and Prajadhipok are at center top and lower right. **Above**, Prajadhipok delivering new constitution.

Beloved Great King. As Rama V, Chulalongkorn was conscious of worldwide democratic trends, but judged his country as yet unprepared for such a change. It is said that he brought progress to Siam through the judicious exercise of his absolute power.

Vajiravudh (Rama VI): King Chulalongkorn's successor, Vajiravudh, began his reign (1910–1925) with a lavish coronation. Oxford-educated and thoroughly anglicized, his Western-inspired reforms to modernize Siam greatly affected modern Thai society.

One of the first changes was a 1913 edict commanding his subjects to adopt surnames. In the absence of a clan or caste system, genealogy was virtually unheard of in Siam. Previously, Thais had used first names, a practice the king considered uncivilized. The law generated much initial bewilderment, especially in rural areas, and Vajiravudh personally coined patronymics for hundreds of families. To simplify his forebears' lengthy titles for foreigners, he invented the Chakri dynastic name, Rama, to be followed by the proper reign number. He started with himself, as Rama VI.

As Thai standards of beauty did not conform to Western ideals of femininity, women were encouraged to keep their hair long instead of having it close-cropped, and to replace their *dhoti* or plus-fours with the *panung*, a Thai-style sarong. Primary education was made compulsory throughout the kingdom; Chulalongkorn University, the first in Siam, was founded, and schools for both sexes flourished during his reign.

Vajiravudh's most significant political contribution was to promote the concept of nationalism. An accomplished author, he used literature and drama to foster nationalism by glorifying Thai legends and historical heroes in plays. Under a pseudonym, he also wrote essays extolling the virtues of the nation.

At the outbreak of World War I, Siam remained neutral, but late in the war, Vajiravudh joined the Allies in 1917 by sending a small expeditionary force to fight in France, thereby securing Siam's admittance to the League of Nations. The then-Thai flag, a white elephant against a red background, was flown with others at Versailles, but the pachyderm was unfortunately mistaken for a small domestic animal. The incident greatly discomfited the king, who then changed the flag to red, white and blue stripes to represent the nation, the religion and the monarchy, elements now recognized as essential to the structure of modern Thailand.

Vajiravudh preferred individual ministerial consultations to summoning his appointed cabinet. His regime was therefore criticized as autocratic and lacking in coordination. Members of his family were dissatisfied because he rarely saw them, enjoying more the company of his courtiers. His extravagance soon emptied the reserve funds built up by Chulalongkorn; towards the end of his reign, the national treasury had to meet deficits caused by the ruler's personal expenses.

Vajiravudh married late. His only daughter was born one day before he died in 1925.

He was succeeded by his youngest brother, Prajadhipok, reaping the consequences of his brother's brilliant but controversial reign.

Prajadhipok (Rama VII): The early death of his elder brother propelled Prajadhipok to royal succession, although being an old Etonian, he would have preferred a soldier's career to that of a ruler's. Once king, however, he stressed economy and efficiency within the government.

Unlike his brother, he tried to cut public expenditure by reducing the civil service and royal household expenses drastically. Prajadhipok's economic policies paid off.

In the early years of his reign, communica-tions were improved by a wireless service, and the Don Muang Airport began to operate as an international air center. It was also during his reign that Siam saw the establishment of the Fine Arts Department, the National Library and the National Museum.

Hard-working and conscientious, Prajadhipok was personally concerned with improving the welfare of his subjects. He was aware of the rising demand for greater participation in government by a small foreign-educated faction, but felt that the Thais were, on the whole, not ready for democracy. In 1927, he publicly commented that the people must first be taught political consciousness before democracy could effectively be introduced.

The worldwide economic crisis of 1931 affected Siam's rice export. By the time Prajadhipok dropped the gold standard, linking the Thai baht to the pound sterling, it was too late to stem the financial crisis. The government was forced to implement further economies by cutting the salary of junior personnel, and by resorting to a retrenchment of the armed services. Thus, discontent brewed among army officials and bureaucrats, who felt promotions were hindered.

Coup d'etat: Rumors and speculation were rampant during the 150th anniversary celebrations of the Chakri dynasty in 1932. Prajadhipok was the last regal representative of traditional Thai kingship to preside over grand pageantry, which featured a royal barge procession. Two months later, a coup d'etat ended the absolute rule by Thai monarchs.

The coup was staged by the People's Party, a military and civilian group masterminded by foreign-educated Thais.

The chief ideologist was Pridi Panomyong, a young lawyer trained in France. On the military side, Capt. Luang Pibul Songram was responsible for gaining the support of important army colonels. With a few tanks, the 70 conspirators sparked off their "revolution" by occupying strategic areas and holding the senior princes hostage. Other army officers stood by as the public watched.

The king was in Hua Hin, a royal retreat to the south, at the time. To avoid bloodshed, he accepted a provisional constitution by which he "ceased to rule but continued to reign."

Left, Plowing Day, 1930. **Right**, King Rama V, or Chulalongkorn.

In 1932, the Chakri dynasty celebrated its 150th anniversary, with the Memorial Bridge, the city's first bridge spanning the Chao Phraya River, was opened – but the air reverberated with calls for change.

Originally motivated by idealism, the People's Party soon succumbed to internal conflicts and competitions. A National Assembly was appointed, but universal suffrage was postponed while the public was to be tutored in the rudiments of representative democracy. The Thai people didn't show much interest, however. They wouldn't voluntarily attend the party's educational rallies, and other parties were initially outlawed.

The party's military factions quickly outmanoeuvred the civilian contingents. They had greater cohesion, and more extensive connections with traditional elite power brokers. The officers exercised their influence when Pridi presented a vague and utopian economic plan in 1933. It called for the nationalization of land, and for the creation of peasant cooperatives. When his opponents attacked the plan as communistic, Pridi slipped into his first overseas exile. The power of Pibul and the army was further strengthened in October of 1933 by the decisive defeat of a rebellion led by Prince Boworadet, who had been King Prajadhipok's war minister.

The king had no part in the rebellion, but he had become increasingly dismayed by quarrels within the new government. He moved to England in 1934 and abdicated in 1935. In a farewell message, he said that he had wished to turn over power to the entire people and not to "any individual or any group to use in an autocratic manner." Sadly, the subsequent history of coups, aborted coups and bloodbaths has caused the king's words to be often quoted. Ananda Mahidol (Rama VIII), a 10-year-old half-nephew, agreed to taking the throne, but he remained in Switzerland to complete his schooling.

The governments of the 1930s had some achievements. Most notably, public primary

education, totaling four years, was extended to many rural areas. Indirect and, later, direct elections to the lower house meant that for the first time representatives from provincial areas had a voice at the national level. After a series of crises and an election in 1938, Pibul became prime minister. His rule grew more authoritarian.

While some Thai officers favored the model of the Japanese military regime, Pibul admired – and sought to emulate – Hitler and Mussolini. Borrowing many ideas from Eu-

ropean fascism, he attempted to instill a sense of mass nationalism. With tight control over the media and a creative propaganda department, Pibul whipped up sentiment against the Chinese residents. Chinese immigration was restricted, Chinese were barred from certain occupations, and state enterprises were set up to compete in industries dominated by Chinese firms. By changing the country's name from Siam to Thailand in 1939, Pibul intended to emphasize that it belonged to Thai (or Tai) ethnic groups and not to Chinese, Malays, Mons or any other minorities.

World War II: When Hitler invaded France

Left, today's King Bhumibol on his coronation day in 1950. **Above**, page from a period book, showing coup d'etat officers.

in 1940, French hold over its Indochinese colonies was seriously weakened. Anticipating that Japan might make a claim, Thailand made its own by invading southern Laos and parts of western Cambodia, in November 1940. Stepping in as a mediator, Japan sided with Thailand. For the previous 50 years, Thai foreign policy had been coupled with Britain's, but these military ventures now meant that the (soon-to-be) Allies thought little of cooperating with Thailand.

On December 7, 1941, (December 8 in Asia) the Japanese bombed Pearl Harbor and launched invasions throughout Southeast Asia. Thailand was invaded at nine points. Despite a decade of military buildup, resist-

with a network in Thailand headed by Pridi. The resistance supplied Allied forces with intelligence, but it never quite reached the stage of operating a guerrilla army.

By 1944, Thailand's initial enthusiasm for its Japanese partners had evaporated. The country faced runaway inflation, food shortages, rationing and black markets. The assembly forced Pibul from office. When the war ended in 1945, Britain demanded reparations and the right to station troops in Thailand. The Thais argued that due to the work of Seni Thai, they were in fact allies. The U.S. supported the Thais, partly because it was then trying to blunt British and French efforts to repossess their Asian colonies.

ance lasted less than a day. Pibul acceded to Japan's request for "passage rights," but Thailand was allowed to retain its army and political administration.

Popular anecdote has it that the Thai ambassador to Washington, Seni Pramoj, single-handedly prevented war between Thailand and the United States by hiding the declaration in a desk drawer. It's not true. Thailand in fact declared war against Britain and the United States. It is true, however, that Seni immediately offered his services in Washington to set up an underground resistance movement, *Seni Thai*. Starting with overseas Thai students, Seni Thai linked up

After the war: Following World War II, Bangkok began to develop its economy along the lines of European countries, with new industries, firm administration and the first of many five-year plans.

Bangkok began to change dramatically in response to the new prosperity. The last of the major canals were filled in to make roadways. The city began its big push to the east, as Sukhumvit and Petchburi roads changed from quiet residential areas into busy, business-filled thoroughfares.

(But it wouldn't be until the arrival of American forces in the late 1960s that would give the city its present look. Large infusions of money resulted in a burgeoning economy, multi-storied buildings and a population that swelled in response to the new jobs offered. The Thai military, which had steadily been gaining power in Thai politics, reached its peak of influence during these years.)

The first few years after the end of World War II were marked by a series of democratic civilian governments. Pridi served behind the scenes, drafting a constitution, and briefly served as prime minister. In 1948, under threat of military force, Pibul took over once again. In the early years, his power was contested. Two coup attempts, supported by the navy, resulted in fierce battles on the streets of Bangkok and along the Chao Phraya

dead of a gunshot in his palace bedroom. (Pridi believed that the king accidentally shot himself.) The charge against Pridi now seems absurd, but with the mass media in Pibul's hands, many people at the time probably believed it.

Ananda was succeeded by his younger brother, Bhumibol Adulyadej (Rama IX), the present monarch, who returned to Switzerland to complete law studies. He did not take up active duties until the 1950s. By then, Thailand was without a king for 20 years.

Vietnam War: In addition to renewed anti-Chinese campaigns, Pibul vigorously hunted out communists. Many of the leaders of the small, outlawed Communist Party of Thai-

River. In the 1950s, Pibul's grip grew tighter. Police power was abused, newspaper editors were beaten, and government critics mysteriously disappeared.

Pibul had also rid himself of his nemesis, Pridi. After attempting a coup in 1949, Pridi fled into permanent exile. (After 20 years in China, he died in France in 1983.) Pibul sealed Pridi's fate by convening an inquiry that implicated him in the death of King Ananda. In 1946, on a visit to Thailand from school in Europe, the young king was found

land were Sino-Thais. Pibul's anti-communist credentials helped win both economic and military aid from the United States. American largesse, with too few strings, has been blamed as cause for the corruption that permeates the police and military to this day. Another cause was Pibul's practice of placing military officers to run state enterprises. Private firms were also encouraged to appoint officers to their boards of directors.

In 1957, a clique of one-time proteges overthrew Pibul. The leader, General Sarit Thanarat, and two cohort generals, Thanom Kittikachorn and Prapas Charusathien, ran the government until 1973. While Pibul had

Left, soldiers taking part in a religious ceremony. **Above**, Democracy Monument, Bangkok.

retained some trappings of democracy, such as a constitution and legislature, Sarit employed martial law. Labor organizations were banned, and educational and cultural groups even found it difficult to associate. The Buddhist *sangha* was co-opted to promote anti-communism and other campaigns.

Unadorned dictatorship did not hinder official relations with the United States. By the end of the 1960s, the war in Vietnam was raging and Thailand was America's staunchest ally. A small Thai contingent served in Vietnam. Total aid was running about $100 million annually. American funds built the first roads in the Northeast, where air bases and other military facilities proliferated. From

a middle class began to emerge, especially in Bangkok. Many Thais were exposed to Western values, partly due to the resident population of 45,000 American servicemen. Yet, the dictatorial trio did not – perhaps could not – anticipate that socioeconomic changes would lead to new aspirations.

The October revolution: In a mystifying burst of generosity, Prime Minister Thanom issued a constitution and held elections, in 1969. His party naturally won most seats, but the general nonetheless quickly bored of slow parliamentary processes. In November 1971, Thanom and Prapas dissolved the parliament and reverted to their old ruling habits. Many Thais felt betrayed, but only students kept up

here, US aircraft bombed Vietnam and Laos.

The Northeast was also the Thai base for forays into Laos. Thousands of Thai soldiers died fighting in allegiance with the Royal Lao Army against Lao communists. Meanwhile, Thai communists had turned to armed conflict in 1965. The original strongholds were in the impoverished Northeast, but by the early 1970s, there were communist areas throughout, including the Muslim south.

Sarit, Thanom and Prapas used their power to accrue enormous personal fortunes, but they also deserve credit for development. Health standards improved. The business sector expanded. Construction boomed, and

low-key protests, despite grave personal risk.

With reasonable demands for a constitution and popular elections, students were able harness public support. The final straw was the arrest of 13 student leaders and professors who had made such demands. On October 13, 1973, a demonstration to protest the arrests attracted 400,000 people to Bangkok's Democracy Monument. The next day, the protest turned violent and at least 100 students were shot by riot police. The two generals discovered that their army had deserted them. They fled to the United States.

Political parties, labor unions and farming organizations sprang to life with very specific grievances. Right-wing and paramilitary organizations sprang up in response. Between 1974 and 1975, the Farmers' Federation was decimated by the murder of 21 of its leaders. Two elections in the mid 1970s produced civilian governments, but the diverse range of parties could not work together for long.

The middle class was originally strongly supportive of the student revolution, as were parts of the upper class. But they came to fear that total chaos or a communist takeover was at hand. The 1976 return of Thanom, ostensibly to become a monk, sparked student protests and paramilitary counter-protests. On October 6, police and paramilitary thugs stormed Thammasat University. Students

required to attend anti-communism indoctrination. Many students and other dissidents joined the communists in the countryside.

Yet another military coup ousted Thanin in October 1977. For the next decade, two comparatively moderate generals headed the government, both endorsing amnesties for the communists.

Fragile democracy: A former general was elected in 1989, but deposed two years later in a bloodless military coup. The junta installed a businessman and ex-diplomat, Anand Panyacharun, as a caretaker premier, but were startled when he exhibited an independent streak and earned a reputation for running the cleanest government in memory.

were lynched and their bodies burned on the spot. A faction of army officers seized power. Self-government had lasted but three years.

Ironically, the civilian judge appointed to be prime minister, Thanin Kraivichien, turned out to be more brutal than any of his uniformed predecessors. Besides outlawing political parties, unions and strikes, he ordered arrests of anyone "endangering society." A curfew was strictly enforced. Teachers suspected of left-wing leanings were

Far left, honoring pro-democracy protestors killed by army, 1992. **Left**, military officers looking sharp. **Above**, awaiting national election results.

As expected, the junta's new party won the most parliamentary seats in the 1992 elections. Unexpected, however, was the public discontent when the coup leader, Gen. Suchinda Krapayoon, assumed the prime minister's post without having stood for election. In the following weeks, students, professors, social workers, maverick politicians, entertainers and the curious public convened in a series of outdoor rallies. On 17 May, more than 70,000 gathered at Sanam Luang, the grassy expanse near the Grand Palace and Democracy Monument. Late in the evening, soldiers fired on the unarmed demonstrators assembled there.

Shootings, beatings, riots, arson and mass arrests continued sporadically for three days. Broadcast media, which were controlled by the government or military, enforced a nationwide news blackout. But owners of satellite dishes, in Thailand and around the world, were glued to footage of "Bloody May." Unrepentant, Suchinda stepped down. The Democrat Party and other prominent junta critics prevailed in the September elections. A rarity in Thai politics, newly elected Prime Minister Chuan Leekpai was not corrupt and lived modestly. He prevailed for three years, setting a record for a civilian, elected government. But by the end, Chuan had lost much of the goodwill of the

democracy forces that had lifted him to office. For many, he was too passive.

No one was prosecuted for the May crackdown. As with the massacres of 1973 and 1976, the numbers and identity of those who died or disappeared in May 1992 are still in dispute. Corruption flourished. Most disappointing, Chuan was deflected in his efforts to push through a law that would have relegated more power to local governments. The coalition collapsed in 1995 when members of Chuan's party were discovered profiting from a land reform program.

Two subsequent elections brought businessman Banharn Silpa-archa, and a former general, Chavalit Yongchaiyudh, to the highest office. Both had unsavoury reputations for their business dealings and campaign expenditures. And both were incompetent in handling the economy.

In fact, the economic rot had set in much earlier. Kick-started by an influx of Japanese assembly plants in the late 1980s, Thailand had become one of the fastest growing economies in the world for almost a decade. Per capita income doubled to US$ 2,000 per year and more than 4 million rural people migrated to urban jobs.

But even as economic growth was slowing down, liberalisation of the financial sector in the early 1990s enabled Thai companies to borrow cheap money. Property firms in particular went on a borrowing binge. The first cracks opened in mid-1996 when two officials at the Bangkok Bank of Commerce fled after embezzling more than US$2 billion. The central bank stepped in with bail-outs that eventually extended to cash-strapped finance companies. More than US$16 billion later, the central bank had covertly carried out the biggest bank bail-out in history.

IMF rescue: Faced with capital flight and a deteriorating balance of payments, in July 1997, the baht was floated from its dollar-weighted peg. It quickly dropped 25 percent in value, dropping even more later.

The Thai government finally sought the help of the International Monetary Fund (IMF). In the following days, on IMF advice, 56 of the nation's 91 finance companies were declared insolvent. IMF loans and credit guarantees came only after stringent conditions were met.

As the economy ground to a halt in Thailand, the IMF was blamed for just about every problem in the country. Chuan Leekpai returned to office in 1998. More pro-active this time, he has made internationally applauded moves to resuscitate Thailand. While many Asian economies continued to falter in the late 1990s, Thailand's economy was held up as an example of an economy that was diligently working its way out of the abyss, but still ever so slowly.

Left, Thais are beginning to demand more responsibility from their political leaders. **Right**, other than economic stability, Bangkok's greatest challenge is to develop a functional and efficient infrastructure.

Underlying that distinctive Thai warmth to visitors – and to life in general – is *sanuk,* a word that can be translated as fun or enjoyable. Indeed, the quantity – and quality – of sanuk, whether in work or play, determines if something is worth pursuing.

Thailand's culture and society has traditionally been centered on agriculture, an activity that nurtures a sense of community, especially during planting and harvest. The shift to urban life has changed much of the countryside's ways, but it is a rare Thai who does not enjoy getting together with friends. Indeed, the notion that one might go off solo to a dinner or on a holiday is considered *mai sanuk,* or not fun. Mai sanuk can apply to one's personal situation, or life in the office. There is a sense of family about Thai activities that does not exclude outsiders. For the visitor invited to join, there is no expectation of reciprocation.

When a visitor encounters a tense situation, it is usually because of language difficulties. In this instance, it is best to adopt another Thai attitude, *jai yen,* or cool heart – to deal calmly with a problem. Indeed, it is difficult to stir a Thai to real anger. But touching a Thai (and never do so on the top of the head), shouting, or threatening the strong sense of independence that Thais have will effect an immediate response.

Closely allied with this is a concept that provides the answer to all life's vicissitudes: *mai pen rai,* a phrase that eludes precise translation, but which is usually rendered as never mind. The Thai would rather shrug shoulders in the face of adversity than to escalate a difficult situation. Solutions that contribute to reestablishing calm are welcomed. In fact, the Thais have survived intact as a sovereign nation by adopting a superb sense of compromise, putting trifling or trivial matters in perspective, or else in the rubbish bin.

Colors of the flag: At eight o'clock each morning, the Thai national flag is ceremoniously raised in every Thai town and city. The

modern flag – introduced in 1917 to replace an earlier red flag emblazoned with a white elephant, the flag of the absolute monarchy – is composed of five horizontal bands of white, red, and blue. The white symbolizes the purity of Buddhism; red, the land and its people; and blue, the monarchy as the force that binds the other two together.

Monarchy: The three colors of the flag are revered as symbols of enduring qualities amidst changes, values evoked in 1992 when Thais rose up against the military's grip on

political power with massive street demonstrations that sometimes turned bloody. King Bhumibol – Rama IX – ended the escalating political crisis between the prime minister and his chief political opponent, which had threatened civil war. The two men prostrated themselves at the king's feet, on live television, where they stayed silent as the king lectured them to bring the country back to a peace. There were free elections.

The king does not govern the country, but of all Thai institutions, he is perhaps the most respected, with considerable influence in government and in society, and is an example of high moral standards.

Preceding pages: royal family at Wat Phra Kaeo. Left, blessing of a commercial airliner. Right, the royal couple preside at a ceremony.

Originating long ago in the ancient city of Sukhothai, the royal symbol has endured through wars, revolutions, the fall of dynasties, the smashing of traditions and governments – both dictatorial and democratic – and through times of tribulations and prosperity. In Thailand the monarch remains the most powerful unifying force in the country, truly respected by all groups.

The current king came to the throne in 1946, the latest monarch in the Chakri dynasty that has produced several enlightened monarchs in the 19th and 20th centuries.

However, the abolition of the absolute monarchy in 1932 had exerted unprecedented strain on the system; the royalty had seemed

Rama V and later regarded as the father of modern medicine in Thailand, was a minor member of the royal family. At his birth, there seemed little chance of Prince Bhumibol becoming king. Between him and the throne, according to the laws of succession, stood Bhumibol's own father and elder brother, Prince Ananda. (Rama VII had borne no sons to take the throne.)

In the nearly five decades since his coronation in 1950, King Bhumibol has proved himself a worthy successor to his celebrated ancestors. With Queen Sirikit, he has traveled to every part of Thailand, the first monarch to visit some parts of the country.

His involvement with rural people began

to lose contact with the people, along with their confidence. There were continuing doubts if the monarchy could survive the turmoil of World War II, when 18-year-old Bhumibol ascended the throne unexpectedly after the fatal shooting of his elder brother, King Ananda, in the Grand Palace, in Bangkok. The king's death was never fully explained publicly, but much later, two royal servants were executed for his murder.

King Bhumibol was born in Cambridge, Massachusetts, in 1927, where his father, Prince Mahidol of Songkhla, was studying medicine at Harvard University, and his mother, nursing. His father, a son of King

with a concerted effort to find new crops for the hilltribes, in order to wean them away from opium cultivation. He incorporated this experience into programs to aid farmers in each of the country's four regions.

He has also turned over his palace grounds to agricultural purposes. Behind the walls of Chitralada Palace, where the king lives (the Grand Palace is for ceremonial and state occasions), the king has transformed gardens into an agricultural research station, with a dairy farm, rice fields, and orchards. A skillful and professional-caliber musician, he plays jazz on clarinet and saxophone.

The king and queen take part, of course, in

the numerous royal ceremonies that punctuate the year – the seasonal robing of the Emerald Buddha, the various Buddhist holy days, the opening of Parliament. Only recently have they cut back considerably on handing out university diplomas, and on the sponsoring of weddings and cremations.

If the Thais revere their king as a symbol, they also respect him as a man, a fact that makes the Thai monarchy stronger now than at any period since King Bhumibol's grandfather, Chulalongkorn (Rama V).

Military: After ousting Gen. Suchinda Krapayoon, perhaps the only lasting effect of the May 1992 demonstrations and killings was an amendment to the constitution man-

disapproval of military dictators than formerly. Thai citizens also increasingly suspect the generals' motives, resulting from scandals and gossip about kickbacks and other corrupt practices.

The military's conviction that might makes right is a puzzling anathema to Westerns and some other Asians. At the turn of the century, the legal system was created after the French model. Since the overthrow of the absolute monarchy in 1932, a parliament has usually had the trappings of Britain's system. Why is it, then, that the military didn't simply transfer its loyalty from the monarchy to a civilian government?

It's probably important to recall that, while

dating that the prime minister be an elected member of parliament. Whether the military has new respect for constitutions remains to be seen over the long haul. Every coup of the past 50 years simultaneously abrogated some form of a constitution.

On the plus side, the military can no longer justify its authority by pointing to the threat of communist insurgency. And like all elite, generals are sensitive to Thailand's image in the world; the last coup, in 1991, revealed that Western leaders were more vocal in their

Left, King Bhumibol at crown prince's investiture. **Above**, Plowing Ceremony, Bangkok.

the group of civilians and officers engineering the 1932 overthrow were French-educated, France of the 1920s and 1930s was churning with ideas and movements espousing the need for strong-man leadership and the suppression of communists, trade unions and dissent. Pibun, the general that wielded power for most of the 1940s and 1950s, was an ardent disciple of German fascism and his influence haunts the present.

With all other avenues blocked, the military in this century became the only way for a poor boy to rise in status and wealth. It still remains the principal path. In theory, all young men are supposed to serve in the military for two years. In practice, the ranks are predominately poor boys, whose primary duty is to defend the borders. The upper ranks have other matters on their minds.

High-ranking military officers sit on the boards of state enterprises and private banks, own hotels and restaurants, and otherwise participate in business even as they actively pursue military careers. This practice contributes to corruption in many ways. For example, if a golf course resort is encroaching on a national forest – as is common – villagers and forest rangers are afraid to complain if a high-ranking officer sits on the board. They assume that such an "influential person" guarantees the resort protection.

military. The military has fiercely resisted efforts to increase civilian oversight in these particular areas.

Government: For most of the past five decades, Thailand has been ruled by military dictators, although in the late 1980s, a far-seeing general, Prem Tinsulanond, willingly shared power with an elected parliament. Since 1992, for the longest period in Thai history, the country has been governed by an elected parliament, from which the prime minister is chosen.

As was the case from 1973–1976, no party has emerged as a majority, so fractious coalitions form and re-form. The trappings resemble the British parliament, with an upper

The much-publicized logging deals between Thai military and their counterparts in Burma (Myanmar) and Laos (and at one time the Khmer Rouge in Cambodia) offer another example. It's probably impossible to distinguish whether the Thais are acting in an official capacity or conducting private deals. Regardless, the fact is that Thailand has lost most of its forests.

The Thai soldier, like the civil servant, belongs to a sprawling and secretive organization with activities that extend far beyond defense. The army runs national television and local radio stations. Basic services, such as ports and airports are the fiefdoms of the

house, or senate, appointed by the prime minister every five years (most recently, appointed in 1996).

In contrast to the late 1940s or mid 1970s, political parties don't pretend to have political platforms. They revolve mostly around the personality and purses of a single man. It's the norm for politicians to jump from political party to political party. Most Thais only hear from their MPs at election time. In between, they resort to protest rallies, which can turn violent.

The tinderbox issues are dam construction and consequent resettlement; land grabbing, land scandals and forest encroachment; lack of price supports and other assistance to poor farmers. When they are consistently frustrated, "troublemakers" bring their protests to the gates of the Parliament building. It can take weeks, but eventually the prime minister or other high official will meet to offer a few soothing words.

The Thai government is very centralized. For the democratic forces, the watchword is decentralization. These comprise some leaders of the venerable Democratic Party, academics, lawyers and local groups, such as environmental organizations and associations of small farmers. In particular, they would like provincial governors to be elected, rather than appointed by the prime minister.

men – in matters of land ownership, marriage or citizenship. For example, while a man can divorce his wife on grounds of adultery, a woman cannot. She must prove that her husband was maintaining another woman as a "minor" wife. In the Thai practice of Theravada Buddhism, a woman cannot take the same vows or perform the same duties that monk can. In the home, a girl must sacrifice so that her brothers can get the better education.

Yet, historically, Thai women enjoyed more power and liberty than, say, their counterparts in India, Japan or China. They worked by the sides of men in the fields, could inherit property and had considerable freedom of

For different reasons, many of the upstart provincial businessmen-cum-politicians ultimately favor decentralization; they already have extensive local machines. For the traditional power brokers – the Bangkok elite and the military – decentralization is a considerable threat.

Women: The status of Thai women is paradoxical. As the prevalence of prostitution attests, women do occupy a subordinate place and are not entitled to the same legal rights as

movement. It's true that noble men acquired scores of concubines. And when Chinese men began immigrating in large numbers during the 19th century, they brought a penchant for prostitutes and, with vast additional wealth, the habit of collecting minor wives. However, for the majority of the population, consisting of peasants living in rural villages, one wife was the norm and prostitutes were unavailable.

Nowadays, with the blessings of their founding fathers from China, Chinese-Thai women have been at the top of big businesses for more than a generation. Thai businesswomen often joke about the difficulties of convincing newly-arrived Japanese business-men that, yes, a woman really is in charge. As can readily be seen in Bangkok, women flourish as market vendors, cooks, and store-keepers. More than half of the laborers in garment and electronics factories are female. At the very bottom, women work alongside men on construction sites (at lower wages).

Women hold prominent positions in academia, the civil service, banking, the professions (notably dentistry), and the tourist trade. The next frontier is a provincial governorship, which seems a possibility now that there is a female general in the military. It's not unusual for the elected "headman" of a village to be a woman.

Women obtained the right to vote at the same time as men, in 1932.

The paradoxes are probably explained by differences in class. Girls born into the top 10 percent of households, encompassing the upper and middle classes, have much the same education and options as their brothers. The university population is almost equally divided between male and female. The elite now are just as likely to send daughters as sons abroad for an education.

Women in the lower ranks, forming the majority of the population, don't have any choice but to work. From a young age, girls are instilled with their responsibility to the family. Given the feckless tendencies of some Thai men, their wives or sisters often end up as the family's sole support. Often, that can begin at the age of 12 or 13, when girls (and boys) finish the customary six years of public schooling.

Too often, that's the age that brothel brokers seek when they descend on villages with dazzling offers for young flesh. While at least half of teenage boys are enrolled in school, the share of the female population is but one-third.

The Chinese: Like every country in Southeast Asia, Chinese merchants have been active in Thailand since the earliest days of commerce. When King Rama I selected Bangkok as his new capital, the site on which he wanted to build the Grand Palace was occupied by Chinese shops. He asked the owners to move a kilometer down the riverbank to Sampeng, where they settled in what is today the Chinese center.

Throughout the l9th century and the first half of the 20th, immigrants from China were denied ownership of land and participation in government, so they naturally drifted towards trade and commerce.

One thing, however, has long distinguished the Thai Chinese from their counterparts in most other Asian countries: they have been assimilated to a remarkable degree into the life of their adopted land. In part this has been due to deliberate government policy. (The Chinese language was not even taught at the university level until a few years ago.)

Chinese and Thais have intermarried freely; it is difficult to say with assurance that someone is "pure" Thai or Chinese. There is no deep-rooted anti-Chinese bias in Thailand, nor have there been any of the serious racial conflicts marring the recent histories of neighboring countries. Only among the older generation are there people who think and speak of themselves specifically as Chinese more so than as Thai.

The younger generation thinks of itself as Thai, speaks Thai as their only language, voices loyalty to Thailand and the monarchy, and has only cursory interests in affairs in China or Chinese culture.

Left, women see the future improving. Right, Buddhism is a communal focus in Bangkok's Chinatown.

In the pale light of early morning, a young saffron-robed monk walks with grave dignity along a city street, a cloth bag over one arm, a metal alms bowl cradled in the other. Silently, he opens his alms bowl to receive the offerings – not handouts – of rice and curries placed in it by ordinary Thais, who have stood for long moments before their homes, awaiting his arrival. He says not a word of thanks, because, according to Buddhist tenets, he is doing them a favor, providing them a means to make merit so they can be reborn in the next life as higher beings. Turning, he continues to walk on bare feet to the next set of alms givers, following the steps of monks before him for 2,000 years.

Buddhism – a philosophy, rather than a religion – has played a profound role in shaping the Thai character, particularly in the people's reactions to events. The Buddhist concept of the impermanence of life and possessions, and of the necessity to avoid extremes of emotion or behavior, has done much to create the relaxed, carefree charm that is one of the most appealing characteristics of the people. Tension, ulcers, nervous breakdowns and the like are not unknown in Thailand, at least not in places like Bangkok. But they are remarkably uncommon, in no small way due to the influence of Buddhism.

Most of the Thai population are supporters of Theravada Buddhism, which is also the main Buddhist sect in Laos, Cambodia, Burma (Myanmar) and Sri Lanka. (Nevertheless, even a casual visitor to temples in these countries will quickly see differences between them. As they have done with most outside influences – Khmer temple decorations and Chinese food, for instance – over the centuries the Thais have evolved a Buddhism of their own cast.)

The oldest of all Buddhist faiths, it is the only one to trace its origins directly back to the teachings of the Gautama Buddha in the sixth century BC. The central doctrines of Theravada Buddhism are based on the temporary nature and imperfections of all forms of beings. Every existence is caught up in the wheel of reincarnation and must be reborn in a new life after death. A new life in turn means new suffering. The root cause of the never-ending cycles of rebirth and life is desire, since all desire gives rise to fresh suffering. The total conquest of desire will end the suffering and lead to the final enlightened state of *nirvana*. The only way to achieve this goal is to practise the so-called Noble Eightfold Path.

With the help of a complicated system of rules, each Thai, whether lay person or monk, tries to achieve spiritual merit in the present life so that it will favorably influence one's next life, thus permitting an existence characterised by less suffering, until ultimately nirvana is reached. Almost all the religious activities that a traveler will experience in Thailand has to do with merit-making. A man who spends some part of his life as a monk will earn merit by living in accordance with the strict rules governing monastic life. So, too, a person who supports the monks on a daily basis by donating food, or visits a temple to pray for a sick person, gains merit.

Strictly speaking, the Buddha image in front of which the prayers are offered provides only a formal background for these activities. Neither the statue, nor the Buddha himself, is worshipped; after all the latter, as every Thai knows, was only a mortal.

In addition to Theravada Buddhism, there is the Mahayana Buddhism practiced by those of Chinese descent. Their shrines can be found throughout Bangkok, and in most towns of Thailand.

Particularly in Chinatown, visitors are likely to spot Mahayana temples. Mahayana literally means "Greater Vehicle" and, according to this doctrine, those who have attained nirvana return to help others reach the same state. The various sects and practices that predominate in China, Tibet, Taiwan, Japan, Korea and Vietnam are classified at Mahayana. It is taught that dissatisfaction is caused by insatiable desires, which the eight-fold path can stem; meditation is essential. But Chinese Buddhism, at least as practiced in Thailand, primarily consists of incense, lucky charms and heaps of other

Preceding pages: a gathering of monks. **Left,** the gold-gilded presiding Buddha, Wat Benjamabophit.

practices. The visitor entering a *sanjao,* or inner shrine of such a temple, will have a chance to shake sticks out of a canister, from which a fortune can be told. At funeral times, paper money and doll-size cardboard houses (complete with paper toy cars) are burned to assist the deceased in his or her next life.

Temple life: Thailand's 300,000 monks typically live in a *wat,* practicing and teaching the rules of human conduct laid down by the Buddha more than 2,500 years ago.

There are literally hundreds of Buddhist wat in the cities and suburbs, usually sited in serene pockets of densely-packed neighborhoods and serving as hubs for spiritual and social life.

The term wat defines a large walled compound made up of several buildings, including a *bot* or hall where new monks are ordained, and one or more *viharn* where sermons are delivered.

It may also contain a belltower, a *ho trai* (library), and *guti,* or monk meditation cells, as well as stupa, called *chedi* in Thailand. Chedi contain the ashes or relics of wealthy donors, emulating the Buddha whose ashes and relics were placed by his instruction in a mound of earth. There may be a government school on the premises to educate the local children. If there is any open space in the grounds, it is a sure bet that it will be filled with happy kids playing soccer or *takraw.*

The total number of monks at Thailand's 28,000 wat varies from season to season, swelling during the rainy season, the normal time for a young man to enter the priesthood. Tradition requires that every Buddhist male enter the monkhood, for a period ranging from seven days to six months, or even a lifetime. Regulations require that government offices and the military give a man time off to enter the monkhood; companies customarily grant leave time with pay for male employees entering the monkhood.

The entry of a young man into monkhood is seen as repayment to parents for his upbringing, and as bestowing special merit on them, particularly his mother. Unlike the case in other countries, women cannot be ordained in the Thai Buddhism. It is thus popularly believed that a son, as a monk, can earn merit for his mother and other female relatives. Enough merit, goes the popular belief, and she can even reach nirvana. Even more alarming, to reformist monks and sects,

such as *Santi Asoke,* is the preeminent belief in merit-making, or the making of donations to monks and temples. While making donations is perfectly admirable, reformers observe that too many Thais believe they can somehow "buy" earthly luck or eternal nirvana for themselves or their relatives. At the same time, these gamblers neglect to practice right living, loving kindness, moderation and other fundamental Buddhist tenets.

Prior to being ordained, the would-be monk is shorn of all his hair. He then answers a series of questions put to him by the abbot, assuring that he is in good mental and physical health. He then moves to a monks' dormitory, or to a small *kuti* or meditation house.

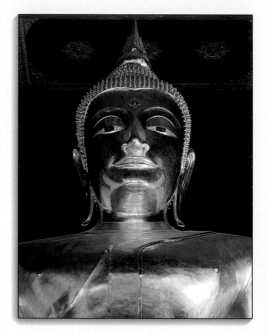

While in the temple, he listens to sermons based on the Buddha's teachings, studies the *Tripitaka,* or Three Baskets (the teaching of Buddha in Pali), practices meditation, and learns the virtues of an ascetic life. He shares in the work of the monastery: washing dishes, keeping the quarters clean. He goes out at dawn to receive his daily meals.

The shaven-headed, white-robed women living at some wat are *mae chee.* They cannot correctly be called nuns, since they cannot take the same vows or conduct the ceremonies that monks do. They chant and meditate separately from the monks, consume the monks' leftover food, and help to maintain the grounds of the wat. Many elderly women retire to these wat as a sort of nursing home, and some eventually become mae chee.

A Buddhist monk must not only abstain from stealing, lying and idle talk, taking life, indulgence in sex, intoxicants, luxuries and frivolous amusements, he must also obey no fewer than 227 rules that govern the minutiae of daily conduct and manners. In practice, however, most monks observe ten basic rules: no possessions except the yellow robe, the alms bowl and a few personal necessities; two meals a day, the first early in the morning and the second before noon; no sleeping on a comfortable bed. Moreover, there is to be no singing or dancing.

Except during the period of Buddhist Lent, from July to October, monks are free to travel from one temple to another at will. Moreover, the wat are open to anyone who wishes to retire to them.

On *wan phra,* a day each week determined by the lunar calendar, Thais go to the wat to listen to monks chant scriptures and deliver sermons. In addition to providing monks with food, the laity earns merit by making repairs on the temple or, even better, replacing an old and derelict building with a new one. At the end of the Lenten season, groups of Thais travel to distant villages to make donations, an occasion filled with as much riotous celebration as solemn ceremony.

Communal center: For all its Spartan life, however, a Buddhist wat in Thailand is by no means isolated from the real world. Most wat have schools of some sort attached to them; for centuries, the only schools were those run by monks. The wat has traditionally been the center of social and communal life in the villages, with monks serving as herbal doctors, psychological counselors, and arbitrators of disputes. Monks also play an important part in daily life, such as the blessing of a new building, or a birthday or funeral.

Left, Golden Buddha. **Above**, offerings for monks outside of Wat Benjamabophit.

Religious tolerance: A little over 90 percent of the Thai people are Buddhist, but religious tolerance is extended to other religions. Around six percent of Thais are Moslem, with the remainder Christian, Hindu and Sikh. Indeed, the national constitution declares that the king is the "upholder" of all religions. In Bangkok and areas to the south, there are hundreds of Moslem mosques, Islam being the second-largest religion in Thailand. The repair or construction of mosques is done with funds from the government.

Christian missionaries have struggled for more than a century to attain converts, without great success. Today, there are only

200,000 Christians in Thailand. King Mongkut, who welcomed missionaries in the 1860s and learned English and Latin from them, is said to have told them: "What you teach us to do is admirable, but what you teach us to believe is foolish." He suggested that Christianity succeeded only with a weak indigenous religion. There are pockets of Christians – notably in Chiang Mai – but few steeples amidst the chedi forest.

Christians have, nonetheless, wielded greater influence than their numbers. They founded the first schools outside of temples, introducing secular subjects such as science. In Bangkok, Catholic high schools and one university (Assumption) are bastions of the

assistance with the unfathomable tragedies of daily life, and certainly no answer to the questions of the supernatural. They thus continued to worship their old deities or spirits to fill in what they saw as gaps in Buddhism.

The variety of *phi* (spirits) in Thailand is legendary, outnumbering the human population many times over. A seductive female phi, believed to reside in a banana plant, torments young men who come near. Another bothersome one takes possession of her victims and forces them to remove their clothes in public. (For some reason, the most destructive spirits seem to be female.)

To counteract the large numbers of spirits and dangers lurking in life, protective spells

elite. In fact, Queen Sirikit attended a Catholic high school. Christians also started the first hospitals, which remain among the best today. Christians also led the way in providing schooling, medical care and other services to hilltribe people.

Spirits and amulets: When Buddhism started to spread across Southeast Asia during in its early centuries of existence, the people in what is now Thailand still worshipped a world of gods and spirits who determined their daily lives down to the last detail.

Buddhism, the new religion of goodness and renunciation, offered promises of a better life, but for farmers, it provided little

are cast and kept in small amulets worn around the necks. The amulet trade is a lively one, and prices for particularly powerful amulets can run into millions of whatever currency one chooses.

Curiously, the amulets are not bought, but rather rented on an indefinite lease from 'landlords', often monks considered to possess magic powers. Some monasteries have been turned into highly profitable factories for the production of amulets. There are amulets against accidents while traveling, bullet and knife wounds, or – very popular amongst sailors – those that transform sea water into fresh water. All this has no more to do with Buddhism, certainly, than the protective blue-patterned tattoos sported by some rural Thais to ward off evil.

No building in Thailand, not even the humblest wooden hut, will be seen today without a 'spirit house', or at least a house altar. In ordinary residences, the small doll-like house may resemble a Thai dwelling; in hotels and offices, it is an elaborately-decorated mini-temple.

In either case, these spirit houses serve as the abodes of the resident spirits. It is within their power to favor or plague the human inhabitants of the real house or building, so the spirit house is regularly adorned with placative offerings of food, fresh flowers

widespread reputation for bringing good fortune to outsiders as well.

A less well-known shrine sits in the compound of the Hilton Hotel. Its offerings consist entirely of phalluses, ranging from small to gargantuan, sculpted from wood, wax, stone or cement, and with fidelity to life. They are left by women hoping to conceive a child, or unable to do so.

Many of the Thais' non-Buddhist beliefs are Brahman in origin, and even today Brahman priests officiate at major ceremonies. The Thai wedding ceremony is almost entirely Brahman, as are many funeral rites.

The rites of statecraft pertaining to the royal family are presided over by Brahman

and incense sticks. If calamity or ill luck befalls the compound, it may be necessary to call in an expert to consult the spirit to determine what is wrong.

One of the most famous spirit houses in Bangkok is the Erawan Shrine, at the intersection of Ratchadamri and Ploenchit roads. This shrine, honoring the Hindu god Brahma, was erected by the owners during the construction of the original hotel in the 1950s, after several workers were injured in mysterious accidents. The shrine soon acquired a

Left, a spirit house. **Above left**, malai, Buddhist flower offerings. **Above right**, spirit house.

priests. One of the most popular and impressive of these, the Plowing Ceremony, takes place each May in Bangkok. To signal the beginning of the rice planting season, a team of sacred oxen is offered a selection of grains. Astrologers watch carefully, as the grains the oxen choose will determine the amount of rainfall, and the degree of success or failure of the year's crops. Afterwards, the oxen draw a gilded plow around the field and seeds are symbolically sown (and afterwards eagerly collected by farmers to bring them luck). The head priest makes predictions on the forthcoming rainfall and the bounty of the next harvest.

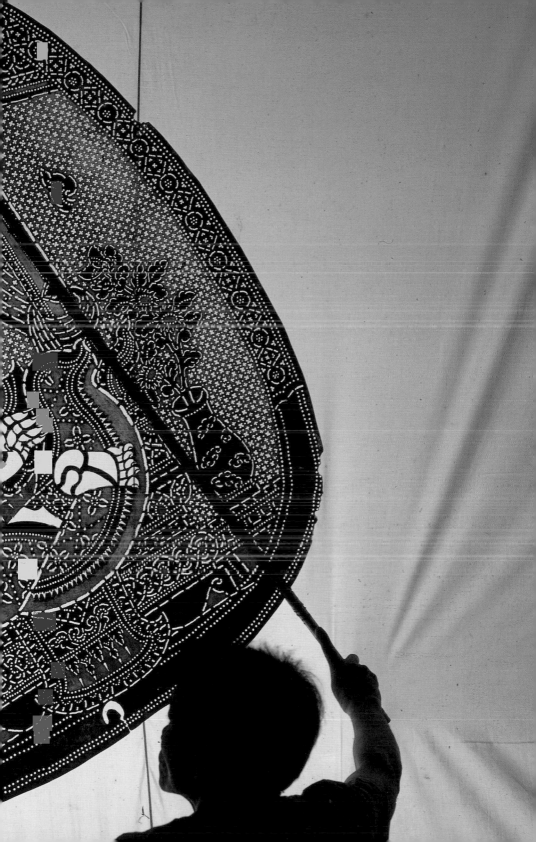

In all of Southeast Asia, the symbols and aesthetics of Thailand's culture are perhaps the most widely recognized by outsiders. Indeed, the Thai people have combined a lively imagination, a superb aesthetic sense and a fine hand to produce some of the most detailed and arresting visual arts found in Asia. And in the performing arts, Thai dance dramas are among the world's most dazzling, with elaborate and colorful costumes, and graceful, enchanting movements.

Drama and dance: When discussing Thai theater, one cannot use the word "drama" without uttering the word "dance" immediately before it. The two are inseparable, as the dancer's hands and body express the emotions that the silent lips do not. In effect, the actor is a mime, with the story line and lyrics provided by a singer and chorus to the side of the stage. An orchestra creates not only the atmosphere, but an emotive force.

It is thought that the movements of dance-drama originated in the *nang yai* performances of the 16th and 17th centuries. Huge buffalo hides were cut into the shapes of characters from the *Ramakien*. Against a translucent screen, which was backlit by torches, puppeteers manipulated these shadow puppets to tell complex tales of good and evil. As they moved the hide figures across the screen, the puppeteers danced the emotions they wanted the stiff figures to convey. It is thought that these movements evolved into an independent theatrical art.

The most popular form of dance-drama is the *khon,* performed by dancers wearing brilliantly-crafted masks. An evening's entertainment comprises several episodes from the *Ramakien.* (The entire *Ramakien* would take 720 hours to perform, slightly longer than even the most feverish theater-goer is prepared to endure.)

The expressionless masks focus the viewer's attention on the dancers' movements, where one sees grace and control of surpassing beauty – a dismissive flick of the hand, a finger pointed in accusation, a foot stamped

Preceding pages: leather fan puppet. Left, the masked khon dancer's personality is unseen. Right, young dancers at a wat.

in anger. The favorite character is Hanuman, in his white monkey mask, whose dance movements would tax even the strongest viewer. Only the characters of Rama, Sita and Phra Lak appear without masks, but features are kept stiff, looking like masks.

The most graceful of the dramatic arts is the *lakhon.* There are two forms: the *lakhon nai* (inside lakhon), which was once performed only inside the palace walls, and then only by women, and the *lakhon nawk* (outside lakhon), performed beyond the palace

walls by men. Lakhon nai is more popular.

Garbed in costumes as elaborate as their movements, the performers glide slowly about the stage; even in the most emotional moments, their faces are impassive and devoid of smiles or expression. The heavily-stylized movements convey the plot and are quite enchanting, though for most foreign visitors, 30 minutes is sufficient to absorb the essentials of the play. Lakhon's rich repertoire includes the *Ramakien,* and tales like *Inao* that have romantic storylines.

There have always been two cultures in Thailand: palace and village. The village arts are often parodies of the palace arts, but more like burlesques with pratfalls and heavy-handed humor. *Likay* is the village form of lakhon. Broad, bawdy humor is its mainstay, played out against gaudy backdrops to an audience that walks in and out of the performance at will, eating and talking and having a good time, regardless of what takes place on stage.

It is possible to glimpse likay at a wat fair, or at Bangkok's Lak Muang, when a troupe is hired by a worshipper to give thanks for a wish granted or a lottery number that has hit. A variant often seen in markets is *lakhon ling*, the monkey theater where the roles are played, as the name suggests, by monkeys.

Bangkok's *ngiew* or Chinese opera thea-

often arranged by major hotels for their guests during the year-end holiday season.

Modern Thai drama has yet to come into its own in a major way. Leading hotels produce stage plays, but they are primarily for popular entertainment – pastiches, soap operas, comedies, and direct translations from plays that were popular in the West.

The counterparts to the grace and beauty of classical dance are the traditional dances performed in villages by farm families. Each region has its own special form.

Harvest, fingernail, candle and fishing dances are performed by groups of women in village costumes. In dances of flirtation, they are joined by male dancers who attempt to

ters have closed their doors forever, victims of television with its unending kung fu programs. Wandering in a market at night, however, one may come across a performance that has been arranged as part of the entertainment during a funeral. (Grief is experienced privately; what one shares with friends is happiness.) They can also be seen at wat fairs during the winter.

Puppet theater has also lost most of its Bangkok audiences to television, but a few troupes remain. *Hoon krabok* puppets, similar to Punch and Judy puppets, tell the story of *Phra Aphaimani*. Delicately crafted, they are charming to watch. Performances are

weave romantic spells around their unsmiling but appreciative partners.

Music: Classical Thai music eludes many finely-tuned Western ears. To the uninitiated, it sounds like a mishmash of contrasting tones without any pattern. To aficionados, it has a very distinct rhythm and plan. The key is to listen to it as one would jazz, picking out one of the instruments and following it, switching to another as the mood moves one. Thai music is set to a scale of seven full steps, but it is normally played as a pentatonic scale (the scale of *Auld Lang Syne*). The rhythm is lilting and steady, with speeds varying according to section. Each instrument plays the same melody, but in its own way and seemingly without regard to how others are playing it. (One might say the same about Thai politics.)

Seldom does an instrument rise in uninterrupted solo; it is always being challenged, cajoled by the other instruments of the orchestra. In a sense, it is the aural counterpart to Thai classical painting, with every space filled and a number of separate strands woven together, seemingly at random but with a distinct pattern.

A classical *phipat* music orchestra is made up of a single reed instrument, the oboe-like *phi nai*, and a variety of percussion instruments. The pitch favors the treble, with the

result that the music sounds airy rather than stentorian. The pace is set by the *ching*, a tiny cymbal, aided by the drums beaten with the fingers. The melody is played by two types of *ranad*, a bamboo-bar xylophone and two sets of *gong wong*, tuned gongs arranged in a semi circle around the player. Another type of orchestra employs two violins, the *saw-oo* and the *saw-duang*. It is usually heard accompanying a Thai dance-drama.

The *ja-kae*, a stringed instrument similar to a Japanese *koto*, sits flush with the floor

Left, girls learn the subtleties of finger movements for dance. **Above**, dance in art.

and is often played as a solo instrument in the lobbies of some of Bangkok's larger hotels and restaurants. A separate type of orchestra performs at a Thai boxing match to spur the combatants to action: four instruments: the *ching*, two double-reed oboe-like flutes, and a drum. It plays a repertoire entirely its own.

Originating in the countryside, but having found a permanent home in the city as well, are the *klawng yao* or long drums. They are thumped along with gongs and cymbals as accompaniment to group singing. Never played solemnly, they lend an exuberant note to any occasion – and for a Thai, it doesn't take much of an excuse to have an occasion. It may be a procession on the way to ordain a new monk, a bus trip upcountry, or a *kathin* ceremony in the late autumn, when groups board boats to travel up-river to give robes to monks at the end of the three-month lenten season.

The klawng yao beat an infectious rhythm, inviting one to join in a *ramwong*, a dance that, despite its simple steps and body movements, eludes most foreigners' attempts to execute. (One's participation, not skill, is important to a Thai. No one will force you; the rewards for joining are laughter and warm acceptance.)

Literature: Thais have always placed a heavy emphasis on oral tradition. It's a lucky thing. Aside from some inscribed steles and stones, most of its classical written literature was completely destroyed when the Burmese burned Ayutthaya to the ground in 1767.

Moreover, as tropical insects relish palm leaf paper on which tales were written, books are manifest – examples of the Buddhist tenet that nothing is permanent. Most of the classical works which survive today are the product of late night sessions during the reigns of Rama I and II when scholars delved into their collective memories and recreated a literature on palace verandas.

At the heart of Thai literature is the *Ramakien*, the Thai version of the Indian classic tale, the *Ramayana*. The enduring story has found a home in the literature, dance and drama of every southeast Asian nation. In Thailand, it is the basis of a dance drama tradition. Familiarity with the *Ramakien* enables one to comprehend a variety of dramatic forms; its significance for the Thai monarchy, which adopted the title "Rama" for kings in the 1920s; and its role as

RAMAYANA AND RAMAKIEN

One of the two great Indian epics informing Thai theatre and dance is the *Ramayana.* (The other one is the *Mahabharata.*) From the Sanskrit meaning romance of Rama, the *Ramayana* is the basis for many of Southeast Asia's epic tales, including Thailand's *Ramakien.* It's a moral tale, full of instructions and examples on how to lead the good life. It praises the rectitude, wisdom and perseverance of the noble *satriya* or warrior class, and stresses faithfulness, integrity and filial and fraternal devotion.

The *Ramayana* acknowledges that the trek along the path of virtue demands humility, self-

sacrifice, deprivation and compassion. It is a cautionary tale – less a battle between good and evil (in which evil must always lose) than a recognition of the perpetual ebb and flow of the spirits of darkness and light.

In its homeland, India, the *Ramayana* has been known for 3,000 years. With the spread of Indian religions and culture through Southeast Asia, the *Ramayana* became part of the mythology of Burma, Thailand, Laos, Cambodia, the Malay Peninsula, and Indonesia. The epic is long and complex.

The characters: In the *Ramayana,* the chief characters are Rama, his wife Sita, his brother Laksmana, the monkey general Hanuman, the demon king Rawana, and Rawana's brother, Wibisana. Rama is semi-divine (an incarnation

of Visnu), and a consummate archer. Rama is of noble birth, for he moves in a refined (*halus*) manner. Even in battle, he is graceful and delicate, using his mind as much as muscles. Rawana, Rama's implacable foe, thrusts and struts upon the stage, every step filled with menace. His head turns sharply with each movement. His face (whether a grease-painted human one, a mask, or a puppet head) is an impassioned, furious red in keeping with his aggressive, hostile nature.

The Story: Rama, Laksmana and their half-brother, Barata, are the sons of the king of Ayodya. An accomplished bowman, Rama wins the hand of beautiful Sita in an archery contest, but through the intervention of Barata's mother, Rama is prevented from succeeding his father as king. Rama, Sita and Laksmana go into exile, refusing Barata's entreaties to return. In the forest they meet a sister of Rawana, king of the demons (*raksasas*); she falls in love with Rama, is spurned, and then turns to Laksmana, who promptly cuts off her nose and ears.

Rawana, determined to avenge this indignity, sends off a servant in the form of a golden deer. Rama stalks the animal and kills it. Its dying cries sound like Rama calling for help, and Laksmana, taunted by Sita, goes in search of his brother. In his absence Rawana appears as a holy beggar and confronts Sita, who refuses his appeals to desert Rama. Rawana assumes his natural terrifying form, abducts Sita, and flies off with her.

Searching for Sita, the brothers meet Hanuman, a general in the kingdom of the apes, who takes them to meet Sugriwa, his king. Sugriwa, who has been usurped by his brother, seeks Rama's aid in regaining his throne. Rama kills the errant brother, and the grateful monkey king places his army at Rama's disposal. Rama and Laksmana set off with Hanuman and the white ape army, and learn that Rawana has carried Sita across the sea to the island of Langka, Rawana's homeland. Hanuman undertakes a daring reconnaissance of Langka and finds Sita in a garden of Rawana's palace. He gives her a token from Rama, and Sita in turn gives Hanuman one of her rings, but Hanuman is discovered by Rawana's guards, captured after a desperate fight, and is sentenced to be burnt at the stake. With the pyre blazing, he wrenches free, his tail a mass of flames, and sets fire to the palace before fleeing from Langka.

Hanuman carries Sita's ring to Rama, and the ape armies gather on the shore opposite Langka and build a giant causeway across the sea. On the island, a tumultuous battle ensues. One of Rama's magic arrows eventually fells Rawana, and the victors return home with Sita to a boisterous welcome. Rama receives the throne from his half-brother Barata. ∎

a model for exemplary behavior. The *Ramakien* is a vivid, epic tale of the god-king Rama and his beautiful wife, Sita, paragon of virtue and model for all wives. Sita is abducted by the nasty 10-headed, 20-armed demon king Tosakan, who imprisons her in his palace on the island of Longka (present-day Sri Lanka). Tosakan begs her to divorce Rama and marry him.

With his brother Phra Lak, Rama sets off in pursuit, stymied by mammoth obstacles to test his mettle. Along the way, he is joined by the magical monkey god, Hanuman, a mischievous but resourceful general who is one of Thai's favorite characters. Hanuman and his army of monkeys build a bridge to Longka.

A classical work, pure Thai in its flavor and treatment, is *Khun Chang*. Khun Phaen, a love triangle involving a beautiful young women with two lovers, one a rich, blad widower and the other, a poor but handsome young man. This ancient soap opera provides a useful insight into Thai manners and morals of the Ayutthaya period.

Written by Sunthorn Phu, the poet laureate of the early 18th century, Phra Aphaimani is the story of a rebellious prince who refuses to study to be king. Instead, he plays the flute, much to the disgust of his father. After numerous exciting adventures, the prodigal son returns home to don the crown and rule his father's realm. These stories or segments of

After a pitched battle, Tosakin is killed, Sita is rescued, and all live happily ever after. Or until the sequel.

The 547 enduring Jataka tales are also of Indian origin. They tell of Buddha's reincarnations before he became enlightened, though some are probably based on tales that existed before Buddha lived. The first tales were translated from Pali to Thai in the late 15th century. They have generated many other popular and classic stories and are still retold like fairy tales to Thai children.

Above, story-telling was both oral and visual, such as this temple painting.

them can be seen in Bangkok drama theaters or in restaurants offering cultural shows.

Although Thais began to translate and loosely adapt Chinese sagas and mediocre Western novels in the latter 19th century, it wasn't until the 1920s that genuine Thai novels were published. Running through the quality novel ever since has been a strong thread of social or political criticism. During the first few decades, novelists moved from trenchant attacks on the old existing elite to the rising military elits.

In the 1950s, however, censorship became so heavy and writers were so harshly persecuted that quality fiction practically disappeared for 20 years. Those writers who were not exiled, jailed or silenced resorted to churning out pulp romance, which Thais dub "stagnant water literature". As the literati lament, Thailand is not a "reading culture" and if Thais read for pleasure at all, this is it.

The overthrow of military dictators in 1973 precipitated a heady, anarchic three years in which burned books were revived and formerly banned writers rediscovered. With Marxism in the air, a work was often judged by how well it advocated the interests of the Thai poor or furthered the way to revolution. Aesthetic merit was a secondary factor. This schism between "art-for-life" and "art-for-art" still lingers in all the arts today, from

in China. The last spent more than five years as a communist guerrilla.

Architecture: It is odd that influences so diverse as those of India, Cambodia and China could be combined to produce an architecture that is unique, bearing little resemblance to its progenitors. Thai architecture does it brilliantly.

The style of Bangkok's classical temples and palaces are the final step in a long process of evolution that saw architectural styles change from massive to light; it is perhaps similar to Romanesque evolving into the Gothic architecture of medieval Europe.

Like the architecture of Angkor Wat, every part of a Thai wat has symbolic significance.

literature to music to painting to sculpture.

After a brief return to the dark ages in the late 1970s, Thai writers since the 1980s have enjoyed almost total political freedom. While they remain social critics, they are striving to create work of literary merit. Probably all the best writers under age 50 today are of modest or dirt-poor origins.

Only a handful of Thai novels and modern short stories have been translated into English, but more are in the pipeline. Look for the names Kularp Saipradit (Seeboorapha), K. Surangkhanang, Chart Korpjjtti and Sila Khoamchai. The first was a courageous journalist who died at the end of a 17-year exile

The capitals of columns are shaped either like water lilies or lotus buds, the lotus symbolizing the purity of Buddha's thoughts, in that it pushes through the muck of swamps to burst forth in extraordinary beauty.

The typical wat (temple) consists of a *bot* (ordination hall) and a varying number of *viharn* (assembly halls) and tower-like structures for the preservation of relics, or *chedi* (also known in Indian-style temples as stupa). The bot, which is reserved for the use of the monks, is surrounded by eight *sema,* or marker stones. Often, the sema are the only distinguishing feature that separate the bot from the viharn, which contains the most important Buddha statues. Temple complexes dating from the Khmer period have a tower-like prang at its center, at the base of which is a sacred phallic symbol (*lingam*). Buddha statues demonstrate one of four symbolic basic positions: sitting (meditation), lying in death (passing into nirvana), standing, and walking. These positions are also differentiated by specific hand positions.

The mingling of Thai-Buddhist and Khmer-Hindu cultures, which occurred from the 10th century onwards, especially in central Thailand, introduced a number of Hindu elements to Thailand's iconography. Popular figures include the four-armed Vishnu; the *garuda* (a half-man, half-bird creature)

"by royal appointment". Every other other element on a wat has roots in ancient myth and legend.

Palace architecture conveys a lightness similar to that of the wat, employing many of the same motifs and materials. Homes for ordinary people share the same sensitive treatment as those for the exalted. Thai-style teak houses, with their inward-sloping walls and steep roofs, seldom fail to charm with their airiness and their marvelous adaptation to tropical climates.

Raised high off the ground on stilts, they are the perfect foil for floods and other intruders, but allow the free-flow of cool breezes. The best example is the Jim Th-

and its female equivalent, the *kinnari;* the eight-armed Shiva; elephant-headed Ganesh; the three-headed elephant Erawan; the ghost-banishing giant Yak; and the *naga,* a snake that appears sometimes as a cobra and sometimes as a dragon.

The *cho-fa* on the end of the temple roof represents the garuda, the vehicle of Vishnu; in its claws it holds two naga, mythical serpents that undulate down the eaves. The garuda is also a royal symbol and companies bearing it on their building facades operate

Left, refined architecture, monk's quarters, Wat Arun. **Above**, lacquer hats, Royal Barge oarsmen.

ompson house, with its superb collection of Thai art; numerous other examples line the banks of the silvery network of canals that crisscross the Thonburi suburbs.

Sculpture: The focal point of the bot and viharn interior of a wat is the Buddha image. The image is not considered a representation of the Buddha, but is instead meant to serve as a reminder of his teachings. The casting in bronze, or carving in wood or stone, of Buddha images constitutes the bulk of Thai sculpture. Buddha images epitomize the zenith of the sculpting art and employ some of the finest artistry (and hence command some of the highest prices) of any arts. Superb examples of bas-relief sandstone carving can be seen around the base of the bot of Bangkok's Wat Po. Delicately executed, the dozens of panels depict scenes from the *Ramakien* drama.

Painting: In similar manner, the inner walls of the bot and viharn are traditionally covered in paintings, usually displaying a high degree of skill. In the days before public education, a wat was the principal repository of knowledge for the common person. Monks were the teachers, and the interior walls of the temples were illustrated lectures.

The principal themes are the life of Buddha and the *Tosachat*, the last ten of 550 *chadok* (incarnations) of a single soul before

he was born as the Buddha, thus ending a long cycle of lives and passing into nirvana.

The back wall generally depicts the *Maravijaya*, or Victory over Mara, in which all the earthly temptations are united to break the meditating Buddha's will and prevent his achieving nirvana. He is guarded by the goddess Mae Toranee, who helps him by wringing out her hair, sending a torrent of water to drown the evil spirits.

The murals at Wat Buddhaisawan in Bangkok's National Museum are among the finest examples of Thai painting. Others include the murals at Wat Suthat and the avant garde 19th-century paintings at Wat Bowon Niwet.

Although restored several times with less-than-perfect accuracy or regard for previous artists' efforts, the *Ramakien* murals in the cloisters that surround Wat Phra Kaeo include wonderful, whimsical scenes of village and palace life.

Minor arts: Thai classical minor arts are marked by a delicacy and sureness of execution. Among the most stunning are the lacquer and gold works that cover the window shutters of most bot and viharn. Thai artists employ the time-honored technique of covering a plank of wood with seven coats of *lac,* the black sap of the sumac tree. A scene is drawn on a sheet of rice paper and a pin is used to prick holes along the outlines. The paper is then laid on the lacquered wood and a bag of ashes or lime is tapped gently against the paper. When the paper is removed, lines of ash-white dots remain to indicate the original pattern.

The artist then paints, with the yellow sap of the *mai khwit* tree, all the areas he wishes to remain black, much the same way a batik artist paints with wax those areas whose color he does not wish to change. When the paint has dried, he covers the entire surface with gold leaf. When the wood is gently washed with water, the gold over the mai khwit-painted areas washes away, leaving the gold figures to gleam against the midnight sheen of the lacquer.

The best examples of lacquer painting can be found on walls of the Lacquer Pavilion, in the Suan Pakkad Palace. It also decorates the ornate manuscript cabinets found at Suan Pakkad and in the Buddhaisawan Chapel.

Mother-of-pearl, as executed by Thai artists, differs from its Chinese counterpart both in the material and the technique used. Thai artisans use the Turban shell, which secretes nacreous material along its outer rim, meaning it will not peel with age.

Moreover, Thai artists cut the patterns in small bits, affix them to a wooden panel and fill the spaces in between with the same black lac used in lacquer and gold artworks. Two of the finest examples are the 200-year-old doors of Wat Po, with scenes from the *Ramakien,* and the doors of Wat Ratchabophit, which depict in tiny detail the royal decorations awarded to nobles of old.

Left, Buddha at a Thonburi factory. **Right**, a lacquered window depicting foreign traders.

Thailand's biological treasures and diverse land forms derive from its geographical position as the crossroads of Southeast Asia. Just as the nation has accommodated many peoples and cultures, so it has served as a conduit dispersing plant and animal life.

Roughly the size of France, Thailand covers some 513,115 square kilometres (198,115 sq mi). The overall shape resembles that of an elephant's head, with the southern peninsula forming the trunk. The most conspicuous landscape features are striated mountains

enclosing cultivated valleys, but there are great contrasts in the six geographical regions that make up Thailand. In the north, extending along the borders of Burma and Laos, great parallel mountains run from north to south, reaching over 2,000 metres (6,500 ft) in height. The valleys have been cultivated for centuries, but until 50 years ago — with the proliferation of slash-and-burn farming — there was considerable forest cover in the higher altitudes.

To the south, the vast valley called the Central Plain stretches 450 kilometres (300 mi) to the Gulf of Thailand. The overflowing tributaries traditionally deposited nutrient-rich silt that created a thriving agricultural rice bowl. The farms these days are supported by intensive irrigation, courtesy of a network of highly controversial big dams. The western region consists mostly of mountain ranges, the source of tributaries of the Mekong, Chao Phraya and Salween rivers. Sparsely populated by humans, this region is the richest repository of wildlife.

The northeast, one of the poorest regions in Thailand, encompasses the broad and shallow Khorat Plateau, which lies less than 200 metres (650 ft) above sea level. This is a land of poor soils, little rain, too many people, and a bit of grass and shrub. The sandstone base has weathered into strange shapes in this harsh environment.

The small, hilly southeast coast is bordered on the north by the Cardomom Range, which protrudes from Cambodia. It includes 80 rocky, forested islands. Intense heat and violent underground pressures created the rubies and sapphires that are mined here. Endowed with the heaviest rainfall and humidity, the south covers the isthmus all the way down to the Malaysian peninsula. Coastal forests were cleared for rubber and palm plantations. But some 275 islands, especially in the western Andaman Sea, support unique species and are surrounded by coral reefs.

The limestone rock so common on the Andaman side was once seabed. Soft and easily eroded, it is limestone that is the basis of the crumbly mountains and jutting islets. Underground streams in limestone have also created the many spectacular caves.

Flora: Sixty years ago, forests covered about 70 percent of Thailand's land area. In 1960, the figure had dropped to 50 percent. Today, probably only about 15 percent of undisturbed forest remains, although perhaps another 15 percent of it has been replanted, often with non-indigenous species, or else turned into plantations growing the likes of palm-oil trees or eucalyptus. Aside from tiny Singapore, the scale and rate of forest loss in Thailand is the greatest in Southeast Asia. Following fatal landslides, logging was finally outlawed in 1989, but trucks ferrying contraband logs are still a common sight.

The country's forests can be classified as either evergreen or deciduous; the latter shed leaves seasonally. There are many subcategories in between, and a single habitat may contain both types of trees. Evergreen forests are, of course, green all year round. They are most abundant in the uplands of both south and southeast Thailand, where rainfall is plentiful and the dry season is brief. Rain forests are generally classified as evergreen forests.

Contrary to many preconceptions, all

as 60 metres (200 ft). Healthy rain forests can be found in the Khao Luang, Koh Surin, Tarutao and Thale Ban national parks, all located in the south.

More common than rain forest is the broad-leaved evergreen forest, which is found at higher elevations. Here are found temperate-zone laurels, oaks and chestnuts, along with ferns, rhododendrons and the yew-like podocarps. A wide variety of orchids also proliferate. Usually, the ground level consists of shrubs and grasses that attract larger

tropical forests are not evergreen, and all evergreen forest is not necessarily rain forest. A rain forest is a four-layered forest harbouring the world's densest concentration of species. Herbs, shrubs, ferns and fungi form the bottom layer. A relatively open layer of palms, bamboos and shrubs is above ground level while mid-level trees, festooned with vines, mosses and orchids, create a 25-metre-high (80 ft) canopy. The well-spaced trees of the upper-most canopy soar as high

Left, limestone hills in north Thailand. **Above**, a particularly beautiful specimen of the 1,200 species of butterflies found in Thailand.

mammals. The leaves of the taller dipterocarps turn yellow and red before shedding in the dry season. A few weeks later, they burst into bright purple, pink, orange and red flowers.

About a hundred years ago, deciduous forests of the north were thick with teak trees, but virtually all were cut long ago.

Fauna: Of the world's 4,000 species of mammals, 287 can be found in Thailand: 13 species of primates, 18 hoofed species, nine of wild cats (including tigers and clouded leopards), two of bear, two of wild dogs and eight of dolphins. Bats are abundant, with 107 species identified so far. Tigers and the larger deer could soon join the list of mammals that have vanished this century – rhinoceros, several species of deer, two otter species, and the kouprey, wild cattle that were discovered in Thailand in the 1930s.

Declared the country's first protected species back in 1921, the Asian elephant is the national mascot, but nonetheless is perilously close to extinction. From well above 20,000 a century ago, fewer than 8,000 survive in Thailand today. Most of these are domesticated, many begging on Bangkok's hard streets. Khao Yai National Park offers the best chance of observing some of the few thousand remaining wild elephants.

Thailand also harbours four types of reptiles

and three types of amphibians. Among 175 species of snakes are deadly cobras, kraits and vipers. No doubt most of the insect species haven't been identified yet, but there are 1,200 variegated butterflies. Beetle species may number in the tens of thousands, but have been so little studied that amateurs occasionally discover a new one.

Visitors of national parks and sanctuaries may not see any large animals, but they will be compensated with sightings of birds. There are around 900 species that are permanent residents of the region. In the north are the colourful montane birds with Sino-Himalayan affinities. The birds of the south

are similar to those of Malaysia. There are also about 240 wintering and non-breeding migrants that pass through.

Marine life: Off the west coast, the flora and fauna of the Andaman Sea are characteristic of the Indian Ocean. Off the east coast, in the Gulf of Thailand, they are characteristic of Indo-Pacific seas. Coral reefs off both coastlines have been little surveyed, but they support at least 400 species of fish and 30 of sea snakes. The corals themselves come in almost 300 species, with the Andaman Sea boasting a far greater diversity. Intact reefs survive only in areas far from human habitation, such as the vicinity of the Surin and Similan islands.

Environment at risk: As many of the aforementioned remarks concerning habitats and wildlife indicate, Thailand's ecology is an environment in danger of irreversible damage. With the destruction of habitats, be they forests or coral reefs, so could disappear many more species of flora and fauna, not only from Thailand, but from the world.

The Forestry Department, which includes the Parks Service, is underfunded and understaffed. In the past few decades, at least 40 rangers have been murdered in the line of duty. Earning less than most factory workers, many rangers also collude with poachers of logs and animals. The country's poorest people inadvertently contribute to the degradation by farming on protected lands. In addition, the demands of Chinese-Thais and Chinese visitors – for both medicinal purposes and gourmet "jungle" dining – further threaten the endangered populations of tigers, bears and deer.

Tourism undoubtedly plays a considerable role in the degradation of Thailand's ecosystems, most visibly when beach hotels spew untreated sewage into the seas. But there are also signs that tourism might conceivably become a positive force in the preservation of what remains of Thailand's ecology. There are encouraging signs that a few Thais – among them trekking guides and local green groups, and even a few progressive politicians – are becoming aware that environmental caretaking will sustain tourism longer than continued destruction.

Plunge into a Bangkok market and one plunges into a vibrant and vigorous grassroots economy, a venue to bargain and feign. Haggling is an essential art, of course, but pursue it in a light-hearted fashion. Don't make an issue over a few baht. You won't win, and, in any case, you'll probably end up paying more than the locals anyway.

Hugging Paholyothin Road, the **Chatuchak weekend market** is situated on over 30 acres of land holding at least 5,000 stall holders. What they sell is the world – a

sizeable portion of it, anyway. Some prices in the market are fixed, others are for bargaining. Afternoons are hot, so it is wise to limit bargaining to the morning hours.

Pratunam market, in the city center, is Chatuchak on a smaller scale and with a smaller selection. Hole-in-the-wall tailoring shops can whip together an outfit copied from a magazine picture. Off the rack, few tourists are likely to be interested in the skimpy sequined bikinis with *Hot* emblazoned on the rear, which go-go dancers examine with the intensity of a sommelier studying a bottle of Mouton Rothschild.

Bangrak market on New Road is another victim of urban change. Vastly reduced in size and relocated in a building behind the original, it has lost some of its flavor but none of its spirit. Its specialties are floral wreaths and garlands, fashioned into stunning works of art through hours of painstaking work.

Located on the banks of Padung Krung Kasem canal, **Thewes market** is the favorite spot for plant lovers. There are crotons and caladiums, dieffenbachia and dendrobia, creepers and climbers – not to mention orchids, thousands of the more than 25,000 orchid species found worldwide.

Another venue is **Chatuchak flower market**, south of the weekend market and across Yan Paholyothin Road.

Pak Klong Talat, at the foot of the Memorial Bridge, is the city's provisioner and the point of entry for vegetables, fruits and flowers, unloaded from boats at the docks and snapped up by restaurateurs and grocers.

Between Yaowaraj and New roads, near the western end of Chinatown, is **Nakorn Kasem**, or **Thieves Market**. A few decades ago, it was the area a householder searched after having been robbed, and where it was likely they would recover their wayward goods, and for a very reasonable price. It later became an antique dealer's area. The antiques, however, have been nudged aside by more prosaic items like automotive parts and cement mixers.

A recent phenomenon is the emergence of **night markets**. Perhaps inspired by the success of Chiang Mai's well-known night market, many entrepreneurs have banded together to turn empty daytime spaces into night-time emporia, selling clothes, art objects, cheap souvenirs, and music cassettes. Knowing that every shopper has limited endurance, many enterprising stall holders have set up bars selling drinks and snacks.

The most extensive markets are at the railway tracks near Soi 1, Sukhumvit Road; on Sukhumvit itself between Soi 5 and Soi 11; on Gaysorn Road near Le Meridien President Hotel; along the upper end of Silom Road; and down the middle of Patpong Road.

Left, Sunday market at Chatuchak. **Right**, flower market at Pak Klong Talad.

Best to diet before coming to Thailand, especially if harboring plans for bikini-and-beach time. Once in Thailand, and especially in Bangkok, there's little chance of tending to one's vanity. The food is simply too tempting, and too available.

While it's true that there are very spicy regional dishes – certain southern Thai curries are notable – most Thai food is not hot at all. Generally, an authentic Thai meal will include at least one very spicy dish, a few that are less hot, and some that are bland, fla-

its own, one of the most flavorful rices in Asia. (The Japanese say its taste is far too strong.) Try a few spoons of plain rice before you get into the meal and discover just how delicious it in fact is.

At the start of the meal, heap some rice onto a plate and then take a spoonful or two of curry. It is considered polite to take only a little bit at a time, consuming it before ladling more onto the rice.

Thais eat with the spoon in their right hand and fork in their left, the fork being used

vored with only garlic or herbs. Usually, purely Thai creations will take their place alongside adapted Chinese and Indian dishes, influences that are easy to spot.

Dishes are placed in the middle of the table and shared by all, so it makes sense to eat with a large group, with more dishes to try.

Thai food is eaten with rice. Traditionally, the curries were secondary to the meal, a means of pepping up tastebuds so one would eat more rice.

Even today, rural Thais eat enormous quantities of rice with nothing more than bits of dried and salted fish. Chilies are also a means of spicing up Thai rice, even though it is, on

primarily to shovel the food onto the spoon for transport to the mouth. Chopsticks are used only for Chinese noodle dishes.

There seems to be some confusion among those who have sampled their first Thai meals abroad, in particular, regarding the proper condiments to add to the food. Much to their surprise, they discover that peanut sauce, an "indispensable" addition to every dish in Thai restaurants in Western countries, is really of Malayan and Indonesian origin; in Thailand, it is used only for *satay*. Similarly, instead of salt, Thais rely on *nam plaa,* or fish sauce, splashing a bit of it on the rice and mixing it in.

Spicy dishes: *Keng* means curry, which includes the spiciest of Thai dishes and forms the core of Thai cooking.

Among the green curries is *keng kiaw wan kai*, a gravy filled with chunks of chicken and tiny pea-sized eggplants. A relative, *keng kiaw wan nua*, has bits of beef in it. *Keng luang*, a category of yellow curries, includes *keng karec*, which is also made with chicken or sometimes beef.

Keng pet is a red curry with beef. A close relative is *penung nua*, a so-called "dry"

generally translated as salad and is as much meat as vegetable. It is also quite hot. Among the non-spicy curry dishes is a favorite among foreigners: *tom ka kai*, a thick coconut milk curry of chicken chunks with lemon grass.

Plaamuk tawt kratium prik tai is squid fried with garlic and black pepper. When ordering, ask that the garlic (*kratium*) be fried crispy (*krawp krawp*). The dish is also prepared with fish.

Keng joot is a non-spicy curry, a clear broth filled with glass noodles, minced pork

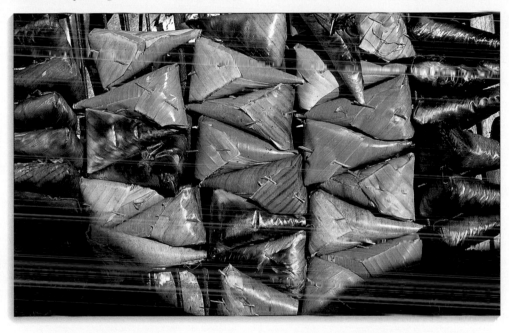

curry with beef in a tasty paste.

Among the fiery favorites is *tom yang kung*, a lemony broth teeming with shrimp. It is served in a metal tureen that is wrapped around a mini-furnace heated by charcoal, so that it remains piping hot throughout the meal. *Po tak* ("the fisherman's net bursts") is a cousin of *tom yang kung* – the broth also has squid, mussels, crab and other seafood.

Keng som is cooked in a sour soup but falls into the category of hot-and-sour soups. It is filled with bits of fish or shrimp. *Yam* is

Preceding pages: Lumpini Park. Left, sometimes spicy. **Above**, street-cooked meals.

and mushrooms. *Muu paat namman hoi* is beef in oyster sauce, with a few chopped shallots to add variety.

Muu paat praw wan, sweet-and-sour pork, is probably of Portuguese origin and arrived in Thailand via Chinese émigrés. It is also possible to order it with red snapper (*plaa krapong*), beef (*nua*) and shrimp (*kung*).

Homok talay is a seafood casserole of fish and shellfish chunks in a coconut mousse, steamed in a banana-leaf cup. *Keng musselman* is an unspiced curry. It consists of pieces of beef or chicken, combined with potatoes and onions in a brown gravy.

Of Chinese origin but having secured a

A CALENDAR OF FRUITS

Bangkok is especially fortunate to have a wide variety of fruits coming in and out of season throughout the year and a number, such as bananas (*gluay*), oranges (*som*), pomelos (*som-O*) and watermelons (*daeng mo*), that are available year-round.

Bananas, for example, are not just bananas – there are over 100 varieties, and are eaten fried, boiled, roasted, and, of course, raw. Watermelons are small but seductively-sweet and juicy. Pomelos are often mistaken for grapefruits; in fact, it is easy to eat, with rich and sweet juices that soothe and cool on a hot Bangkok day. Any fruit that can be peeled is a great street snack.

A calendar of fruit follows:

March–June: **Papaya** (*malagaw*). Especially tasty after the advent of the hot season. Thais like to squeeze lime juice on them to add a bit of tang. Shredded papaya is the main ingredient in *som tam*, a fiery salad popular in Northeastern Thailand.

March–July: **Sapodilla** (*lamood*). A surprisingly sweet, soft pulp fruit eaten peeled or halved and its sampled with a spoon. Beware of the big black seeds.

April–May: **Lichee** (*linchee*). Only a decade ago, this small fruit with its thin, hard shell was regarded as sour and not tasty. It is now grown to nearly twice its former size and sweetness. Resembling, the rambutan, the whitish flesh conceals a big black seed.

April–June: **Mango** (*mamuang*). Mangoes have lush yellow flesh is sweet, often bordering on tart. There are many ways of serving them but the old standard *khao niew mamuang* (mango and sticky rice) reigns supreme. They enjoy a strange relationship with the durian: if it is a good year for mangoes, the durian crop will be bad and vice-versa.

Durian. The durian is either hated or loved. The most expensive of Thai fruits, the durian is recognized by its hedgehog skin, the heavenly aroma (or disgusting stench to some) of its flesh, and by the rather mushy consistency of its meat. Try it in a coconut milk sauce on sticky rice. The durian has a reputation for producing gas, for heating up the one's innards. It is a small price to pay. Persevere and you will be rewarded.

April–July: **Pineapple** (*saparot*). Thailand is a top exporter of tinned pineapple and for good reason: its pineapples are sweet, with low acidity. Thais eat it sliced and garnished with salt and ground chilis which, odd as it sounds, enhances its natural sweetness.

Rose Apple (*chompoo*). The pink and green-skinned *chompoo* is pried apart with the fingers to reveal a crispy white meat with the texture of a delicate pear.

May–August: **Custard Apple** (*noi-na*). This light green hand-grenade with its knobby surface, can also be pulled apart by hand. The pulp is soft, often mushy, very sweet and very tasty. The pulpy fruit conceals long black seeds.

July–August: **Longan** (*lamyai*). A relative of the lichee and rambutan, it resembles the langsard with its thin yellow skin but has the lichee's sweetness.

July–September: **Rambutan** (*ngor*). Similar to the lichee, its skin is covered in thick red hairs. There is a technique to squeezing it open to avoid squirting oneself with its juices; any Thai can demonstrate. The flesh is translucent and sweet.

August–September: **Jackfruit** (*khanoon*). Dividing this enormous fruit into its myriad sections is best left to the experts. The rich yellow sections resemble buttercup blossoms, are waxy-textured and semi-sweet.

August–October: **Langsard**. The langsard's brownish-yellow skin conceals a fruit that is somewhat bitter and breaks into sections like a garlic cloves. **Mangosteen** (*mangkut*). The hard deep red shell conceals soft pulpy sections that ooze with sweetness. A favorite Thai game is to ask visitors to guess the number of sections it contains without breaking it open. (Count the number of "petals" in the woody flower on the bottom of the fruit.)

October–February: **Green Plum** (*putsa*). Shaped like a plum, putsa resemble green apples in color and pulp texture. ∎

place in Thai cuisine is *plaa jaramet nung kiem bueh*, steamed pomfret with Chinese plum and bits of ginger.

Pu paat pong karee is pieces of unshelled, steamed crab slathered in a curry sauce laden with shallots. *Hoi malang pu op moh din* is a thick, savory coconut milk gravy filled with mouthwatering mussels.

Noodles and others: Most noontime dishes are derived from Chinese cuisine, and noodle dishes, a Chinese invention, have been adopted by the Thais. Those served at streetside, open-front shops come in two varieties: wet and dry. When ordering either, specify the wetness by adding the word *nam* or *heng* to the dish's name. Thus, a wet *kuay tiaw* would be *kuay tiaw nam*.

Kuay tiew is a quick favorite: noodle soup with balls of fish or bits of beef. *Baa mii* is egg noodles with bits of meat and vegetable.

The rice based lunchtime dishes are also Chinese and include *kao mun kai*, boiled rice topped with slices of chicken and bits of ginger; *kao moo deng*, the same dish with pork slices; and *kao ka moo*, stewed pork with greens on rice.

Then there are the variants using noodles. *Kuay tiaw rawt naa* is broad white noodles boiled and served in a dish with morning glory. *Paat tai* is noodles fried in a wok with tofu and bits of vegetables. *Mii krawp* is crisp-fried noodles coated in honey and served with bits of vegetables.

Served late at night and early in the morning are two soup-like dishes filled with boiled rice. The rice in *kao tom* is watery and is augmented by bits of minced pork and shallots. A close relative is *jok*, in which the rice has been cooked until the liquid becomes viscous like a porridge. Into this mix is tossed ginger, coriander and bits of meat.

Each of Thailand's three regions has its own cuisine. Northern and northeastern cuisine are related to Lao dishes, which are eaten with glutinous rice. Southern food is flavored with the tastes of Malaysian and Muslim cooking.

Northern cuisine: Northern specialities are generally eaten with *kao niaw* or sticky rice, which is kneaded into a ball and dipped into various sauces and curries.

Sai oua (also called *naam*) is an oily, spicy

Left, some of the luscious fruits. **Right**, roadside service.

pork sausage that epitomizes northern cooking. The sausage is roasted over a fire fueled by coconut husks, which impart an aroma to the meat. Although it is usually hygienically prepared, it is best to buy it only at better restaurants. Beware the *prik kii nuu* chilies that lurk inside, waiting to explode on the tongues of the unwary.

Kao soy originated in Burma. This egg-noodle dish is filled with chunks of beef or chicken, then lightly curried in coconut cream and sprinkled with crispy noodles.

Nam prik ong combines minced pork with chilies, tomatoes, garlic and shrimp paste. It is served with crisp cucumber slices, parboiled cabbage leaves, and pork rind (the

latter is also a popular northern snack).

Laap is a minced pork, chicken, beef or fish dish that is normally associated with northeastern cuisine. While northeasterners traditionally eat it raw, northerners cook it thoroughly. It is served with long beans, mint leaves and other vegetables that contrast with its mellow flavor.

Keng hang lay, another dish of Burmese origin, is one of the spiciest of northern dishes and should be approached with caution. Pork and tamarind flesh give this curry a sweet-and-sour flavor. The curry is especially suited to dipping with a ball of sticky rice, quick and nifty.

Mieng, or fermented tea leaves, is also Burmese and is eaten as an hors d'oeuvre.

Northeastern cuisine: Northeastern food is simple and spicy. Like northern food, it is eaten with sticky rice, which *Isaan* (northeastern) diners claim weighs heavily on the brain and makes one sleepy.

Kai yang, or northeastern roasted chicken, has a flavor found in no other chicken. Basted with herbs and honey, it is roasted over an open fire and chopped into small pieces. Two dips, hot and sweet, are served with it.

Nua yang is beef dried like a jerky. One can chew for hours on a piece and still extract flavor from it. *Som tam* is the dish most associated with the northeast. It is a spicy

salad made from raw shredded papaya, dried shrimp, lemon juice and chilies.

Southern cuisine: *Kao yam* is rice with *kapi* (a paste made of fermented shrimp). *Paat pet sataw* looks like a lima bean but has a slightly bitter yet pleasant flavor. This dish is cooked with shrimp or pork, together with a sprinkling of chilies. *Kao mok kaj*, a Muslim dish, puts roasted chicken onto a bed of saffron rice and mixes it with ginger, which has been fried lightly to make it crisp.

Kanom chin is found throughout Thailand, but the south claims to have created it. Tiny bits of minced beef are stewed in a red sauce and then served atop rice noodles. It is gen-

erally sold in markets in the early morning.

Nam prik kung siap, or dried prawn on a stick, is grilled and served with chilies, *kapi* (fermented shrimp paste) and lime.

Keng tai plaa was created by bachelor fishermen who wanted a dish that would last them for days. Fish kidneys, chilies and vegetables are blended in a curry sauce and stewed for up to seven days. *Homok kai plaa* is made from fish roe that are stirred into a coconut mousse, wrapped in leaves and then cooked by steaming.

Chinese: Most Thai Chinese are of *tae-chiew* (*chiu chow* to a Hong Kong Chinese) descent, so the typical Thai Chinese restaurant serves *tae-chiew* dishes with a distinct Cantonese flavor. *Tae-chiew* is famed for dishes such as thick shark's fin soup, goose doused in soy sauce, and dried blood recipes that are not to everyone's taste. Fruits and teas are integral parts of every meal. Poultry, pork and seafood are essentials, as are a huge variety of fungi and mushrooms.

Other Chinese cuisines are well represented in Thailand. Shanghai food is typified by dishes that are fried in sesame or soy sauce for a long time, making them sweeter and oilier than other cuisines.

Liquids: The local beer is Singha, or, more popular with visitors, Kloster. Both are excellent, although some people claim that Singha can leave a more fearsome hangover. The local cane whiskey is called *mekhong* and packs a wallop for the unsuspecting. A bit sweet, it is drunk neat, or more popularly, mixed with club soda and lime.

Thailand has its own special coffee, mixed with a thick black melange of coffee, chicory and who knows what else, strong enough to set a dead person's heart beating. In the markets, Thais fill the bottom of the glass two fingers high with sweetened, condensed milk and pour the coffee over it. Ask for it black (the iced version is called *oliang*) to gain the full flavor of this exotic mixture.

Thai desserts: In Bangkok, desserts and sweets *(kanom)* come in a bewildering variety – from light concoctions through to custards, ice creams and cakes, along with an entire category of confections based upon egg yolks cooked in flower-scented syrups. Bananas and coconuts grow everywhere in Thailand, and if they were to be removed from the list of ingredients available to the *kanom* cook, the entire edifice of Thai dessert cookery would come crashing down. And woe to the traveler should such happen.

The heavier Thai confections are rarely eaten after a big meal. Desserts, served in small bowls, are generally light and elegant. *Kluay buat chii*, a popular after-dinner sweet, consists of banana chunks stewed in sweetened, slightly salted and scented coconut cream, and served warm. Another favorite, *taap tim krawp*, is made from small balls of tapioca flour, dyed red and shaped around tiny pieces of water chestnut. These are served in a mixture of sweetened, fragrant coconut cream and ice.

Anyone walking through a large Bangkok market is bound to come across a sweets

Excellent kanom of various types can be bought from roadside vendors, who prepare them on portable griddles. One such sweet is the *kanom beuang,* or "roof-tile cookie", which consists in one version of an extremely thin crispy shell folded over taco-style, and then filled with coconut, strands of egg yolk cooked in syrup, spiced and sweetened dried shrimp, coriander and a sugary cream.

In buying Thai sweets, picking what looks good is usually pretty disappointment-proof. *Sangkhya maprao awn* is a magnificent custard made from thick coconut cream, palm sugar and eggs, then steamed inside a young coconut or a small pumpkin. *Kao laam* is glutinous rice mixed with coconut cream,

vendor selling anything from candied fruits to million-calorie custards made from coconut cream, eggs and palm sugar. They are generally sold in the form of three-inch squares wrapped in banana leaves. Such snacks are good for a quick boost.

Many of these sweets are startlingly inventive, putting familiar ingredients in surprising surroundings. You might find yourself finishing off a rich pudding, for example, before realizing that its tantalizing flavor came from crisp-fried onions.

Left, night markets offer everything. **Above**, Thai sweets, many of Portuguese origin.

sugar and either black beans or other goodies, all of it cooked in bamboo segments, then slit open and the rice eaten. *Teng taai nam kati* consists of a Thai melon cut into small cubes and mixed with ice and sweetened, flavored coconut cream. *Kanom maw keng* is a custard-like sweet, again made with coconut cream and eggs, but this time with soybean flour to thicken it and baked in square metal tins. *Kluay kek* uses bananas sliced lengthwise, dipped in coconut cream and flour, and deep fried until crisp and tempting.

If you sample nothing else, try a dish of *katit*, a rich and heavenly coconut ice cream.

Dining is one of life's joys for Thais. The aesthetic sense they have brought to their arts has been extended to food as well, creating one of the world's finest cuisines with an infinite variety of dishes. One chef's *keng khieo waan gai* (chicken in green curry) is quite unlike that of another chef.

The Thai love of good food has acted as a magnet for the chefs of other lands to open restaurants in Bangkok. One of the surprises for visitors is the cornucopia of cuisines: Lebanese, Korean, Burmese, Arab, Mexican and all the European cuisines.

There are seafood markets where fresh fish and shellfish are laid out on ice for selection. Riverside restaurants offer ever-changing views of passing boats – one of the most interesting facets of Bangkok life. And, in fact, floating restaurants cruise the river serving Thai meals during the voyage.

There are restaurants in the middle of bustling markets. There are small boats that paddle to canal-side diners to serve noodle dishes, and small noodle restaurants along the street where one pulls up a chair at a folding table and feast until dawn.

Last but not least, there are the noodle vendors with an entire restaurant on their three-wheeled bicycles.

Restaurants conform to high government health standards, and it is rare that one experiences an upset stomach over anything more than overindulgence. (Easy on the raw seafood, however.) The drinking water and ice at the larger restaurants is bottled under health department supervision. The water at shophouse restaurants and markets may not be so pure. It is best to stick to bottled soft drinks or hot tea.

Singha is a local beer whose reputation for quality extends beyond Thai borders. Kloster, another home-spawned beer, is also well-liked by drinkers. The local cane whiskey is called *mekhong* and packs a wallop for the unsuspecting. A bit sweet, it is drunk neat or, more popularly, mixed with club soda and lime, the drink of the tropics.

Preceding pages: art for the tourists. **Left,** hotels offer classy cultural performances. **Right,** Bangkok's social venues are numerous.

Thais have their own special coffee, mixed with a thick black melange of coffee, chicory and god knows what else – the amyl nitrate of coffees, nitroglycerin brewed from a bean, strong enough to set a dead man's heart beating. Forgot your pacemaker? Down a cup of Thai coffee. Thais fill the bottom of the glass two fingers high with sweetened condensed milk and pour the coffee over it. Ask for it black (Thais call the iced version *oli-ang*) and you will gain the full flavor of this exotic mixture.

Tea time: In Bangkok, drinking tea seems to be associated with nostalgia, as the city's tea rooms all are trimmed with decor from another era. The Oriental Hotel's Author's Lounge, for example, is an unabashed throwback to the days of Joseph Conrad. This is not to say it isn't authentic; it was originally the courtyard of the original hotel and one can easily imagine a 19th-century gentleman and his escort enjoying the air while sipping piping hot Darjeeling or Earl Grey.

Today, the air is chilled by air-conditioning and the open sky is shut out by a fiberglass canopy. Tall, slender bamboo trees reach high along white-washed stucco walls that are covered in photographs of Thai royalty at the turn of the century. Guests sit on wicker sofas to sip a variety of teas and filtered coffees, and to snack on pastries under the shade of brightly-colored parasols.

In the Dusit Thani Hotel, Library 1918 offers similar fare as one sits in high-backed Regency chairs to enjoy the view of the gardens, and of the waterfall that tumbles down through them.

The Regent of Bangkok was originally called the Peninsula Hotel, and its lobby was modeled on that of the incomparable Peninsula Hotel in Hong Kong, one of the classic establishments of Asia. The present management has maintained the traditional tea hours

barges are paddled homeward in the glow of the setting sun. The terraces of five hotels offer superb views of river life: the Marriott Royal Garden Riverside, the Menam, the Shangri-la, the Oriental, and the Royal Orchid Sheraton.

During the monsoon season, step in out of the rain for a late afternoon drink at the lobbies of The Oriental and The Regent of Bangkok, which ring with the sound of strings early each evening, ensembles that serenade patrons with baroque melodies.

Into the evening: In an area of Sukhumvit Soi 21 called Washington Square is a cluster of American-style bars. The bars along Soi Sarasin, on the north edge of Lumpini Park,

of its predecessor, along with providing a string orchestra in the balcony to shower soft melodies down upon guests.

Evening drinks: Daytime Bangkok is hard on the nerves and by the (roughly) four-hour rush period; many people prefer to sit and wait out the horror and sip a cool drink.

The terraces of major hotels along the Chao Phraya are the best places to watch the sun go down. In the cool of the evening, order a colorful tropical drink or a tall glass of beer, sit back and watch the drama taking place on the river before you. At this hour, ferries move commuters between the banks, tugboats cruise up and downstream, and

are somewhat similar, but they transform into live music venues as the night progresses. Bangkok is just discovering wine bars. There are outlets of Suk's Vinotheque on Sukhumvit Soi 24 and in the basement of Galleria Plaza, near the east end of Silom Road.

Royal City Avenue (RCA), which connects Rama IX and New Petchburi roads, sports scores of theme bars. This is the mecca for the city's trendy set, but besides nightclubs, there are cafes, restaurants and quiet bars. None of the proprietors seem to know that 2am is the official closing time. Sukhumvit Soi 4 is a good bet for late-night restaurants.

Restaurants: Thais tend to dine early and restaurants accommodate them by opening early and closing equally early, which puts a crimp on those suffering from late-evening hunger pangs. Later than that, finding a quality restaurant isn't easy. However, fluorescent lights will signal makeshift sidewalk restaurants, and there's no need to settle for noodles alone. You should be able to discover quite hefty meals, complete with whiskey or beer, until early in the morning.

Just as there is no business district in Bangkok, there is no restaurant row. In general, European restaurants are tucked into back lanes off Sukhumvit Road, Indian restaurants are off New Road between Silom

dishes come under the heading of *larb*; *som-tam*, a fiery salad made from shredded raw papaya, dried shrimp and chilies; and strips of beef jerky.

Isaan chicken is the speciality of a group of restaurants behind the Ratchadamnern Boxing Stadium. A few Northeastern restaurants are to be found in the lanes behind Chancaras Restaurant on Soi Lang Suan, 250 meters in from Ploenchit Road. Northern cuisine with its cold rice in water (*khao chae*) is often served by restaurants offering Thai classical dancing performances. Southern food is virtually unheard of in Bangkok.

Chinese: With a country and culture as diverse as that of China, it is not surprising

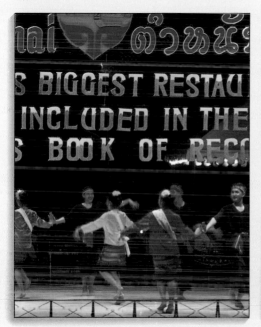

and Soi 11, Japanese are on Thaniya Road, Middle Eastern are on Soi 3 and Soi 4 of Sukhumvit Road, while fast food chains are at Ratchaprasong, near the Erawan Shrine, and at the head of Silom Road, near the Dusit Thani Hotel. Everything else – Thai, Chinese, and other Asian – are scattered all over.

Thai: Most of the dishes found in Bangkok are from the Central Plains. Northeastern (*Isaan*) food is quite hot and features such items as chicken basted and roasted as only the Isaan people know how – minced meat

Left, some evening socializing. **Above**, dinner offerings of every sort.

that its chefs would have created an enormous variety of dishes. Most Thai Chinese are of *tae-chiew* (*chiu chow* to a Hong Kong Chinese) descent, so the typical Thai Chinese restaurant serves tae-chiew dishes with a distinct Cantonese flavor. Tae-chiew is famed for dishes such as shark's fin soup, goose doused in soy sauce, and dried-blood recipes that are not to everyone's taste.

For this reason, the more widely acceptable Cantonese influence is apparent in Thai Chinese cooking. Fruits and teas are integral parts of every meal. Birds, pork and seafood are essentials, and the variety of fungi and mushrooms is enough to make the senses reel. Cantonese cooking emphasizes the fast-frying approach to bring dishes to the peak of their natural taste and color.

Other Chinese cuisines are well represented in Thailand. Shanghainese food is typified by dishes that are fried in sesame or soy sauce for a long time, making them sweeter and oilier than other cuisines. Although not as varied as their southern cousins, Pekinese dishes such as Peking duck, Mongolian hot pot, and wheat dumplings justify their world renown. Pekinese dishes have been enriched by the wealth of Thailand's vegetables, although the Peking duck available here takes on the guise of a goose. This shouldn't affect enjoyment of the dish,

taurant's name the type of food on its menu, especially as the restaurants will often serve a mix of several cuisines.

Restaurants are often denoted as Muslim, which means they do not serve pork. Neither is their food strictly Middle Eastern nor is it Thai, and their patrons are normally Thai Muslims, or Indian and Pakistani Muslims.

Continental: At the top Continental-style restaurants, the dishes are near carbon copies of those one would find on, naturally, the Continent. If the meats and seasonings available in the local market do not meet high hotel standards, they will be imported. Not to be ignored are the gourmet restaurants, European and Thai, in the large hotels which

however, as it is the skin that's important.

Indian: The cuisine is of the northern portion of the sub-Continent and runs strongly to *tandoori*, *korma*, and *masala* served with rice, *chapati* or *nan,* with *lassi* to wash it down. Madrasi and southern Indian food is served at only one or two restaurants (off Silom Road), a shame because, despite its extreme spiciness, it is delicious.

Middle Eastern: This is a tricky category. Aside from the very decidedly Arabian restaurants along Soi 3 and Soi 4 on Sukhumvit, which cater almost exclusively to Arab visitors, and the Lebanese food served by The Cedars, it is difficult to know from the res-

serve excellent meals complemented by equally high-quality wines.

In restaurants whose menus are dominated by Thai food, Continental dishes tend to be approximations. Thus, a Cordon Bleu (or Blue or Blew, as it appears on some menus) can be an anemic slab of pork stuffed with slices of processed cheese.

It is a Thai conviction that Western food is inherently *jute* (bland), and thus a cook will often try to make it as bland as possible. If dining or having breakfast in anything other than a restaurant specializing in a particular European cuisine, be prepared for some interesting surprises.

Vegetarian: Strange in a land of Buddhists, but nearly every Thai dish contains meat. The exception is during a three-week period in October, when Chinese vegetarian food is easily found in restaurants and markets. Whole Earth, with locations on 93/3 Soi Lang Suan and 71 Sukhumvit Soi 26, offers but a few meat dishes, excelling instead at Thai-style vegetarian food. The ambience is also very conducive to relaxed dining, much more so than the many Indian restaurants, which also always have a good choice for vegetarians.

Vegetarian Cottage, on the sixth floor of the World Trade Center, is nearby to six movie theaters. The cafeteria of the Bangkok most outdoor restaurants are along the Ratchapisek Highway, beyond the Asoke-Din Daeng intersection. They take full advantage of their rural setting, erecting Thai-style pavilions around ponds and artificial waterfalls. The largest, Tum Nak Thai, features the foods of all of Thailand's regions. It seats 3,000 patrons, served by waitresses on roller skates.

Thai entrepreneurs have finally discovered that food lovers enjoy dining by the edge of the river, and so in recent years have begun building riverside restaurants. Most major riverside hotels also have terraces serving Continental and Asian food.

Lord Jim's in the Oriental Hotel lets you

Adventist Hospital serves no meat at all – nor coffee, tea or soft drinks. Most of the big hotels have caught on to the Western taste for salad bars. Several Western fast-food outlets also have them. If you go to Chatuchak weekend market, try to have lunch at the cheap and good vegetarian restaurant run by the strict Buddhist Santi Asoke sect.

Outside and riverside: Bangkok's balmy evenings and tropical setting invite one to sit down to a dinner under the stars. In addition to the luxury hotels along the Chao Phraya,

Left, self-service seafood emporium. **Above**, sparkling night along the Chao Phraya.

survey the river while enjoying seafood lunches and dinners. The Oriental's Rim Naam Restaurant across the river, the Shangri-La's Salathip, and the Dusit Thani's Dusit Rimtam Seafood Restaurant, in the riverside Supakarn Shopping Center, all have Thai-style decor and dishes.

There are also restaurants built on floating platforms moored along the river. They are reached by gangways and set gently swaying by each passing wave, making it somewhat difficult to know when one has had too much to drink, or eat. Most of them serve only Thai cuisine. There are several on Phra Athit Road, near the Phra Pinklao Bridge, that are popular places with both Thais and travelers. If diners like the river so much, why not seat them on it rather than alongside it? That bright revelation has spawned a dozen boats that cruise up and down the river while serving a set-menu Thai dinner. The Tassaneya Nava was the first to float the idea, but it has been joined by others including the ornate Ayutthaya Princess.

Markets: Having attracted an increasingly sophisticated clientele, market restaurants have moved upmarket, even to the point of encasing their premises in glass and air-conditioning them. This does not detract from the high quality of the food, and inflates the bill just a bit.

sive and offer the ambience of market stalls.

The seafood-market concept has become so popular here that it has been copied elsewhere. In most, like the Seafood Market Restaurant, on Sukhumvit Road across from Soi 21, the diner pushes a shopping cart along freezer counters laden with an array of seafood. Purchases are totted up at a cash register and then taken away to be cooked according to instructions. A cooking fee is charged. Lots of fun, but it can be expensive.

Dinner-and-cultural shows: Many visitors opt for sampling Thai cuisine and culture in the same sitting. Diners are seated in a Thai-style house, on cushions or chairs around a table and upon which are placed dishes of

Pratunam market is very popular for its fresh seafood. You choose your items and they are prepared in one of a hundred delicious ways, usually Chinese-style, although they can be spiced up to suit one's taste. Most of the restaurants in Pratunam are open-air, creating an atmosphere of relaxed conviviality that, as much as their food, has been responsible for their popularity.

Bangrak market off New Road, between Silom and Sathorn roads, is somewhat downscale. There is nothing fancy here, just good food as eaten by ordinary Thais. Seafood restaurants in Samyan (intersection of Phay Thai and Rama 4 roads) are inexpen-

Thai food. This is a good opportunity to sample several cuisines of Thailand and then settle back to experience the elegance of Thai classical dancing.

Baan Thai, Pimarn, the Maneeya Room, Sala Norasingh and Sala Rim Nam all offer excellent introductions to Thailand and should be considered for your first night in town. The Siam Inter-Continental has a Thai night daily in its garden, with a buffet of Thai food and a cultural show.

Traditional dance and boxing: Most short-term visitors usually want to attend one of two standard evening activities (other than the sex venues): traditional dance performances or the finesse of Thai kick-boxing.

There are *lakhon nai* dance shows at about half a dozen hotels and restaurants every night. Most hotels and guesthouses sell tickets that include transportation and a traditional Thai meal. Travel agencies can do likewise. Indeed, most of the audience will be other tourists and travelers, but the performances do provide an authentic taste of Thai culture.

On the other hand, at a boxing match you will easily be outnumbered by raucous Thai fans. With origins as a battlefield martial art, Thai boxing (*muay Thai*) employs not only fists, but elbows, feet, knees and nearly every other part of the body. A high-pitched or-

But because it is so huge, **Royal City Avenue (RCA)** will probably remain trendy for a good while. Inconvenient to just about everything, RCA links Petchburi and Rama IX roads. At first glance, the outdoor cafes and restaurants seem to be filled with the idle teenage children of the very rich. But in the scores of bars and restaurants housed in the shophouses and high-rises is a more diverse clientele. The major theme is theme bars. House bands churn out high-quality music, ranging from Thai ballads to jazz to indie rock. Many of the proprietors are the older idle children of the wealthy elite, or else well-known Thai singers or actors. Large dance clubs are in the works.

chestra wails an accompaniment. A stylized dance precedes each bout on a 10-fight card. For those who find the fighting too brutal, it's also entertaining to watch the audience, which consists of emotional bettors. Bouts take place every night at either Lumpini Stadium, on Rama IV Road, or else at Ratchadamnern Stadium, near Democracy Monument.

Nightlife and entertainment: Bangkok's venues for music and Western-style dancing pop up and evaporate with the blink of an eye.

Left, night market in Pratunam. **Above**, quick feet in Thai boxing.

One of the oldest and flashiest discos is the Nasa Spacedrome, on Ramkamhaeng Avenue. It has a dance-floor capacity of 500 and can attract more than 1,000 people on a good night. At midnight, a huge spacecraft descends to the floor. Elsewhere, in the area of Silom Soi 2 and Silom Soi 4, is the site for hipper DJs and dancers, as well as accomplished drag shows. But some are wagering that these will eventually migrate to RCA.

In a more quite mood are a string of music bars along Soi Sarasin, in the northern edge of Lumpini Park. Here, one can catch Thai jazz bands with foreign vocalists. Another dependable stand-by is the Saxophone Pub

HER FATE, OR CHOICE?

Thailand has a prostitution problem. It is of neither recent nor imported vin tage. Contrary to the impression of many foreigners, prostitution has been illegal for over thirty years. Social scientists and non-governmental organizations (NGOs) estimate that there are between 300,000 and 2 million Thai prostitutes in Thailand and overseas in places like Japan. In Thailand, no truck stop or town with a population of 20,000 would be complete without a few ramshackle brothels.

According to a Thai newspaper editor, except for the area surrounding the Grand Palace, there is not a single neighborhood in Bangkok where

sex is not for sale. The venues include brothels, hotels, nightclubs, massage parlors, bars, barber shops, parks, karaoke lounges, tea houses and even golf courses. At the top are private member clubs, advertised in the glossiest magazines. At the bottom are locked brothels, where the women – and young girls – are virtually enslaved. As measured by compensation and working conditions, the tawdry bars serving foreign men are somewhere in between.

There is no single reason why Thailand has more prostitutes than many poorer countries. The traditional explanation of poverty, however, carries less and less weight. While it's true that the wealthiest have chiefly profited from the economic boom of the last decade, benefits have trickled down to the poorest. At least in Bangkok, there are jobs in domestic service or construction for any person.

With increased prosperity, many Thais assumed prostitution would diminish. Instead, the numbers of prostitutes and venues are ballooning. Demand is on the rise. With more money in their pockets, Thai men are buying more sex. While most patrons of Thai prostitutes are Thai men, foreigners also contribute to the demand. Besides the infamous sex tours from Japan, Germany and elsewhere in Southeast Asia, there is also a sizable community of Western men, notably in Pattaya and Phuket, who live in Thailand solely because of the cheap sex, child sex or teenage wives.

Agents kidnap young girls or trick them (with offers of factory jobs) from remote provinces. These girls may end up in locked brothels, from which they may eventually be smuggled to other Asian countries.

It's hard for poor families to resist the blandishments. Particularly at April "harvest time", when 12- and 13-year-old girls finish the customary six years of schooling, agents flock to villages, where they offer parents hundreds of dollars or dazzling electric appliances in exchange for pretty daughters. A girl typically has to work off a debt that is twice her sale price, although she may have to start over if she is resold before reaching her goal.

The commoners religious beliefs – an amalgam of superstition and debased Buddhism – does little to discourage prostitution. Genuine Buddhism, of course, in no way sanctions prostitution. According to its most basic tenet, all human discontent stems from insatiable desires. To achieve inner peace and break the cycle of rebirth, we must learn to control wants.

When asked why she became or remains a prostitute, a young woman will usually talk about luck or fate. Yet true Buddhists believe in neither, and don't subscribe to predestination.

Feminist NGOs don't focus their primary efforts on extricating girls and women from prostitution. They have found that regardless of how women were originally lured into prostitution, few are strongly motivated to get out. The work is easy, the money is too good, the family pressure overwhelming. It is their "fate".

Instead, the advocates concentrate on prevention. They try to teach marketable skills and encourage girls to remain in school. After they initiated scholarships to help keep vulnerable girls in school beyond the sixth grade, the government began a small program. Still, only a few thousand girls are reached this way every year.

Prostitution is probably the principal reason why the AIDS epidemic is so extensive in Thailand. Random blood testing indicates that just under 1 million men, women and children are now infected with AIDS. ∎

and Restaurant, at Victory Monument. The menu is blues and jazz. Visiting musicians are welcome to sit in with the band, but they had better not be neophytes.

At the southeastern intersection of Petchburi and Phyathai roads are a clutch of clubs featuring a heavy favorite among young Thais: heavy metal bands. The British-style Bobby's Arms Pub, on Patpong Soi 2, has for many years hosted a popular Dixieland band every Sunday evening. The Oriental Hotel usually has a sophisticated pianist and jazz singer from the United States.

Although it's waned in popularity among Thais, many foreigners are intrigued by "songs-for-life" music. The sound is folk-rock incorporating traditional Thai instruments; the lyrics are socio-political critiques. Again, the venues change and may be far-flung. If you can't see a band, cassette tapes are readily available.

Movies: Bangkok has seen a blossoming of new movie theaters in recent years, most of them multiplex cinemas in new shopping centers. English-language movies are either subtitled or dubbed in Thai; check before buying a ticket.

The largest concentration of these are shown in the Siam Square area, with over two dozen screens. The World Trade Center also has several cinemas.

Of the 350 to 400 movies shown in Bangkok every year, about half are American imports. Second in the running are Hongkong Chinese films. Although Thailand is a popular location for filming American movies, Thailand itself produces only about 50 to 60 films each year. The themes are similar to the Hongkong variety. If one doesn't understand Thai, they still are easy to follow – mostly body language with lots of kicks and jabs.

The Alliance Francaise and Goethe Institute regularly run high-quality French and German films, with English subtitles.

And then there's S-E-X: For too many foreign visitors, not to mention rambling or stray men on the prowl, Bangkok nightlife is associated with **Patpong**.

The sex on display and sold in Patpong tells nothing about Thai notions of sexuality or prostitution, but it does reveal that manner

in which many Western men wish to see women, in general or Asian women in particular. Originally a red-light district for American troops on leave during the Vietnam War, Patpong is now an area specializing in vending sexual services and amusements to foreign tourists and residents.

Located in a prime business area not far from Lumpini Park, Patpong actually consists of three narrow streets linking Silom and Surawong roads. Patpong 1 caters to heterosexual men, Patpong 2 to gay men. The clientele on the third street, Soi Thanlya, is exclusively Japanese, who come to Bangkok on tour company-packaged sex tours.

Street-level on Patpong 1 are the so-called

go-go bars, where the bar girls, primarily from the impoverished northeastern part of Thailand, can be "bought out" for the evening. They then must negotiate a price for their services. On the upper floors, young men and women perform live but lifeless sex shows; the women eject ping-pong balls and smoke cigarettes with their vaginas, all for foreign audiences.

Increasingly, these audiences include silver-fox, senior-citizen tour groups, men and women alike, who come to watch on escorted tours of Bangkok's nightlife. Mostly, however, Patpong is the haunt of men with nothing more useful to do.

Left, many young women must pay off family debts by working in Bangkok's sex industry. **Right**, party time on Silom Road.

Over the past few years, a hotel construction spree of epic scale has given Bangkok a choice of deluxe hotels unsurpassed anywhere else in Southeast Asia. And not only do rates remain among the lowest in the region, Thailand's seasonal tourism business means that decent discounts can be had during off-season periods.

In terms of style and ambience, Bangkok's offerings could probably satisfy the most finicky, obsessive, neurotic or simply demanding of guests.

as offices, hotels and restaurants are concerned. And in a move back in time, four of the leading hotels on the Chao Phraya river – Oriental, Shangri-La, Royal Orchid Sheraton and Marriott Royal Garden Riverside – have combined to use the river, rather than the roads, to get guests to their rooms in a reasonable amount of time. A deluxe jetboat service shuttles to and from a pier near the airport and down the river to the hotels.

In any narrative of Bangkok's hotels, one necessarily begin with the **Oriental Hotel**,

One advantage that Bangkok's hotels have over other regional destinations is the time-honored Thai sense of hospitality – and it is a natural warmth, unpretentious, which makes a stay at any Thai hotel, no matter how many rating stars or other guests, a genuinely pleasurable experience.

What the visitor to Bangkok must remember, however, is that the city's traffic has now become so bad that one's choice of hotel often must often be based upon its location, rather than the hotel name. This is especially true for the business traveler on a schedule.

Bangkok therefore has started to coalesce into a series of urban villages, certainly as far

one of the fabled hotels of the East and which, despite the best efforts of its competition, consistently rates amongst the world's best hotels. The original wing, with its literary associations from the lengthy stays of Joseph Conrad and Somerset Maugham, is a charming colonial-style remnant, and afternoon tea here in the Authors Lounge is evocative of a more gracious age. Not to be missed also is a drink or meal on the terrace overlooking the Chao Phraya. Unlike other Bangkok hotels, however, the Oriental rarely needs to compete in price wars.

A short way down river (although the tight little maze of riverside streets makes the walk a challenging one) is the plush and expansive **Shangri-La Hotel**. This has the longest river frontage of any of the hotels, and the lush gardens here are a joy in which to relax. The lobby, with its great glass walls, is also a superb place from which to watch the river life pass by. The hotel's decidedly luxurious Krungthep Wing is almost a separate hotel, with its own lobby, business center and restaurants.

Thonburi, on the other side of the Chao Phraya and further down-river, is less hectic,

parts of the city. The hotel is built along the lines of a resort, and is an exceptionally peaceful property.

On the other side of the Oriental and up river a bit, the **Royal Orchid Sheraton** is a major venue for incentives and conventions, as well as a popular hotel. The Sheraton has fine leisure facilities and is also directly – and in Bangkok, conveniently – adjacent to the River City Shopping Complex.

The **Holiday Inn Crowne Plaza** is within walking distance of the water, but has the

and thus many major companies are shifting their headquarters into new premises that are being built near the river here; the residential market is also growing.

The **Marriott Royal Garden Riverside** is ideally placed for this market, and for those travelers seeking urban respite. Its location – with easy access to both the highway network and the river – makes it easy to reach the heart of the business district, or other

Left: most of Bangkok's deluxe hotels are central and offer lofty views. **Above**, hotels along the Chao Phraya River offer convenient transport connections.

advantage of being located right on Silom Road, the spine of the blossoming central business district. The hotel's lobby is exceptionally cool and spacious, and calming down here with a cold drink is an ideal antidote to the heat and hustle of the city outside.

Around ten minutes walk away is the **Monarch-Lee Gardens Hotel**, another ideally located place for business travelers and tourists alike. The restaurant facilities on the 38th floor offer spectacular views.

At the top end of Silom Road is the **Dusit Thani**, a long-established landmark famous for its banquets and other events, and with a huge selection of restaurants, including an extremely well-patronized roof-top restaurant and bar. Close by is the **Montien Hotel**, another graceful landmark that has been well established for many years.

On the corner of Rama IV Road and Silom rises the 32-story **Pan Pacific Hotel**, the ultimate executive hotel. With seven meeting rooms, an executive boardroom and business center, the Pan Pacific also offers a special business package. Pagers, mobile phones, a call-referral service and free local telephone calls are supplemented by the installation of a fax machine in guest rooms of corporate clients. The lobby is actually several floors above ground level, with an understated entrance at ground level. Nearby are Lumpini Park and Patpong.

To the north, the area around the picturesque Erawan Shrine, with its garlands of flowers, swirls of incense, and traditional Thai temple dancers, is very much modern Bangkok, with a concentration of shopping malls and cinemas here.

The **Grand Hyatt Erawan** is located on Ratchadamri Road, close to the intersection (called Ratchaprasong) where Rama I Road becomes Ploenchit Road and where the Erawan Shrine itself is located. The lobby, with its lush jungle and cool stream, is Grand Hyatt luxurious. The hotel is noted for hosting evening events, and it also has a highly popular restaurant and entertainment center.

A few yards down Ratchadamri Road is the elegant **Regent of Bangkok**. The lobby here is high and wide, and its ceilings are exquisitely painted with traditional murals. This is another must for afternoon tea, with small a orchestra playing in an upper gallery and a welcome sense of relaxation in the air. The hotel also has a cool and green atrium that is a perfect refuge from the busy outside.

Le Meridien President is on the other side of the Erawan Shrine, and is another long-established hotel. The lobby has a clubby and friendly feel, and the dining facilities are excellent.

North from Ratchaprasong, past the giant World Trade Centre and where Ratchadamri turns into Ratchapraop Road, is the bustling garment market called Pratunam (Water Gate), an area that is developing into a business and commercial district. A gleaming new landmark here is the **Amari Watergate Hotel**. The hotel has exceptionally fine restaurants and views.

Going eastward from Ratchaprasong along Ploenchit Road leads past office buildings and the intersection with Wireless (Witthayu) Road, home of several embassies and the **Hilton International**. A low-rise building set within extensive tropical gardens, the hotel actually has three atrium lobbies. Glass walls make this a restful spot for visitors to its coffee shop and French restaurant.

Continuing along, as Ploenchit becomes Sukhumvit Road, is a prime tourist area filled with small shops and clothing stalls. A long-established hotel here, **The Ambassador**, describes itself with perfect accuracy as a self-contained city. In addition to its 1,000-plus guest rooms, it has huge convention

facilities and an almost countless number of restaurants and bars. Especially noteworthy is the food center, which features cuisines from around Asia.

The **Landmark**, on the other side of Sukhumvit Road, is another property with a huge number of facilities and a good shopping mall. An excellent piano lounge and restaurant are located on top of the hotel, accessed by an outside elevator – a ride that makes even seasoned Bangkok hands catch breath with pleasure.

The **Mansion Kempinski**, in contrast to its giant neighbors, is a tiny gem of a hotel tucked away in the streets behind the Ambassador. It has a beautiful lobby with a sweeping staircase, large guest rooms, and a fine restaurant within a glassed-in terrace.

On the corner of Soi Asoke, and ideally placed for the Queen Sirikit National Convention Center, is the unmistakable boat shape of the **Delta Grand Pacific Hotel**, which has excellent shopping facilities. Directly opposite, meanwhile, is the **Imperial Queen's Park Hotel**, another 1,000-plus guest room property, with full exhibition and convention facilities.

For many people, the lodging in Siam Square won't be too remote. This large shopping area at the intersection of Rama I and Phyathai roads is the home to many small

Siam Inter-Continental. Set in 26 acres of old royal land, and with streams and duck ponds in its lush gardens, this traditionally-styled building might as well be in the countryside. In Bangkok, it's an oasis.

Ratchadapisak is one of Bangkok's newest shopping and restaurant districts, which only a handful of years ago was better known for its used car lots and its elephant training school. The latter is long gone, while the former are quickly disappearing to make way for open-air restaurants serving great seafood, and giant department stores. The **Emerald Hotel** is a luxury property along this strip, and is particularly noted for its tennis courts and fine dining facilities.

restaurants, fast-food outlets and several cinemas. To the south are the expansive grounds of Chulalongkorn University. Continue west to Soi Kasemsan 2, where the elegant Jim Thompson's House is located. On the quiet Soi Kasemsan 1 are about a half-dozen small hotels favored by Europeans visitors.

The **Novotel** is located adjacent to Siam Square, and has a very comprehensive entertainment complex, plus superb fitness facilities. Also located near Siam Square is the

Further north, in the direction of the airport – and thus convenience – is the Japanese-owned **Hotel Nikko**. Naturally popular with Japanese travelers, it has one of Bangkok's best Japanese restaurants. The large **Central Plaza** is even further out, but the expressway is close and well situated for travel into the business district. There is also a shopping complex adjacent to the hotel.

The area around the **Malaysia Hotel** is especially well-known for guesthouses, and the Khao Sarn Road area is another center for budget travelers and is especially convenient to the river, and for tourist sites such as the Royal Palace and Wat Arun.

Left, chartering a boat at the Oriental Hotel, with the Sheraton in the background. **Above**, swimming pools erase the day's heat and dust.

300/4

300/y

With the artistry that 19th-century craftsmen lavished on temples, 20th-century artisans now employ in creating a wealth of beautiful products that have made Bangkok a place to seek out art, crafts, clothing and jewelry.

Bargaining is meant to be fun, not a clash of wills, and it is generally accompanied by casual bantering. If the price does not suit you, smile and walk away. Chances are you will be accosted to return and your offer will be accepted. If not, you may find the price you want just down the block. Remember

ceptance for its nubbly texture and shimmering iridescence. Within a few years, silk had become a major Thai industry.

Thai silk is thicker and stiffer than Chinese and European silks, but it holds its own when transformed into a suit, for example. It looks better on women, of course, than men, and it can be turned into superb evening attire or a business suit by one of Bangkok's tailors. It is also turned into pillow slips, scarves, ties, and bags. *Mudmee*, a Northeastern silk, is a form of tie-dye wherein the threads are dyed

that when making several purchases at the same shop, bargain down the price for each item, and then try to bargain down the total; you can usually knock a little extra off the overall price. On the other hand, don't descend into the absurdities of trying to knock off a few cents or bahts just for the righteousness of it.

Thai silk: For decades, silk languished in the remote regions of the country, shunned by the Thai aristocracy who preferred imported cloths. In fact, silk production was a dying art when it was revived by American entrepreneur Jim Thompson, who promoted it abroad, where it quickly gained wide ac-

before they are strung on the loom. It is characterized by a very subtle pattern of zigzagging lines and tends to somber hues like dark blue, maroon and deep yellow. It makes a very elegant woman's dress or suit, or a handsome *rajaprathan* highly favored by Thai officials.

Cotton is made into dresses and most of the items into which Thai silk is rendered. A surprising number of visitors arrive with measurements for sofas and windows.

Northern hilltribes each have their own distinctive patchwork and embroidery designs, mainly in bright blues, magentas and yellows. The embroidery is either appliqued on clothes, or else sold in short lengths. Although a major textile producer, Thailand imports a large amount of Chinese and Japanese silk, Chinese satin, denim, linen, poplin, wool (surprising for tropical Thailand), and polyester blends. Look for them in Pahurat market (Pahurat Road), Sampeng Lane, Pratunam market, Chatuchak weekend market and major department stores.

Tailoring: Bangkok has taken over men's tailoring from Hong Kong, which simply priced itself out of the market. Select from a

elsewhere or selected from a wide variety in the shop. Generally, men are more successful at getting a good fit than are women.

Leatherware: Well tanned and durable, Thai leather products are generally of good quality, even the counterfeit brand names. Beware of the "brass" fittings, which are often a plated metal that quickly tarnishes.

Crocodiles are no longer the hunters, but the hunted. Crocodile and, to a lesser extent, cobra, skin is a popular material for wallets, purses, shoes, belts, and even briefcases.

wide range of imported or local cloth to make three-piece suits, pants, and shirts. Some shops can complete the work in 24 hours, but if you have sufficient time, it is best to go back for one or two fittings before the final stitches are put in place. Most of the deluxe hotels and nearby shopping centers have high-quality tailors. They will keep measurements on file, if asked, so that clothes can be ordered later by post. Similarly, women's fashions can be crafted from cloth bought

Preceding pages: silk for sale. **Left**, Thai silk in the making. **Above**, Thailand's middle class is increasingly doing more than window-shopping.

Gems and jewelry: Thailand mines its own rubies and sapphires (with some also coming from neighboring Burma), and is the world's leading cutter of colored gems.

Rubies range from pale to deep-red (including the famous "pigeon's blood" red); sapphires come in blue, green and yellow, as well as one associated with Thailand, the Star Sapphire. Many zircons have been heat-treated to change them from red to colorless, enhancing their beauty but lowering their overall value.

Thai craftsmen turn gold, white-gold silver, and platinum into handsome jewelry settings. Local creations tend towards traditional patterns; modern designs are imported from abroad and crafted here. The standard of workmanship is generally good.

A word of warning, however. The stones are often not of the quality and weight advertised, and some shopkeepers are less than scrupulous in ensuring that the gold content of the settings is of the carat stated.

Shops offer guarantees of the authenticity of each piece, but these cannot always be believed. Once you have paid, it is difficult to get refunds or restitution. It is best to shop at a larger store or one that comes solidly recommended.

Gold can be found in shops along Chinatown's Yaowarat Road. Gold shops are eas-

Thai hilltribe women are known for the elaborate and detailed jewelry that they wear. The pieces bear something of a resemblance to American Indian jewelry, with a multitude of small parts intricately linked together and flat pieces etched with tribal patterns. Silver content is a few percentage points shy of 100, but their raw beauty compensates.

Jade is easily available in Thailand by merit of its having Burma as a next-door neighbor. Most of it is smuggled across the border, with very valuable pieces shipped abroad; the lesser grades are cut and sold in Thailand. Rare is the nephrite or mutton-white jade prized by the Chinese.

Most common is jadeite, the bright-green

ily recognized – they seem stamped out of the same mold, with glass fronts, upswept ceilings, vermillion lacquer surfaces, acres of display cases and a policeman on guard out front. Rings, earrings, bracelets, anklets and other items are sold with plain surfaces, etched with designs, set with precious or semi-precious stones and as linked chains. The gold content is generally accurate. Chiang Mai makes attractive silver necklaces, bracelets and other accessories that are sold in Bangkok shops. In addition, there are purses, boxes, betel-nut sets, teapots and much more made by Khmer, Lao, Shan, Burmese, and Chinese craftspeople.

jade familiar to European buyers, and the less expensive types in a rainbow of earth colors. Beware of other stones such as jasper that are often passed off as jade.

Pearls: Heavily-guarded farms off the southern island of Phuket produce fine cultured pearls, including what is reputed to be the largest pearl ever created. Pearl necklaces, earrings and other fashion accessories are offered in many Bangkok jewelry shops. Imported Mikimoto pearls are also sold.

Metalwork: Northern silversmiths pound out a variety of bowls, which they coat with an extract of tamarind to make them shine. They also weave stout silver strands into baskets. Among the more intriguing items are Cambodian silver animals. Charming elephants, chickens, horses and others are, in fact, shells that can be pulled apart and small items stored inside. Most items are replicas of antiques, but their quaint beauty makes them very popular. Thailand is one of the world's leading producers of tin, the prime constituent in pewterware. This gray metal makes handsome vases, plates, mugs, and other practical items with a matte or burnished silver sheen.

Bronze Buddha images cannot be taken out of the country, but there are statues of classic drama figures that make handsome decorations. Most modern bronze pieces are

large noodle cabinets that vendors sling on bamboo poles and carry as they trudge through the back lanes. There are also brass lanterns and small cabinets. Brass items and bronzeware with brass coatings are generally protected by a silicon layer to preserve their sheen.

Antiques: Thai and Burmese antiques are among the finest in Asia – if they can be found. Most of the good Thai pieces were long ago snapped up by collectors, but it is still possible to discover a treasure. Most things in antique shops are beautiful and even perhaps old, but rarely true antiques. One doesn't buy them for investment value, only aesthetic value. (Most of the so-called

designed to decorate a living room. Subjects range from recumbent deer from the *Ramakien* to modern figures of flowing grace. The bronze pieces are generally annealed with a brass skin to make them gleam.

Small bronze temple bells can be hung in the house eaves to tinkle in the wind. Expensive and rare are the Laotian frog drums (also called rain drums), which are often covered with sheets of glass and used as tables.

Brassware includes items as elegant as the

Left, Chinatown is noted for its numerous gold merchants. **Above**, Bangkok offers both art lover and antique buyers plenty to consider.

antiques are produced in antique factories in Burma, then smuggled across the border in exchange for refrigerators and stereos. Don't underestimate the skill and ability in making something fake look very, very old.)

It is a rare dealer who does not know the value of the pieces he sells, so forget bargaining or trying to find a bargain. Dealers usually keep the best pieces in the back.

For years, upcountry wooden temples and their art objects have been disappearing with alarming rapidity, sold by abbots tired of battling leaky roofs and termites. The abbots are content to tear down the old structures and, with the proceeds from selling antiques, tend to the maintenance of their temples. The Fine Arts Department of Thailand maintains fairly strict control over the export of religious antiques. Thus, Thai Buddha images are allowed out of the country only under very special circumstances. As a result, most antique shops now deal almost exclusively in Burmese Buddha images, which for some undefined reason are not covered by the export law.

Antique dealers can clear the buyer's purchases through the Fine Arts Department, obtaining the export permits and shipping them abroad. The buyer can also handle it, but the process is lengthy and time-consuming, and certain to cause indigestion.

pieces. Ayutthayan cabinet-makers produce wooden cabinets with glass doors and old-style grandfather clocks.

The craftsmanship of these fakes can be of a surprisingly high caliber. Most reputable dealers will not try to pass off the pieces as true antiques.

Crafts: Thai craftsmen are supremely skilled at setting oyster shells aglow in black lacquer backgrounds to create scenes of enchanting beauty. Because Thai mother-of-pearl is made from the Turban shell, it does not separate and flake as the Chinese varieties do. Check to ensure that the lacquer is really lacquer and not black paint, as is sometimes used. The difference is in the sheen; if it shines, it

European antiques like the hanging Dutch lamps, old brass fans (and recent replicas) and photographs left over from the 19th century can be found in antique shops and in Chatuchak market.

Thai shopowners have been quick to recognize that while many people are interested in antiques, they are reluctant to pay large sums of money. Instead, they want "antique-looking" pieces as home decor items. As a result, an entirely new industry has grown up to produce them. Centered in Chiang Mai and Ayutthaya, craftsmen turn out wooden art objects like deer, celestial deities and others, most of them modeled on Burmese

is lacquer; if not, it's paint. (If the shopkeeper says that lacquer normally cracks with age, mention Wat Po, where the lacquered doors have stood exposed to the weather for 200 years and not even begun to show signs of cracking.)

Thai craftsmen also excel at lacquerware, the art of overlaying wooden or bamboo items with glossy black lacquer, and on this black "canvas" painting scenes in gold leaf. Many shops carry Burmese lacquerware, which is made by applying a matte red lacquer over bamboo or wicker items. Simple designs are painted on this with black lacquer. Handsome and often large baskets and trays are the main items sold. One of Thailand's lesser known arts is nielloware, which involves applying an amalgam of black metals to etched portions of silver or, to a much lesser extent, gold.

Pottery and ceramics: If archaeological evidence is correct, Thais have been throwing pots for 5,000 years with a considerable degree of skill. Said to date from 3600 BC, the red whorl pottery of Ban Chiang, the prehistorical site in the Northeast, is considered to be historical artifacts and export is prohibited. Copies abound, however, and can be taken out of the country.

Other historical items are Sangkhaloke ceramic plates, with their distinctive twin walls between the 14th and 18th centuries. Either the sailors were an extremely careless lot or were the originators of the throwaway economy – judging from the number of pieces offered for sale, there seems to have been more pottery than water under the ship's hulls. Treat with a large degree of skepticism any claims to the contrary.

Among the most beautiful stoneware items are those with a light jade green or dark-brown glaze called celadon. Said to have originated in China and been recreated in northern Thailand in the 13th century, celadon glaze, created from wood ash (no dyes added), is characterized by a highly polished surface overlaying fine crazing. Pieces include

fish resembling the Pisces sign, from kilns near Thailand's 13th-century capital at Sukhothai. Originally produced for export to China, they keep turning up in shipwrecks discovered in the Gulf of Siam. Few are now available on the open market, but there are numerous copies.

Various ceramic pieces are claimed to have been brought up by divers from the river that flows around Ayutthaya. Dealers insist that the pieces were dropped overboard from ships moored outside the city

Left, painted umbrellas continue to sell well.
Above, one of Bangkok's many shopping malls.

dinnerware, lamps, serving platters, statuary and others.

Bencharong is a style of ceramics that originated in China and was later developed by Thai artists. Its name describes its look: *bencha* is Sanskrit for five, and *rong* means color. The five colors – red, blue, yellow, green and white – appear on delicate porcelain bowls, containers, ashtrays and decorative items. There are a few, but not many, antique Bencharong pieces.

Although it originated in China, blue-and-white porcelain has been produced extensively in Thailand since ancient times. There aren't many antique pieces around, but craftsmen are prolific in turning out a wide range of items, with quality ranging from superior to barely passable.

There must be millions of elephants wandering around Thailand's jungles minus their tusks if the number of ivory items in shop windows is any indication. More than likely, the ivory is either bone or a plastic compound. In any case, the trade of ivory and its export and import is banned in virtually every country of the world. Nonetheless, the workmanship on the fake ivory is superb. Long trains of elephants, classical Chinese scenes, globes within globes, snuff bottles, letter openers and others can be found.

Most wood products made of teak or other

woods have been crafted in Chiang Mai. Products range from practical items like breadboards, serving and cutting boards, dinner sets and salad bowls to decorative items such as trivets and headboards. There are also statues of mythical gods, angels and elephants, some standing a meter high. Teak is an extremely heavy wood; *mai daeng*, substantially inferior to teak and lacking the beautiful grain, is cheaper and lighter. Rosewood is usually employed in Chinese-style furniture (normally inlaid with mother-of-pearl). Its fine grain and satin sheen gives it a warm glow in low light.

Bangkok is a doll collector's heaven, with everything from dolls dressed in classical dance or hilltribe costumes to rag dolls in contemporary clothes. *Tukata chao wong*, the tiny, painted clay dolls belonging to royal daughters in former days, are generally sold as sets depicting everyday scenes.

Burmese puppets and *kalaga* (cloth wall-hangings) have gained a wide popularity in the past few years, to the point that whereas five years ago they were rarely seen, today, one cannot walk into a shop without tripping over them. Nearly all are copies of antiques.

The intricate umbrellas from Chiang Mai, with their bamboo struts and strings, are engineering works of sheer genius. They are sold in sizes ranging from parasols to large beach umbrellas, and usually have flowers and scenes painted on them. The masks used in *khon* masked dramas are crafted both full sized and in miniature.

Counterfeits: Bangkok has an unfortunate reputation as a center for copying and selling fake world-famous, trademarked products. It would be remiss not to mention them, as they appear on every street corner in the city. Fake Rolex watches, for example, virtually indistinguishable from the real thing are offered by touts. They are more decorative than functional, but do seem to work with a surprising degree of accuracy.

All the notable designer names can be seen on bags, briefcases and purses, which are generally of high quality but which may differ from the original enough to cause problems with customs officials.

Where to buy it: The Tourism Authority of Thailand produces shopping guides with listings that are impartially determined and are generally reliable. Its criteria for selecting a shop is based not only on the quality of goods carried, but on the shop's willingness to put the customer's interests, if not first, at least high on the list. Shops recommended by the Tourism Authority of Thailand display a sticker on their doors or windows.

After an initial browse through the markets, many people prefer to do their serious shopping in shopping malls. Bangkok does not disappoint. The prices are higher than in the street markets, but they are fixed and the quality generally guaranteed.

Left, finely-crafted dolls of traditional Thai dancers. **Right**, a farang tries her hand in the fine art of bargaining.

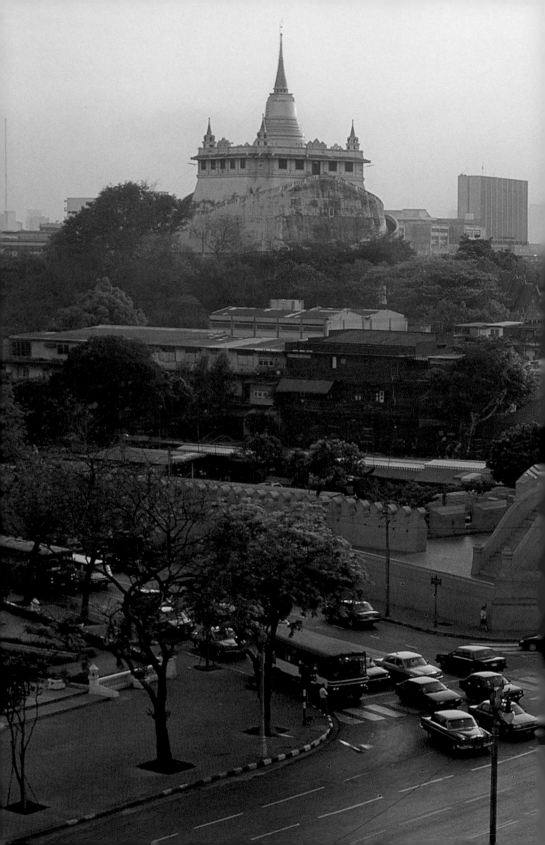

BANGKOK

At first glance, this metropolis of over ten million people seems a bewildering melding of new and old and indeterminate, and of exotic and commonplace and indescribable, all tossed together into a gigantic urban fuss. Years after that first glance, it usually still appears that way. More so than most metropolitan areas, navigation around Bangkok requires a few anchors for the traveler's – or resident's – mental map of the city.

Most obvious for such an anchor is the Chao Phraya, the river that kings throughout the centuries have used to define their royal cities, first to the north and eventually Bangkok itself. In part for the symbolism and in part for defensive concerns, the kings would take a twist in the river, dig a canal or two between two of the river's bends and thus slice off a parcel of land into an artificial island. In Bangkok, the royal island became known as Rattanokosin. After one's hotel, it is here that visitors typically seek. Its highlights are many, including the Grand Palace, Wat Po, and the National Museum.

As outside threats diminished, the kings often established palaces in the suburbs, which were just beyond Rattanakosin. Dusit to the north and the regions to the east – rural countryside at the time – were popular. Today, one finds the current king's residence, a number of parks and the zoo in Dusit. To the east are the main boulevards and blossoming shopping malls of modern Bangkok.

South of the royal city are the several enclaves where foreigners settled, such as Chinatown, or Sampeng, and the Silom Road area. This is where the Oriental Hotel and several other luxury hotels now hug the Chao Phraya's waters. Silom Road itself, at one time girdled by swamps, is increasingly becoming a business and corporate center. At its eastern end, near the green oasis of Lumpini Park, side streets (*soi*) lead to the not-so-humble sexual rumble and tumble of Patpong.

All of this is on one side of the Chao Phraya. On the other side is Thonburi, the royal capital before Krung Thep. Thonburi hasn't been paved over as much. Canals still thread through the neighborhoods, old wooden houses clinging to the canals. The growth that intrinsically defines Bangkok to the east of the Chao Phraya lacks the same intensity in Thonburi.

Growth in most of Bangkok has left a confusion, most clearly substantiated by the city's world-class traffic snarls. But like cities anywhere, Bangkok in no way represents the country as a whole. Bangkok is a distinct entity unto itself, and that is its unique and compelling interest to travelers.

Preceding pages: sunset over the Golden Mount; detail of Grand Palace; Loha Prasada; kites at Sanam Luang. **Left**, old-fashion market, Thonburi.

Bangkok

400 m / 440 yards

134

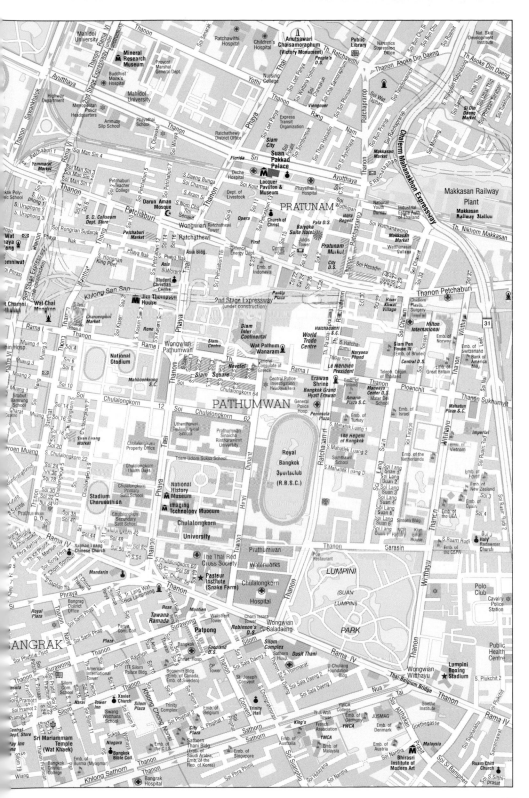

135

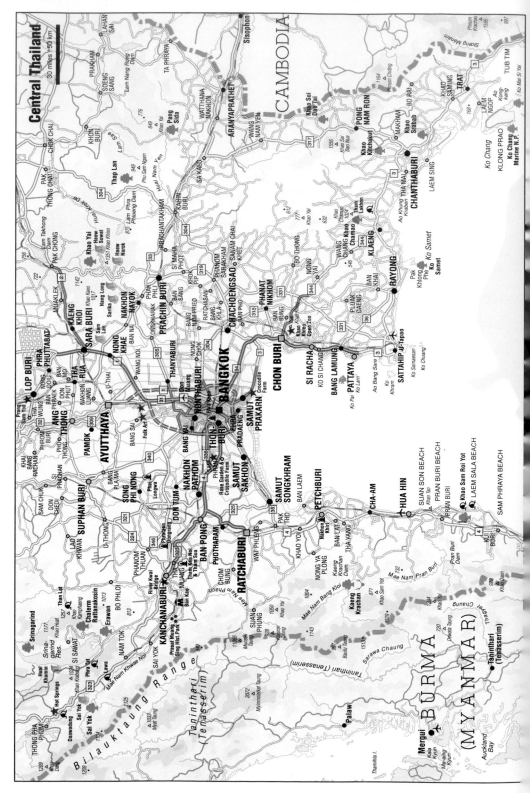

Central Thailand

30 miles • 50 km

RATTANAKOSIN: ROYAL BANGKOK

At Bangkok's heart is the royal center, **Rattanakosin**, an artificial island with most of the principal royal and religious buildings of the city. Search for the Chao Phraya River on the left-hand side of any map of Bangkok. To its right is Khlong Lawd, a canal leaving the river on the north and re-entering it on the south. Together, river and canal define the island called Rattanakosin, upon which Bangkok was born. (A similar militarily-defensive technique was used at Ayutthaya.) An exploration of Bangkok should begin here.

Approach this island from the Democracy Monument on Ratchadamnoen Avenue (Chulalongkorn's version of the Champs Elysees). The tree-rimmed lawn of Sanam Luang will appear ahead. At its far end is Wat Phra Kaeo, a sight so majestic that it will stir even the most jaded traveler.

The official center of Bangkok is **Lak Muang**, a gilded pillar erected by King Chakri (Rama I) in the late 1700s, joined later by a second pillar, blessed with the city's horoscope and placed there by King Vajiravudh (Rama VI). Similar to the Shiva *lingam* that represent potency, the Lak Muang is regarded as the foundation stone of the capital, where the city's guardian deity lives and the point from which the power of the city emanates. Distances within Bangkok are measured from this stone.

Sheltered by a graceful and renovated shrine, Lak Muang and its attendant spirits are believed to have the power to grant most wishes. Floral offerings pile high around the pillar, and the air is laden with the fragrance of incense. Devotees bow reverently in front of the pillar before pressing a square of gold leaf to the monument.

In an adjoining *sala*, a performance of Thai *lakhon* classical dance and music is usually underway. The troupe is hired by supplicants whose wishes have been granted; for spectators, the performance is free.

The 1.5-square-kilometer grounds of the **Grand Palace**, open to visitors who are dressed properly, occupy part of a larger compound that also includes the royal chapel, the Royal Collection of Weapons, the Coin Pavilion and a small museum containing artifacts from the Grand Palace.

Similar in layout to the royal palace in Ayutthaya, the palace compound embodies Thailand's characteristic blend of temporal and spiritual elements. Surrounded by high, crenellated walls and entered by the huge double gate, the Grand Palace was begun by Chakri in 1782. Almost every king since then has added to it, so that today the complex is a melange of architectural styles ranging from Thai to Italian.

After the palace death of King Ananda in 1946, his brother, the present King Bhumibol, moved to the more modern and comfortable **Chitralada Palace**, a few kilometers away in the Dusit area. Today, the Grand Palace is used only for state banquets and other royal and state ceremonies.

The grandest of the buildings was the last to be built. The triple-spired royal residence that commands the courtyard is the **Chakri Maha Prasad**, the audience and reception hall.

This two-story hall set on an elevated base, of which visitors are allowed to see only the reception rooms, was constructed during Chulalongkorn's reign (1868–1910) to commemorate the hundredth anniversary of the Chakri dynasty, in 1882. An impressive mixture of Thai and Western architecture (an influence resulting from the king's journeys to colonial Singapore and Java), the lower part of the building was designed by a British architect; the distinctly Thai spires were added at the last moment, following protests by purists that it was improper that a hallowed Thai site be dominated by a building with a European style.

The top floor, under the tall central spire, contains golden urns with ashes of the Chakri kings. The pair of spires on either side hold the ashes of princes of royal blood. The large reception rooms are decorated with pictures of past kings, busts of foreign royalty (most of whom King Chulalongkorn met on his trips abroad), and a quantity of *objets d'art,* most of them European. The central hall is the magnificent **Chakri Throne Room**, where the king receives foreign ambassadors on a niello throne under a nine-tiered white umbrella, originally made for Chulalongkorn. Outside, the courtyard is dotted with ornamental ebony trees cut in Chinese style.

To the left of the Chakri Maha Prasad, a door leads to the **women's quarters**, an area where the king's many wives used to live. The king himself was the only male above the age of 12 allowed to enter the door, which led to the harem's lovely garden of cool fountains, pavilions and carefully pruned trees; it was guarded by armed women. Even today, this inner section is closed to visitors, except when the king throws a garden birthday party for diplomats and government officials.

North of the women's quarters lies **Borom Phiman Hall**, built in a French

Drawing room, Chakri Maha Prasad

style by Chulalongkorn as a residence for the then Crown Prince Vajiravudh, who later became Rama VI. It was in this building that the young King Ananda died in 1946.

The **Amarin Vinichai Hall**, just east of the doorway leading to the former harem, is another of the palace's few remaining original buildings. It is the northernmost of the three-building group known as the Maha Montien, and served as the bedchamber for Rama I, or Chakri; the three-room building originally served as a royal residence, the bedroom lying just beyond the main audience hall.

In the early days of Bangkok, the building was also the royal court of justice, where cases were heard and adjudicated by either the king or his ministers. Today, the audience hall is used for coronations and special ceremonies. During these ceremonies, the boat-shaped throne is at first concealed by two curtains, called *phra visud*. The king takes his seat unseen by those in the hall. Fanfare on conch-shell trumpets

precedes the parting of the curtains, with the king appearing resplendent in royal regalia. Moreover, by tradition, each new king spends the first night after his coronation here.

The building to the west of the Chakri Maha Prasad is the **Dusit Maha Prasad**, built by Chakri (Rama I) in 1789 to replace an earlier wooden structure, the Amarindrabhisek, which was struck by lightning. As the flames crackled and brought down the building, Chakri personally carried out the heavy teak throne. A splendid example of classical Thai architecture, its four-tiered roof supports an elegant nine-tiered spire. The balcony on the north wing contains a throne once used by the king for outdoor receptions; the last occasion was when Vajiravudh (Rama VI) received the oath of loyalty from his court after his coronation in 1911. Deceased kings and queens lie in state here before their bodies are cremated on Sanam Luang, called more formally for this occasion the Phramane Ground.

Just in front of the Dusit Maha Prasad

Dusit Maha Prasad, Grand Palace.

is Thailand's most exquisite pavilion, the **Arporn Phimok Prasad**, or Disrobing Pavilion. It was built to the height of the king's palanquin, so that he could alight from his elephant and don his ceremonial hat and gown before proceeding to the audience hall. It was reproduced by Chulalongkorn at Bang Pa-in, the summer palace just to the south of Ayutthaya.

Wat Phra Kaeo, or **Temple of the Emerald Buddha**, adjoins the Grand Palace and serves as the royal chapel. Unlike the rest of the kingdom's 28,000 *wat*, no monks live here. Wat Phra Kaeo ranks among the world's great sights: a dazzling, dizzying collection of gilded spires, sparkling pavilions and towering mythological gods, both awesome and delightful. It is what most foreigners expect to see when they visit Thailand, and it is the single most powerful image they take away when they leave.

The wat deserves at least two visits. The first should be on a weekday, when the compound is relatively uncrowded and one can inspect its treasures. The second visit should be on a public holiday, when ardent worshippers fill the sanctuary, prostrating themselves on the marble floor before the golden altar. The air is alive with the supplicants' murmured prayers, heavy with the scent of floral offerings and joss sticks. Bathed in an eerie green light high on its pedestal, the small **Emerald Buddha** looks serenely down on the congregation.

Wat Phra Kaeo was the first permanent structure to be built in Bangkok. Begun by King Chakri in 1782, in imitation of the royal temple of the Grand Palace in Ayutthaya, it was created especially to house the 75-centimeter-high (30-in) jade Emerald Buddha, the most celebrated image in the kingdom. The Emerald Buddha was apparently found in Chiang Rai, in the early 1400s. It was moved around a lot in the subsequent decades, including a 200-year stop in Vientiane. The future King Chakri retrieved the image during battle; it was placed in the wat in 1784.

Today, the Emerald Buddha sits atop

Left, the Emerald Buddha. **Right**, ornate entrance of Wat Phra Kaeo.

an 11-meter-tall (36-ft) gilded altar, protected by a nine-tiered umbrella. Crystal balls on either side represent the sun and the moon. Three times a year, at the beginning of each new season, the king presides over the changing of the Emerald Buddha's robes: a golden, diamond-studded tunic for the hot season; a gilded robe flecked with blue for the rainy season; and a robe of enamel-coated solid gold for the cool season.

The walls of the cloister that surround the temple courtyard are painted with murals telling the *Ramakien* story, the Thai version of the Indian *Ramayana* epic. The murals were originally painted during the reign of Rama III (1824–1850), but have been restored several times. The story begins on the left as one walks around the cloister. Epic battles, processions, consultations and other elements from the *Ramakien* story crowd the murals, along with depictions of daily life. Marble slabs set in pillars in front of the paintings are inscribed with poems relating each episode of the story.

On a broad, raised marble terrace are the **Prasat Phra Thep Bidom** (Royal Pantheon), the library (*mondop*), and a golden *chedi* erected by King Mongkut. The Royal Pantheon contains life-sized statues of the Chakri kings and is open to the public only on Chakri Day, April 6. In front of it stand marvelous gilded statues of mythological creatures.

The original pantheon was built in 1855, but was destroyed by fire and rebuilt in 1903.

Behind the Pantheon to the west is the library, surrounded by statues of sacred white elephants. (The white elephant, which once roamed the kingdom, are symbols of royal power.) The library was erected to hold the *Tripitaka,* the holy Buddhist scriptures. The original building too was destroyed by fire, ignited by fireworks during festivities to celebrate its completion. It is a delicate building rising skyward, and its glory is the multi-tiered roof fashioned like the crown of a Thai king.

Nearby is a large, detailed model of the famous Khmer temple of Angkor Wat. The model was built by Mongkut

to show his people what the temple looked like during the 16th century, when Thais ruled it.

Beyond the wat: North of Wat Phra Kaeo is a large oval lawn known as **Sanam Luang** (Royal Field), and, more formally, as **Phramane Ground** (Royal Cremation Ground). Originally, the palace (now the National Museum) of the so-called second king – a deputy king of sorts – occupied the northern half. It is written that when the Vietnamese threatened an invasion, King Rama III ordered the area be planted in rice. Vietnamese generals, told that the Thai army could hold off indefinitely with such supplies of food, called off the invasion.

The ground has served as the cremation site for high royalty, most recently the 1996 ceremony for King Bhumibol's mother. In a significant departure from tradition, the bodies of those killed in the 1973 revolution were given a royally-sponsored cremation in the field. The annual Plowing Ceremony, an ancient Brahmanistic ritual, is held here each May (on an astrologically-auspicious date) to mark the official beginning of the rice-planting season.

It is also a place for recreation. Thais come here to *pai dern len* (take a leisurely stroll), or to picnic in the late afternoon. Impromptu soccer games are played and children chase each other around the trees. From around mid-February through April, vendors set up racks decorated with dozens of styles and sizes of kites.

Off in the northeast corner of Sanam Luang is the intriguing **statue of Mae Toranee**. A key figure from the Buddha's life, Mae Toranee's image was erected by King Chulalongkorn at the turn of the century as a public water fountain. In the stories, the goddess wrings torrents of water out of her hair to wash away evil spirits threatening the meditating Buddha. It is an apt symbol, perhaps, in a city that submerges beneath the monsoon-swollen Chao Phraya's overflowing waters.

To the northwest is the **National Museum**, in several buildings housing art and ethnology exhibits. (There are **National Museum.**

more than 30 branches of the museum throughout the country.) Besides housing a vast collection of antiquities, the museum has an interesting history of its own. The oldest buildings in the compound date from 1782 and were built as the palace of the "second king", a sort of deputy ruler, a feature of the Thai monarchy until 1870. Originally, the palace included a large park that went all the way to Wat Mahathat and covered the northern half of the present Phramane Grounds, or Sanam Luang.

The first building to the left of the entrance is the **Sivamokha Biman Hall**, which was originally an open-sided audience hall. It now houses the prehistoric art collection, in particular, the bronzes and some of the handsome painted earthenware jars found in northeast Thailand.

Directly behind the entrance is the **Buddhaisawan Chapel**, built in the late 1700s by the second king as his private place of worship. It contains some of Thailand's most beautiful and best-preserved murals – 28 scenes from the Buddha's life and dating from the 1790s. Above the windows, five bands of *thep* (angels) kneel in silent respect to Thailand's second most-sacred Buddha image, the famous Phra Buddha Sihing, a bronze Sukhothai-style image. The image is paraded through the streets – empty of cars – of Bangkok each year on the day before Songkran.

Also in the museum compound is the **Tamnak Daeng**, or Red House. Originally located across the river in Thonburi, where the capital was once situated, it was the residence of an elder sister of Chakri and was formerly located in the grounds of the Grand Palace. It has a fascinating collection of furniture used by early royalty.

The finely-proportioned old palace of the second king, which formerly held the museum's entire collection, is now reserved for ethnological exhibits of elephant *howdah*, ceramics, palanquins, royal furnishings, weapons and other old objects. The Buddhist art collection, in the new wings on either side, includes sculptures from other Asian countries,

Buddhaisawan Chapel.

but its main exhibitions are of Thai art and sculpture.

Wat Po (sometimes spelled Pho) is the popular name for Wat Phra Chettuphon, the **Temple of the Reclining Buddha**. The oldest and largest temple in Bangkok, it is located just south of the Grand Palace and is divided into two sections, one containing the living quarters of 300 resident monks and the other, a variety of religious buildings. The two sections are separated by the narrow and easy to miss Chettuphon Road.

There are 16 gates in the huge, massive walls of Wat Po, but only two of them, both on Chettuphon Road, are open to the public. Each of the 16 gates is guarded by giant demons.

While the temple compound is large, it is crammed with a multitude of buildings, pavilions, statues and gardens.

The first temple building on this site was built in the 16th century, but the wat did not achieve real importance until the establishment of Bangkok as the capital. Wat Po was a particular favorite of the first four Bangkok kings, all of whom added to its treasures. The four large chedi to the west of the main chapel are memorials to them, the earliest being the green-mosaic chedi built by Chakri, and the last being the blue one built by Mongkut in the mid-19th century. Around the chapel are 91 other chedi. The wat contains 1,000 bronze Buddha images, retrieved from ancient ruins in Sukhothai and Ayutthaya.

The vast quantity and variety of things to be seen at Wat Po are more meaningful if you bear in mind that the early kings regarded the temple as a primary source of public education; it is sometimes called Thailand's first university.

Objects were placed in the compound as a way of letting people acquire knowledge, and not necessarily connected with Buddhism. Murals illustrated treatises on such diverse subjects as military defense, astrology, morality, literature and archaeology. Twenty small hills around the compound serve as a useful geology les- **Reclining Buddha feet.**

son, displaying stone specimens from different parts of Thailand.

Wat Po's *bot* is considered to be one of Bangkok's most beautiful. Girdling its base are sandstone panels superbly carved and depicting scenes from the *Ramakien*. The equally-striking bot doors are also devoted to *Ramakien* scenes, brilliantly rendered in some of the finest of mother-of-pearl work found in Asia. Moreover, the cloisters surround it contain some of Bangkok's finest Buddha images.

Wat Po is still regarded as a center for traditional medicine. The building to the left is the headquarters for Bangkok's traditional medicine practitioners. The dozen stone statues of hermits that sit under trees or on rocks were used as diagnostic tools by herbal physicians. The patient pointed to the statue depicting the pain he was feeling; the physician prescribed a remedy. Each day, in the late afternoon, people flock here for herbal treatments.

Traditional Thai massage has nothing to do with the services offered in the gloomy salons of Patpong. The authentic massage is based on reflex massages, yoga and acupuncture. It originated from the 1,000-year-old Indian therapies that accompanied Buddhism to Thailand. Strong thumbs dig deep into tense muscles and work at the body's energy points. Fingers are stretched until the joints crack, and the masseurs bring their full body weight to bear as they rub vigorously up and down on either side of the spinal column. When the pressure from hands, feet and elbows ceases, the pain gives way to pleasant relief. (It's worth the experience.)

Wat Po's big attraction is its gigantic **Reclining Buddha**, in an 1830s *viharn*. The largest in Thailand, the 46-meter-long (150-ft) and 15-meter-high (50-ft) image is covered entirely with gold leaf, and it depicts a dying Buddha entering *nirvana*. The soles of the Reclining Buddha's feet, just over five meters high, are inlaid with mother-of-pearl designs, depicting the 108 auspicious signs for recognizing a Buddha. It was commissioned by Rama III.

Vat Po: one-stop shopping nd entrance.

ACROSS THE RIVER

On the Thonburi bank of the Chao Phraya River, opposite Wat Po, **Wat Arun** is probably the most-remembered image of Bangkok. (Except for the traffic, perhaps.) It is reached by taking a ferry from the Tha Tien landing, just behind the Grand Palace.

Dating from the Ayutthaya period, this Temple of the Dawn started as a short *prang* next to an old temple called Wat Cheng. In the early 19th century, King Rama II enlarged the temple and raised the height of the central tower from 15 meters (50 ft) to its present 104 meters (345 ft) with a base of 37 meters (125 ft), one of the tallest religious structures in the country.

But, at first, the soft earth defeated the royal engineers. It was not until the reign of Rama III that a solution was found: hundreds of *klong* jars were turned upside down and the prang was erected on this floating support. It worked, and Wat Arun has stood to this day with only minor repairs – in 1971, after lightning split a portion of the upper spire.

The great prang (rounded spire) represents Mount Meru, with its 33 heavens. Its decoration is a mosaic of multicolored Chinese porcelain embedded in cement. The builders ran out of porcelain for this large edifice, compelling Rama III to call upon his subjects to contribute broken crockery to complete the decoration. Artisans fashioned the pieces into flower petals, or used them to decorate the costumes of the small gods and mythical figures that ring each tier, guarding it from evil.

It's possible to climb about halfway up the central tower by one of four steep staircases for a fine view of the temple and river. The niches at the foot of each stairway contain images of the Buddha in the four key events in his life: birth, meditation (while sheltered by a seven-headed *naga* serpent), preaching to his first five disciples, and at death. The four outer prang hold statues of Phra Phai, god of the wind.

The complex is guarded by mythical giants called *yaksa,* similar to those that protect Wat Phra Kaeo. Some good murals cover the inside of the *bot*.

A short distance upriver, in an open space opposite the Grand Palace, is **Wat Rakang**, the bell wat. It has a lovely collection of bells, which are rung each morning. Behind it are three wooden houses, now collectively called Tripitake Hall, which once belonged to the future King Rama I when he was a monk, and when Thonburi was the capital of Thailand. The wat's treasure is its library, sitting directly behind the bot. Superb murals dating from 1788 depict scenes from the *Ramakien* and the *Traiphum* (Three Worlds), the Buddhist cosmology.

A visit to Wat Arun can be combined with one to the **Royal Barges**, on the north bank of Khlong Bangkok Noi, which opens into the main river at the Bangkok Noi Railway Station. These splendidly-carved boats are used during the rare Royal Barge Procession, when the king makes a royal *kathin* at the end of the rainy season, taking robes and gifts to the monks of Wat Arun.

His Majesty rides in the largest of the 51 barges, the magnificent *Sri Supannahong*. Nearly 45 meters (150 ft) long, it requires a crew of 54 oarsmen, two steersmen, two officers, one flagman, one rhythm keeper and one singer, who chants to the cadence of the oars. Two seven-tiered umbrellas are placed in front of and behind the golden pavilion that shelters the king. The gilded bird's head that forms the prow of the barge represents a *hong*, or sacred swan. It is a spectacle that, if the opportunity presents itself, must be seen.

But this spectacle is so costly that it is only rarely held, the last occasions being for the Chakri dynasty's bicentennial celebration in 1982, and the king's 60th birthday in 1987.

A short distance away is **Wat Suwannaram**, rarely visited. Erected by Rama I in the late 18th century, it has been extensively renovated. Interior murals of the ten lives of Buddha, commissioned by Rama III, are thought by many to be Bangkok's best.

Wat Arun, across the Chao Phraya

BANGKOK TRAFFIC

Is Bangkok traffic always this bad? No, sometimes it's worse. It's especially bad in the middle of a heavy rainy season when small, low-lying streets may be under water for weeks. The worst must be after a sudden rainy season downpour when commuters and schoolchildren don't struggle home until midnight. But on normal days, many children rise at dawn in order to take a string of buses to school.

The traffic keeps getting worse – that is, slower – because there are no restrictions on buying, registering or driving new vehicles. The speed of traffic during morning and evening peak periods continues to drop. It's somewhere below 2 kilometers per hour, which is equivalent to walking speed. Evening peak period runs from about 4pm to 9pm. Before Thailand's economy crumbled in the late 1990s, the number of new vehicles registered varied from between 300 and 500 new cars each weekday. Still, with about 2.5 million cars in the city, it's long been true that if every one were on the roads at once, there wouldn't be enough road space to contain them.

Economists estimate that traffic congestions leads to losses of millions of dollars in productivity everyday, due to wasted time and health costs. But that doesn't take into account the potential foreign investors who automatically shelve any plans for joint ventures after a single confrontation with traffic jams.

No one seems to want to contemplate the future health costs. A few Chinese cities could challenge claims that Bangkok is the most polluted city in the world, but it is securely among the top 15. Of course, motor vehicles are not solely to blame for the city's air pollution; exhaust from diesel vehicles and motorcycles is the chief culprit. They spew out levels of carbon monoxide, lead, dust particles, benzine and toulene that would have Western environmentalists committing sabotage.

For example, congested areas have clocked up carbon monoxide levels that exceed the city safety standard by 25 percent; but this city standard already allows twice the level of carbon monoxide that a US city would deem unhealthy. In an average year, airborne particulate matter exceeds 230 micrograms on 97 days. In New York, particulate matter never reaches that level on any day.

The health risks are considerable for traffic police. About one-third suffer from respiratory problems and another one-quarter have damaged hearing. Exposure to lead hits children hard and can cause permanent nerve damage, but there are no estimates of the number of pre-school children who spend the day beside their parents at sidewalk stalls or shops.

So what is Bangkok doing to solve this mess? Sad to say, not very much. That few Bangkokites seem to know or care may seem odd, given that they say in surveys that traffic is the city's number one problem (the environment being second). But over the years, residents have observed many ballyhooed mass transit plans collapse and fail time and again. During the boom years, work began on several mass transit projects and elevated expressways in Bangkok. Unfortunately, the recent economic crisis has put many of these projects on hold. When they will be completed is any one's guess, but visitors will see half-completed work everywhere in Bangkok.

Moreover, about twice a year, some government official swears to improve traffic with a few band-aid solutions, such as computerizing traffic lights or applying traffic laws even to "influential persons" in expensive imported cars. Six months later, someone else makes the same promises.

Traffic engineers, both foreign and Thai, say that, even if enforced, such band-aid methods wouldn't be enough to alleviate the crisis. They say that traffic won't improve until a comprehensive approach is adopted. Contrary to the promises of politicians, they say that a rail or subway system won't miraculously cure congestion. It's inevitable: the number of cars allowed on the roads must be restricted.

At least a half-dozen city and national agencies have claims over transit, construction and vehicle ownership. They are more concerned about protecting turf than cooperating. Finally, there are the social factors of restricting the number of cars.

Car ownership in Thailand has always been one of the most important symbols of status. Before the economic crisis ravaged the country, the wealthy used to boast about the number of Mercedes cars they owned. Ironically, traffic is noticeably less congested in Bangkok these days, but not because its citizens have suddenly become more conscious of the environment. With massive job layoffs, and loss of purchasing power, a shiny new car is the furthest thing from the average Bangkokite's mind.

THE OLD CITY AND DUSIT

This section of the old city holds temples whose beauty rivals those in the royal palace area. Many of the principal administrative and religious buildings of the original center of Bangkok lie between the first and second canals, **Khlong Lawd** to the west and a canal with two names – Banglampoo on its northern half and Ong Ang on its southern half – to the east. Along the latter canal were 14 watchtowers; only two have survived, at the canal's northern mouth on Phra Sumen Road and at the intersection of Ratchadamnoen and Maha Chai roads, in the shadow of the Golden Mount.

Wat Ratchabophit, located near the Ministry of Interior, east of Khlong Lawd, is easy to recognize by its distinctive doors, carved in relief with jaunty-looking soldiers wearing European-type uniforms. Built by King Chulalongkorn in 1870, the temple reflects the king's interest in blending Western art with traditional Thai forms.

The design of the principal structures is a departure from the norm, making it unique among Thailand's religious buildings. At the center of the courtyard stands a tall, gilded *chedi* enclosed by a circular cloister, like that encircling the Phra Pathom Chedi in Nakhon Pathom. Built into the northern side of the yellow tile-clad cloister is the *bot*, or chapel, itself covered in brightly-patterned tiles in a variety of hues.

The windows and entrance doors of the bot are works of art. Tiny pieces of mother-of-pearl have been inlaid in lacquer, in an intricate rendition of the insignias of the five royal ranks. In a recess beside one of the doors is a bas-relief of a god named Khio Kang, or Chew Hard, "the one with long teeth," who guards this sanctuary. Four chapels, connected to the central gallery by small porticoes, further enlarge this colorful temple.

The doors open into one of the most surprising temple interiors in Thailand.

Instead of the murals and the dark interior normal in Thai temples, this one has been rendered like a gothic European chapel, with all the light and delicacy of a medieval cathedral combined with a Versailles salon. Wat Ratchabophit was built before Chulalongkorn made his first trip to Europe; its design is remarkable. The king mixed the indigenous and the foreign even further when, 30 years later, he built Wat Benjamabophit.

Bamrung Muang Road, beside the Ministry of the Defense, heads east and – three name changes and several kilometers later – becomes Sukhumvit Road. Before the second canal, directly ahead, is the tall, gate-like structure known as **Sao Ching Chaa (Giant Swing)**. Bamrung Muang, on either side, is filled with shops selling religious objects for temples and homes.

The swing itself consists of two tall red poles in the center of a wide square, bounded on the north by the city hall and on the south by Wat Suthat. The Swinging Ceremony, no longer held, was a popular Brahmanist ritual held in honor

Left, lighted candles and lotus buds, Wat Benjamabophit. Right, Wat Suthat.

of the god Phra Isuan, who was believed to visit the earth for ten days every January. Teams of men pumped back and forth to set the swing in motion, struggling to snatch a bag of gold hanging from a tall pole. Miscalculations sent many plummeting to the ground below. The ceremony was suspended in the 1940s.

The Brahman temple, the only one in Bangkok, is a plain building on Dinsor Road, just northwest of the Swing.

Since the 14th century, the long-haired, white-robed Brahman priests have been a permanent fixture in Thai royal life. They are in charge of conducting royal statecraft and rite-of-passage ceremonies. They have also introduced the pantheon of Hindu gods, such as Siva, Brahma, Indra and others who reappear in Thai art and architecture.

Wat Suthat, which faces the Giant Swing, was begun by Chakri (King Rama I) and finished during the reign of Rama III. It is noted for its enormous bot, said to be the tallest in Bangkok, and for its equally large *viharn*, both of them surrounded by a gallery of gilded Buddha images. Cast in 14th-century Sukhothai, the Buddha image's size and beauty so impressed Chakri that he brought it down by river to Bangkok. The murals that decorate the walls date from the reign of Rama III; most intriguing are the depictions of sea monsters and foreign ships on the columns.

The bot's doors – of teak and 5.5 meters (18 ft) high, 15 centimeters (six in) thick – are among the wonders of Thai art. Carved to a depth of five centimeters, they follow the Ayutthayan tradition of floral motifs, with tangled jungle vegetation hiding small animals. Accounts vary as to whether Rama II only designed the doors or actually carved them himself, but when they were finished, he ordered the chisels to be thrown into the river so that no one could duplicate them.

The courtyard is a museum of statuary with stone figures of Chinese generals and scholars. They came as ballast in Thai ships returning from rice deliveries to China. Given to merchants who

Dawn awakens on Wat Suthat and the Giant Swing.

had no space for them, they were in turn donated to temples, including Wat Po and Wat Arun. Even more beautiful are the bronze Chinese horses.

Democracy Monument was erected to commemorate the nation's first constitution, in 1932. It has been a rallying point for public protests, including the civil demonstrations of 1992.

Almost due north of Wat Suthat, past the Democracy Monument, is **Wat Bowon Niwet**. It was built by Rama III for Rama IV (Mongkut) when he was still a monk, and it was here that he reformed many of the Buddhist texts, ridding them of their superstitious elements. Since then, it has served as the temple where kings are ordained as monks; King Bhumibol donned the saffron robes here after his coronation. (Interestingly, Catholic theologian Thomas Merton died here.)

Nothing of note marks the buildings, but the bot contains some of the most unusual murals in the kingdom. They were painted by an innovative painter named Krua In-khong, a man who had never traveled outside Thailand but who understood the concept of Western perspective. Unlike the flat, two-dimensional paintings of classical Thai art, these recede into the distance and are characterized by muted, moody colors. Interesting are the subjects: antebellum southern American mansions, race tracks, people dressed in the fashions of 19th-century America.

Gilded Chinese carvings surround the entrances to the bot and viharn – wealthy Chinese opium dealers once hoped that the gods would ignore their earthly business. The mouths of the temple guards at the doors were smeared with pitch so that they could not gossip. Royal crowns on the gables of the T-shaped bot refer to Mongkut and confirm the temple's royal connections. Inside, the Jinasri Buddha stands on a plinth beneath a gilded baldachin, one of the finest works of art from the Sukhothai period. Behind it, adopting the same pose in a mystical half-light, stands an even larger gilded Buddha figure, from Petchaburi.

Hidden away in the two viharn on

Democracy Monument.

either side of the huge bodhi tree are more Buddhas. The site is dominated by a 50-meter (160 ft) golden chedi.

The paintings on the double row of columns running from back to front of the bot relate the progress of humanity from barbarous to exalted state, in accordance with Buddhist precepts. The murals are unique in Thai painting.

Across Maha Chai Road from the watchtower below the Golden Mount is **Wat Ratchanadda** and its **amulet market**. Thais are believers in the protective powers of amulets, wearing them around their necks and taking great care in selecting precisely the right one.

The majority of images, often pressed into terracotta, are of Buddha, but there are amulets imprinted with portraits of monks renowned for their wisdom. Also found on amulets are other deities who are supposed to protect the wearer from harm. A ten-eyed deity, for example, protects not only from the front, but from the back and both sides as well. There are amulets that attract women to men, and vice versa, and amulets that ward off bullets and car accidents, and most forms of bad luck that one might encounter or imagine.

Behind Wat Ratchanadda is one of Bangkok's most unusual and most interesting structures, the **Loha Prasad**. Built by Rama III, the multi-tiered building is modeled on an ancient monastery in Sri Lanka. Loha Prasad rises in six tiers to a height of 35 meters (110 ft). Iron spires crowning its dozens of towers lend the name of Loha (metal) Prasad.

The most prominent monument in the area is the **Golden Mount** (**Phu Khao Thong**), for many years the highest point in the city. Ayutthaya had a large artificial hill, and King Rama III decided to reproduce it in Bangkok. Because of the city's soft earth, however, he was never able to raise it to the desired height, and it was not until the reign of Mongkut that the hill and the chedi topping it were completed.

Standing 78 meters (256 ft) high, the top level is reached by a stairway of 318 steps that ascends around the base of the hill. The gilded chedi contains relics of **Golden Mount.**

158

WATERWAYS

For centuries, the river and *khlong,* or canal, served as the transportation arteries of Thailand. In a land that flooded whenever the monsoon-swollen river overflowed its banks, it made little sense to build roads that would be washed away. Rivers and canals also provided natural defenses as moats against invaders.

In the Central Valley, and especially at Ayutthaya, master engineers diverted a river to turn Ayutthaya into a fortified island. Later, in Bangkok, engineers dug a canal across a neck of land between the present site of Thammasart University and Wat Arun, thereby eliminating a long roundabout route to the mouth of the Chao Phraya. Erosion eventually widened the canal, which has now become the river's main course. The original river loop became the khlong of Bangkok Noi and Bangkok Yai.

When King Rama I established Bangkok, he had three concentric canals constructed, turning the royal city into an island. Other canals were dug to connect them. In the 19th century, it was estimated that more than 100,000 boats plied the canals.

The most extensive rural canal expansion came during the reign of King Chulalongkorn. His engineers mapped the Central Valley, and the monarch gave farm land to he who would – or could – dig the section of canal passing his property. Within a few years, thousands of kilometers of canals crisscrossed the Central Plains. The magnitude of this enormous project can only be appreciated from an airplane.

In the mid 20th century, Bangkok shifted from boats to cars. Canals were filled in to create roads, and houses were built on solid ground. The result is evident: congested and noisy streets in the hot season, flooded streets in the monsoon season.

Zipping along at water level in a *rua hang yao,* or long-tailed boat, is one of the coolest ways to tour the city. The rua hang yao is a particularly Thai invention, born of necessity. In engineering terms, it is simplicity itself: A car or truck engine is mounted on a pivot at the stern of a long, low and narrow boat. A long shaft, or "tail", extends from the back of the boat, the small propeller spinning furiously in the water, spitting a rooster tail and propelling the boat at quite rapid speeds. In the narrow canals, the pivot allows the boatman to turn the craft in a very tight radius.

A lovely 90-minute route zips upriver to Khlong Bangkok Noi. A short way beyond the Bangkok Noi Railway Station is the Royal Barge Museum. If asked, the driver will stop for a few minutes for a tour of the museum. Continue up the canal, turning left into Khlong Chak Phra, which soon changes its name to Bang Kounsri and eventually to Bangkok Yai.

One of the most scenic khlong in the eastern section of Bangkok is **Khlong Saen Sap**, dug to carry troops to Chachoengsao to fight invaders from the east, and to join the Bangpakong River for a journey into the sea. The canal begins at Pratunam, but the water is filthy and fetid there. It is better to start at the Ekamai Bridge or at Phrakanong Khlong Tan Bridge, off Sukhumvit Road. The canal is straight and unshaded, so it's less attractive than the twisting Thonburi canals, but it passes through lovely rice country.

The Chao Phraya River also offers possibilities for exploration. The cheapest and most common form of transport are the *rua duan,* or express buses, that run between the Krung Thep Bridge, south of Bangkok, and Nonthaburi, an hour north of the city. The boats make frequent stops along the river, allowing stops to explore, then board another boat later. ∎

the Buddha given to Chulalongkorn, in 1877, by the Viceroy of India, Lord Curzon. The climb is fairly exhausting. Until World War II, it served as a watchtower, with guards armed with signal flags to watch for enemy invaders. During the war, sirens howled from its heights during air raids by British bombers, the Thais having sided with Japan.

At the bottom of the Golden Mount, **Wat Saket** was built during the Ayutthaya period, and was originally called Wat Sakae. Upon returning from Laos in 1782 with the Emerald Buddha, Gen. Chakri stopped here and ceremonially bathed, before proceeding on his way back to Thonburi to be crowned King Rama I. The name was later changed to Saket, which means "the washing of hair."

The temple is also associated with a more grisly history. Commoners were once cremated here. An epidemic during the reign of Rama II killed 30,000 people; their bodies were taken out of the city through the Pratu Pii, or Ghost Gate, and laid here. Soon the sky was black with vultures. The scene was repeated during plagues in 1873, 1881, 1891, and 1900, each killing around 10,000 people.

North to Dusit: Crossing the khlong, Ratchadamnoen Avenue turns into a pleasant, tree-lined boulevard that leads to a square in front of the old National Assembly. The square is dominated by a statue of Chulalongkorn, on horseback, who was responsible for much of this part of Bangkok. On the anniversary of his death each October 23, the square is crowded with students and government officials honoring him by laying wreaths at the base of his statue.

To the left of the square is **Amporn Gardens**, a spacious park with fountains and trees. It is the setting for many royal social functions and fairs. At the back of the square stands the former **National Assembly (Parliament)** building, an Italian-looking hall of gray marble crowned by a huge dome. It was built in 1907 by Chulalongkorn as his Throne Hall, only later becoming the Parliament building. Special permission

Parliament Building, gloriously decked out with strings of lights, in honor of the King's birthday.

is required to go inside the building, decorated with huge murals depicting famous events in Thai history. In 1974, Parliament moved to new premises a short distance north.

Behind the old National Assembly is **Vimarn Mek**, billed as the world's largest golden teak building. Vimarn Mek, or Cloud Mansion, was built in 1901 by King Chulalongkorn as a cooler, rustic getaway home in what was then the Bangkok suburbs. The interesting melange of Italian, Victorian and Thai architectural styles is especially appropriate because of the objects and photographs displayed. Chulalongkorn was the first Thai monarch to visit Europe; here, one can see the kinds of things that caught his eye: Faberge eggs, chinaware, and perhaps the country's first Western-style bathtub. Demonstrations of traditional dancing and Thai boxing take place on the grounds of the house. A collection of historical photographs depict, among many things, one of the last times in Thailand that elephants were used in battle during war. There are also photographs taken by the king himself. Visitors must be escorted through the building.

East of the National Assembly building is **Dusit Zoo**, also known as Khao Din – Mountain of Earth – for the small hill it holds. There are entrances both here and on Ratchawithi Road. Dusit Zoo is the city's main animal park and one of the most popular places in Bangkok for family outings. A lake with boats for rent is surrounded by cages containing the exotic wildlife of Asia: gibbons, Sumatran orangutans, an aviary, snakes and a host of other animals.

White elephants: Among the most interesting are the king's white elephants. By tradition, every white elephant found in Thailand belongs to the king. To newcomers, white elephants look nearly the same color as normal gray ones. It is only by a complicated process involving an examination of skin color, hair and eyes by court officials that the elephant's albino traits are discovered.

Historically throughout Southeast Asia, the white elephant has denoted

Studio in Vimarn Mek.

regal power. Buddha's mother is said to have dreamed of a white elephant touching her side with his trunk, causing her to conceive. Buddha, in one of his previous incarnations, was expelled from his palace after giving a white elephant to a rival kingdom.

The number of white elephants a king owned signified his power; the more he had, the more powerful he was. Wars were fought over ownership of white elephants. One could not own a white elephant without providing all the care their exalted status demanded – special quarters and rare foods were necessary. If the king suspected that a minor prince was becoming too powerful, he would give him a white elephant. The prince would go bankrupt trying to feed and house it; hence, the term "white elephant" that denotes a gift or project costing dearly to maintain.

East of the zoo is **Chitralada Palace**, where the king and queen now reside. It is, of course, not open to the public. Nevertheless, keen observers might note some seemingly unroyal things on the

grounds. The king has long had a deep interest in improving the agricultural well-being of his subjects, especially those in poorer areas of the country. He spends considerable personal time involved in agricultural research, on the palace grounds, and at his own expense.

To the south of the Chulalongkorn statue is **Wat Benjamabophit**, the Marble Wat, the last major temple built in Bangkok. Started by Chulalongkorn in 1900, it was finished ten years later.

The wat was designed by Prince Naris, a half-brother of the king. A talented architect, Naris made a number of departures from the traditional style. The most obvious of these must be the enclosed courtyard; the Carrara marble, from Italy, used to cover the main buildings; and the curved, yellow Chinese roof tiles. Also unique for the time are the bot's stained-glass windows.

The king was quite delighted with the result, writing, " I never flatter anyone, but I cannot help saying that you have captured my heart in accomplishing such beauty as this."

The bot's principal Buddha image is a replica of the famous Phra Buddha Jinnirat of Phitsanulok (which is said to have wept tears of blood when Ayutthaya overran the northern center of Sukhothai, in the 14th century). The base of the Buddha image contains the ashes of King Chulalongkorn. Behind the bot is a gallery holding 51 Buddha images from around Asia. The gallery serves as instruction in the ways that the Buddha has been depicted throughout Asia.

Through the rear entrance of the courtyard is a huge Bodhi tree, approaching a century in age, and said to be derived from a tree that came from Buddha's birthplace in India. Nearby is a pond of turtles, which are released there by people seeking to gain merit.

The wat is most interesting in the early morning, when Buddhists gather before its gates to give food to monks. By giving food to the monks, believers gain merit in their quest to reach nirvana. It is also a popular gathering place for Thais on the Buddhist holidays.

The Dusit area is typically overlooked by travelers, but is worth visiting.

Left, forging a monk's bowl. Right, gilded stucco at Wat Ratchabophi

CHINATOWN

Despite the seeming homogeneity of its population, Bangkok was built by a multitude of nationalities. Small neighborhoods of these people still remain, but many of their residents have moved on, now living side by side with ethnic Thais. Muslims, for example, have integrated into Bangkok's social fabric, yet still prefer to cluster in small communities around mosques. The Burmese traders and Khmers who dug the canals have been completely assimilated, as have the Laotians.

Indians have also blended into the community, and except for the turbans worn by some, are as Thai as Thais. Many are now cloth merchants.

Chinatown, or **Sampeng**, began its life in an area to which the Chinese merchants moved in the 1780s after vacating the land where the Grand Palace now stands.

In 1863, King Mongkut built **New Road**, the first paved street in Bangkok, and Chinatown soon began to expand northwards towards it. New Road, or Charoen Krung, runs over six kilometers, from the Royal Palace to a point where it drops straight into the river, just south of the Krung Thep Bridge. Chinatown was followed at Krung Kasem Canal by a Muslim district that, in turn, was followed by a *farang* area (where the Oriental Hotel now stands). Later, a third road, Yaowarat, was built between Charoen Krung and Sampeng, becoming the main road of Chinatown and the other name for the area.

The area has had a somewhat rowdy history. What began with mercantile pursuits soon degenerated into a lusty, earthy entertainment area. By 1900, alleys led to opium dens and houses whose entrances were marked by green lanterns (*khom khiew*). A green-light district was like a Western red-light district, and while the lanterns have disappeared, the term *khom khiew* still signifies a brothel. Eventually, Sampeng was tamed into a sleepy lane of small shops

House, car and money for the afterlife.

selling goods imported from China. **Sampeng Lane** begins on Maha Chai Road and is bound at either end by Indian and Muslim shops. The western end, Pahurat, has a warren of tiny lanes filled with Indians and Sikhs selling cloth. Across the canal is Sampeng proper, with shops selling inexpensive jewelry, tools, cloth, clothes, toys, shoes and novelties. The prices are low; this is where ordinary Thais shop.

After crossing Chakrawat Road, turn right a short distance to the entrance of **Wat Chakrawat**, an odd amalgam of buildings. Dating from the Ayutthaya period and thus predating Chinatown, it has a small grotto with a statue of a laughing monk. Myth says that it is the likeness of a monk who was once slim and handsome, so handsome he was constantly pestered by women. His devotion to Buddhism led him to the unusual remedy of eating until he grew so gross that the women lost interest.

The *wat* in Thailand normally serve as a humane society. Thais with a litter of puppies or kittens they cannot feed leave them at the wat, to be fed the leftovers from the monks' daily meals. This wat is a departure from the norm, as the animals it houses are crocodiles.

These crocodiles are the descendents, it's said, of an old one-eyed crocodile named Blind Old Guy, who was a fearsome beast over half a century ago. Unwary bathers in the canals just outside of town could suddenly find themselves on the dinner menu. The old guy fell on hard times, however, and the abbot of the wat took pity and gave him a home. He finally died, the loser in a battle with a younger crocodile.

Back on Sampeng, continue east. Halfway down on the left is a handsome building that once served as the gold exchange. In the side alleys are quiet Chinese temples; farther down on the right are sweet-scented shops selling slabs of cinnamon and other spices. Here and there are small and dark wet markets that throb with life at dawn and are dead by mid-morning.

Near the end of Sampeng, notice that the shops bear Muslim names. The mer-

Wholesale market, west end of Chinatown.

chants here trade gems. Marking the eastern end of Sampeng is **Wat Pathuma Kongkha**, also called Wat Sampeng and another temple from the Ayutthaya period. One of Bangkok's oldest temples, it was here that criminals of royal birth were executed for crimes against the state.

At places, **Yaowarat Road** looks like a Hong Kong street with its forest of signs. It is best known for its gold shops, all of which seem to have been designed by a cookie cutter, so alike they look. Daily prices are scrawled on the windows of shops painted red for good luck. Mirrors and neon lights complete the decor. Prices are quoted in *baht*, an ancient unit of weight measurement.

Yaowarat is also an old entertainment area. Halfway down on the north side of the street is the famous "Seven Storey Mansion" that flourished well into the middle part of this century. It was designed so that those interested only in dining could do so on the ground floor. As the evening progressed, one would ascend the stairs, floor by floor, to more sybaritic delights; unrepentant hedonists headed straight for the top floor.

Between Yaowarat and New roads, near the west end of Chinatown, is **Nakhon Kasem**, or **Thieves Market**. A few decades ago, it was the area a householder searched after being robbed, a likely place where one might recover stolen goods for a very reasonable price. It later became an antique dealer's area, but the antiques have been nudged aside by more prosaic items such as cement mixers and automobile mufflers. Nevertheless, it is still possible to find a few shops selling pottery and Buddha images.

Near the eastern end of New Road is Chinatown's biggest Mahayana Buddhist temple, **Wat Monkhonkamalawat**, normally shortened to Wat Monkhon. From early in the morning it is aswirl with activity and incense smoke reminiscent of old China.

The most interesting lane is **Isara Nuphap**, which runs south from Phlab Phla Chai Road. It begins near a busy Mahayana Buddhist temple called Wat Hong Kong, and passes a Thai temple called **Wat Kanikaphon**. Its predecessor was built by a former brothel madam named Mae Lao Fang to atone for her sins. Better known as Wat Mae Lao Fang, the wat's name of Kanikaphon means "woman who sold women".

Around the entrance to Isara Nuphap are shops selling miniature houses, Mercedes-Benz cars, household furniture and other items – all made of paper. These are for the Chinese *kong tek* ceremony. The items are taken to the temple and burnt to send them to deceased relatives. Other shops sell the bright red-and-gold-trimmed shrines the Chinese install in their homes.

Hua Lamphong railway station is a rather old station, with its tall roof built in 1890 and modeled on one of the main-line terminals in Manchester, England. The first line went as far as Nakhon Ratchasima (Korat), and 30 years later, it was extended to Chiang Mai and Singapore. Nowadays, trains leave to most parts of the country. (The Oriental Express also terminates here.)

Just east of the point where Yaowarat

Appeasing ghosts at wholesale market.

Road meets Charoen Krung Road (not far from Hua Lamphong station) is **Wat Traimit** and the famous **Golden Buddha**, found by accident in the 1950s at a riverside temple. A construction company was extending its dock, and the huge stucco figure was too heavy for the sling as it was being moved. It snapped and, to the horror of all, smashed to the ground, breaking one corner. A close examination showed a glint of yellow through the crack. Further investigation revealed that stucco was only a thin coat and that inside was an image of solid gold weighing over five tons. Like many similar statues, it was probably made elsewhere in Thailand during the Ayutthayan period. To preserve it from Burmese invaders, it was covered in stucco to conceal its true composition and rested undetected for centuries.

South of Wat Traimit along New Road, mementos of the European *farang* era are found in the many old buildings that line the river. Where Klong Krung Kasem enters the Chao Phraya is the **River City Shopping Center** and the Royal Orchid Sheraton Hotel. Just to the south of the boat pier, the Portuguese embassy and lush gardens hide behind tall walls, what's left of a time when villas belonging to merchants and foreign embassies overlooked the river. (The **General Post Office** sits atop the former site of the British Embassy.)

The **Oriental Hotel** is consistently rated as one of the world's finest hotels. The old wing, where many notable luminaries and celebrities have stayed, retains much of its old charm (but guest rooms are now in a newer tower). Next to the hotel is a building once occupied by the Danish East Asiatic Company nearly a century ago. Behind it rises the tower of the Catholic **Assumption Cathedral**, a white-and-brown stone colonial-looking building. English-language masses are held on Sundays. Associated with it is a college regarded as one of Thailand's top schools.

While the land along this part of the river is still covered by luxury hotels, much of the commercial activity is now along Silom Road.

House along Chao Phraya.

MODERN BANGKOK

Travelers may find it tempting to stay in the old royal part of the city, Rattanokosin, with its many temples and traditional sights that are protected by canals from the outside. But there is another Bangkok beyond the canals, expanding and fussy and modern. Yet even within the modern Bangkok, there are gems that await to be seen.

On Khlong Maha Nag at the end of Soi Kasemsan II, across from the National Stadium on Rama I Road, stands **Jim Thompson's house**. This Thai-style house is, in truth, a collection of seven Thai houses joined together by the remarkable American, an intelligence officer who came to Thailand at the end of World War II and revived the Thai silk industry. In 1967, while on a visit to the Cameron Highlands in Malaysia, Thompson mysteriously disappeared; despite an extensive search, no trace has been found of him.

Besides his contribution to the silk business, Thompson is remembered for his fabulous collection of Asian art, and for the house in which he displayed it. Several teak houses were moved from Ayutthaya and reassembled at the edge of a canal. (Thai houses are built in panels attached to pillars by wooden pegs, so are eminently transportable, if one wishes to do so.) The garden around the house is a luxuriant tropical mini-jungle. His heirs have decided to keep everything as he left it. "Not only have you beautiful things," Somerset Maugham once wrote Thompson after dining with him, "but what is more rare, you have displayed them beautifully."

Shopping excess: The intersection of Rama I and Phaya Thai offers some of the city's best shopping opportunities. On the southwest corner next to the National Stadium is the air-conditioned **Mahboonkrong Shopping Center**, one of Bangkok's biggest complexes. Five floors of shops sell low-quality goods, but MBK offers a glimpse of what Thais actually buy, not just window-shop.

To the east across Phaya Thai is a sprawl of stores and streets known as **Siam Square**. This area encompasses movie theaters, bookstores, and a wealth of restaurants offering Thai, Chinese, Japanese and Korean cuisines. Most popular are the dozen American fast-food joints (hardly offering a cuisine, however). Especially on the second-story level, close to Phaya Thai, are small shops and stalls selling pirated T-shirts, jeans and so on. At the southern edge of the square, on the campus of Chulalongkorn University, are the new premises of the British Council, which has a library and British newspapers.

Just beyond on Rama I stands **Wat Pathum Wanaram**, whose name means "The Lotus Temple" because of the great number of lotuses and water lilies blooming in the large pond behind it. The temple was built by King Mongkut in a large park that also held a palace, in which the king could escape the summer heat of the Grand Palace. The palace is gone, the trees have been cut and the ponds filled in to build the World Trade Center complex.

The temple's *bot* contains attractive murals painted during the reign of Rama V (1868–1910). Just before it is a lovely stone stele bearing a bas-relief of the Buddha's face. If the style looks un-Thai, it is because the stele was carved by an Italian sculptor who resided at the wat a few years ago. Wat Pathum Wanaram is the most popular temple in Bangkok among taxi drivers, who drive here to have their vehicles blessed against accidents.

To the south, along Henri Dunant Road (still called by Thais by its old name of Sanam Ma, or Race Course Road) are found two important old Bangkok institutions.

On the left, walking south from Siam Square, is the **Royal Bangkok Sports Club**, a multinational private club with sports facilities, golf course, and horse racing on alternate Sundays during all but the rainiest months. The club is closed to nonmembers, but the race course is open to the public.

Across the road stands the temple-like buildings of **Chulalongkorn Uni-versity**, the country's oldest and most prestigious institution of higher learning. The campus extends from Henri Dunant to Phaya Thai Road and holds 14 faculties.

Built in a mixture of Thai and Western styles, with spacious yellow-roofed pavilions, an open gallery and an assembly hall, the university was founded by King Vajiravudh (ruled 1911–1925) and named after his father, King Chulalongkorn.

South of the university is the **Pasteur Institute** or, as it is better known, the **Red Cross Snake Farm**. The entrance is on Rama IV Road directly opposite the Montien Hotel. Operated by the Thai Red Cross, its primary function is to produce antivenom serum to be used on snakebite victims. One may also obtain internationally-certified cholera, smallpox, rabies and typhoid fever inoculations here. The Snake Farm, the second oldest of its kind in the world, produces serum from several types of snake, including king and Siamese cobras, and numerous vipers.

Erawan Shrine and an evening crowd of believers.

Technicians milk Siamese cobras of their venom. Small doses of this venom will then be injected in horses at a farm near Si Racha. After a period, the horses' blood will be extracted in small amounts. The antigens separated from this blood will form the serum that will be distributed to hospitals around the country.

Other non-poisonous snakes, like pythons, are also exhibited. Of most interest to visitors is the deadly king cobra, which can grow up to five meters (15 ft) in length. While the workers are somewhat casual in handling the Siamese cobras and kraits, they concentrate intently when handling the king cobra, and for good reason.

At the end of Rama I is **Ratchaprasong intersection**, where the street intersects with Ratchadamri Road and briefly changes its name to Ploenchit Road before metamorphosing into Sukhumvit Road. The attraction here is the **Erawan Shrine**. To improve their fortunes or pass their exams, believers make offerings at a statue of the Hindu god, Brahma.

Originally erected by the Erawan Hotel, now the Grand Hyatt, to counter a spate of bad luck, the shrine is redolent with incense smoke and jasmine. To repay the god for wishes granted, supplicants place floral garlands or wooden elephants at the god's feet, or hire a resident troupe to dance. Day or night, the shrine provides a fascinating spectacle, an enclave of peace amid the din of one of the city's busiest streets.

Across the street, to the north of Erawan Shrine, is the Gay Sorn Plaza, yet another shopping center catering to the wealthy. To the west, the huge granite block called the **World Trade Center** is yet another shopping center, quite modern, quite comprehensive, and with restaurants and cinemas – and an ice rink for those in need of exercise.

North, still on Ratchadamri, is the government's handicrafts store, **Narayana Phand**. It has an excellent selection of goods and is worth exploring, if for no other reason than to learn about the wide variety of Thai crafts.

Continue up Ratchadamri to **Ratcha-**

Twilight blankets downtown Bangkok.

damri Arcade and Bangkok Bazaar. Both have the air of markets with numerous small shops crammed into a small space and vendors spilling off the sidewalks. One can often find some good handicraft bargains at small shops in Ratchadamri Arcade.

The pair serve as a link between the chic shops of Ratchaprasong and the bazaar atmosphere of a vast, sprawling Pratunam, one block north, a favorite shopping place for many Thais. *Pratunam* means "Water Gate," referring to the lock at the bridge to prevent Khlong San Sap, to the east, from being flooded by the one to the west, which leads to the Chao Phraya River. The noodle shops of Pratunam market are popular late-night eateries after the bars and movie theaters close.

Garden escapes: There are private gardens that can be visited for a respite from the city's fuss. One of the prettiest is Suan Pakkad, at 352 Sri Ayutthaya Road (north of downtown, just east of the intersection with Phaya Thai Road). The splendid residence belonged to the late Princess Chumbhot, one of Thailand's leading gardeners and prolific art collectors.

The beautifully-landscaped grounds (*suan* means garden, *pakkad* means cabbage) contain numerous plants the princess brought from all over the world, as well as varieties found in the Thai jungle.

The gardens are only one reason for visiting Suan Pakkad; another is its superb art collection. Five old traditional Thai houses overlook gardens, ponds and lawns, around which pelicans strut imperiously. In the open-walled houses are antique lacquer book cabinets, Buddha images, Khmer statues, old paintings, porcelain, musical instruments, the regalia of the late Prince Chumbhot, and other art objects.

At the back of the garden stands an exquisite little lacquer pavilion, which Prince Chumbhot discovered in a temple near Ayutthaya, brought to Bangkok, and had carefully restored. The pavilion's black and gold panels are considered masterpieces.

Other buildings at Suan Pakkad con-tain collections of seashells, mineral crystals, and pottery and bronze objects from the prehistoric burial ground at Ban Chiang, in northeast Thailand.

On the other end of Ratchadamri, at the intersection with Rama IV Road, is Lumpini Park, central Bangkok's only park. In the morning, it's Chinese. In the afternoon, Thai.

Wander into the park as the sun is rising and see elderly Chnese practice *tai chi chuan* exercises, the ancient, slow dance that had its origins as self-defence. Sturdy old men perform graceful maneuvers with swords. Middle-aged ladies tango to the strains of old music. Joggers pound along the pavement on a 2.5-kilometer circuit, an effort of either merit or folly, given the city's air pollution.

Just outside the fence on Soi Sarasin, vendors offer snake blood cocktails, slaying and skinning cobras on the spot and mixing the blood with brandy in huge tulip snifters. An early morning pick-me-up.

(It's advisable to vacate the park at

Late afternoon at Lumpini Park

dusk, when every level of low-life, including human, takes control.)

To the south of Lumpini Park – the Rama IV Road side – is the eastern end **Silom Road**, which extends west to New Road, near the Oriental Hotel. Silom Road has developed into one of Bangkok's more important and upscale commercial areas.

In the same area is the well-known **Patpong** area of sex shows and sex, more than you can shake a big stick at.

The **Siam Society** on Soi 21 (Soi Asoke), east of downtown off Sukhumvit Road, is a royally-sponsored foundation established in 1904 to promote the study of Thai history, botany, zoology, anthropology and linguistics. It publishes a scholarly journal containing articles by experts on those subjects, and also special books on specific subjects such as Thai orchids, Thai customs, and gardening.

Any visitor interested in the culture of northern Thailand should visit the **Kamthieng House**, in the Siam Society compound. This lovely old house, which is about a century and a half old, was the ancestral home of a prominent family in Chiang Mai. It was dismantled, brought to Bangkok and carefully reassembled in a garden composed mostly of traditional Thai plants. It has been converted to an ethnological museum devoted to folk art and implements of the north. (The National Museum in Bangkok has no such collection of northern ethnology.)

Notice, in particular, the beautifully carved teak lintels from traditional domestic houses, which are fast vanishing in the north. These were placed over the doorway leading to the inner main room of the house and are called, in northern dialect, *ham yon*, or sacred testicles; the inner room was believed to contain not only the ancestral spirits of the family, but also the virility of the present inhabitants. When an old northern house is dismantled, or when a new owner moves in, the *ham yon* are often symbolically castrated by beating them severely to destroy the powerful accumulated magic under the old owner.

Bus stop.

WEST OF BANGKOK

Before setting out from Bangkok by road, one should seriously consider one's schedule, and, too, the time of day. Nonetheless, outside of Bangkok there are numerous excursions well worth venturing into the suburbs, and beyond.

Less than an hour's drive from Bangkok, the **Rose Garden** is the brainchild of a former lord mayor of the capital. Known as Suan Sam Phran in Thai, the garden lies 30 kilometers (20 mi) west of the capital on Route 4, en route to Nakhon Pathom. Its large area of well-landscaped gardens contains roses and orchids, and includes accommodations, restaurants and a golf course.

Its premier attraction is a daily Thai cultural show at the garden. In a large arena, beautifully-costumed Thai actors demonstrate folk dances, Thai boxing, a wedding ceremony, cockfighting and other rural entertainment. Outside, after this show, elephants put on their own performance, moving huge teak logs as they would in the forests of the north. The elephants then carry tourists around the compound for a small fee.

One demonstrated sport is *takraw,* which can be seen played in parks and temple courtyards throughout Thailand using a small rattan ball. In the basket form of the game, they pass the ball back and forth, using their feet, knees, elbows and heads — everything except their hands. After several of these passes, they propel the ball upwards, trying to place it in the basket. After a set time period, during which the players try to score as many baskets as possible, it's the opposing team's turn. Takraw is a graceful game requiring great agility; a match proceeds languidly, but there are many special or showy moves that keep it interesting.

In the second form, two teams of three men each stand either side of a net stretched head high, as in badminton. A server lobs the ball over the net. Back and forth it goes, until it touches the ground, a losing situation. Many consider this the more exciting of the two styles, as there are many flashy moves, including a somersault kick that sends the ball across the net at great speed. Semiprofessional takraw teams put on excellent performances at temple fairs and parties.

Just 50 kilometers (30 mi) west of Bangkok, beyond the Rose Garden on Route 4, is the town of **Nakhon Pathom**. Notable is a colossal landmark rising from the flat countryside: **Phra Pathom Chedi**, at 130 meters (420 ft) in height the tallest Buddhist monument in the world, and the oldest in Thailand, dating from 300 BC.

The original Phra Pathom Chedi was small, built more than a thousand years ago by the Mon empire, whose culture flourished in Burma and Thailand. They established Nakhon Pathom as a religious center. In 1057, King Anawrahta of Burma besieged the town, leaving it in ruins for the next hundred years.

It was not until King Mongkut visited the old *chedi,* and was impressed by its significance as the oldest Buddhist monument in Thailand, that restoration of the temple began in 1853. The original structure was in such a state of collapse that repair proved impossible; a new chedi was built, taking 17 years to finish and covering the older one, originally built in the 4th century. Unfortunately, this too collapsed in a rainstorm, and eventually the present structure was completed by King Chulalongkorn.

Set in a huge square park, the massive chedi rests upon a circular terrace accented with trees associated with the Buddha's life. In November of each year, a huge fair in the temple grounds attracts crowds from far and near.

In former times, a royal visit to Nakhon Pathom was more than a day's journey, so it is not surprising that a number of palaces and residences were built there.

One of them, **Sanam Chand Palace**, has a fine *sala,* a meeting pavilion now used for government offices, and a building in a most unusual Thai interpretation of English Tudor architecture, used appropriately as a setting for Shakespearean drama. In front stands a statue of Yaleh, the pet dog of King

eceding
iges:
mple in
icient City.
ft, Phra
ithom
iedi,
ikhon
ithom.

Vajiravudh, who commissioned the palace. The fierce dog, unpopular with the court, was poisoned by the king's attendants. (Even as a statue, Yaleh looks insufferable.)

A good way to approach the coastal port of **Samut Sakhon** is by a branch railway connecting it with Thonburi, Bangkok's sister city. The line, called the Mae Klong Railway, runs at a loss, but it is subsidized because of its usefulness to the population of the three provinces west of Bangkok. The 40-minute journey first passes through the suburbs, then through thriving vegetable gardens, groves of coconut and areca palms and rice fields.

A busy fishing port, **Samut Sakhon** (also called Mahachai) lies at the meeting of the Tachin River, the Mahachai Canal and the Gulf of Thailand. The main landing on the river bank has a clock tower and a restaurant serving excellent seafood. Nearby, fishermen at the **fish market** unload fish, crabs, squids and prawns from their boats.

At the fish market pier, it's possible to hire a boat for a round-trip to Samut Sakhon's principal temple, **Wat Chom Long**, at the mouth of the Tachin River. Most of the buildings are modern, except for an old *viharn* immediately to the right of the temple's river landing. The viharn dates back about a century. The extensive grounds overlooking the water are charmingly laid out with shrubs and flowering trees. There is also a bronze statue of King Chulalongkorn commemorating his visit to the temple. His homburg hat does not in the least detract from his immense dignity.

From Samut Sakhon, cross the river to the railway station on the opposite side. Here, board a second train for another 40-minute trip to **Samut Songkhram**, on the banks of the Meklong River. The journey goes through broad salt flats, with their picturesque windmills revolving slowly in the sea breezes. Samut Songkhram is another pretty fishing town; wandering its wharf is an olfactory and a visual experience. Return to Bangkok along the same rail

Fishing boats anchored at harbor.

route or hire a long-tailed boat for a trip up the Meklong River to Ratchaburi.

River Kwai: Established in the early 1800s, thus making it a young city by Thai standards, **Kanchanaburi** is about 120 kilometers (75 mi) northwest of Bangkok, past Nakhon Pathom, and not far from the Thai border with Burma. It prospers from gem mining and a teak trade with Burma. The world's smallest species of bat, about the size of a bumblebee, was discovered near an odd-looking railway bridge crossing the Meklong River, also known as the Kwai Yai, a few kilometers outside of Kanchanaburi. The bridge is contoured with a series of elliptical spans, with an awkwardly rectangular center.

This is the so-called **Bridge on the River Kwai**. In fact, it's not. The bridge that spanned the mightier Kwai River and inspired the novel and film was farther north. Of course, the original bridge no longer exists.

Seeking to shorten supply lines between Japan and Burma in preparation for an eventual attack on British India, the Japanese began work on a railway between Thailand and Burma in 1942. For a large part of its 400-plus kilometers (260 mi), the railway followed the river valley; although the logistics of doing so were often nightmarish, following the valley allowed construction of the railway simultaneously in different areas. At the end, there were nearly 15 kilometers of bridges alone completed.

The Japanese forced 250,000 Asian laborers and 61,000 Allied prisoners-of-war to construct 260 kilometers (160 mi) of rail on the Thai side, leading to **Three Pagodas Pass** on the border. It is estimated that 100,000 Asian laborers and 16,000 Allied prisoners lost their lives from beatings, starvation, disease and exhaustion. In Kanchanaburi, graves mark 6,982 of those Allied soldiers.

There are two cemeteries in Kanchanaburi. The larger is on the main road nearly opposite the railway station; the second, Chungkai, is across the river on the banks of the Kwai Noi. Both hold the remains of Dutch, Australian, British, Danish, New Zealander and other

Allied prisoners-of-war; American war dead were removed to Arlington Cemetery, in Washington, D.C.

An appreciation of the enormous obstacles the prisoners faced is provided by the **JEATH Museum**, near the end of Lak Muang Road. (The museum's name derives from the first initial of those nationalities involved in the construction.) Established in 1977 by the monks of **Wat Chaichumpol** (Wat Chanasongkhram) next door, the museum is constructed like the bamboo huts in which the war prisoners lived. Utensils, paintings, writings and other objects donated by prisoners who survived share some of the horror of their hell-like existence.

Although the current memorial bridge is mistaken for the one made famous in print and film, it is worthwhile visiting from an historical point of view. It can be reached by boat or *samlor* from Kanchanaburi.

The bridge has lost some of its mystery and awe with commercialization, but walking across it is a sobering experience. (Niches between the spans provide an escape in case a train passes by.)

The entire railway was bought by the Thai government from the Allies for 50 million baht. Actually, the British had already dismantled several kilometers of track at the Burmese border, and the whole line was in need of considerable repair – the prisoners had done their utmost to make the worst possible job of constructing the railway.

Shortly before the end of the war, British bombers succeeded in destroying the fourth, fifth and sixth spans of the bridge. As war reparations, the Japanese replaced these three spans with two larger ones; the made-in-Japan signs on the newer girders strike an irony.

Today, the quiet little railway runs peacefully from Kanchanaburi to the terminus at Nam Tok, a 50-kilometer (30 mi) journey taking about one-and-a-half hours across one of the shakiest bridges in the world; the wooden pillars and sleepers creak and groan as the train moves slowly across them.

A steam locomotive used shortly after the war is displayed beside the

River Kwai tragedy reenacted with a sound and-light show.

tiny Kanchanaburi station platform, along with an ingenious Japanese supply truck that could run on both roads and rails. Floating restaurants and hotels line the banks of the attractive river.

The Asian Highway now runs from Kanchanaburi to the Burmese border at Three Pagodas Pass, a distance of 250 kilometers (150 mi). Sporadic fighting between the Burmese military and ethnic groups sometimes makes the area unsafe to visit, but there are many other interesting stops along the way.

The river and its branches are dotted with waterfalls. **Erawan** (or Elephant) **Falls**, 70 kilometers (40 mi) north of Kanchanaburi, is one such sight. Near Nam Tok are the **Khao Phang Falls**, where the water sluices down a series of limestone steps. From here, it is a three-hour boat ride to the **Sai Yok Falls**, where the water plunges into the river.

Nearly the entire length of the river is now dappled with resorts, most of them perched on bamboo rafts. These resorts provide an unusual form of accommodation and a starting point to explore Mon and Karen villages, waterfalls, caves and bamboo forests that lie either side of the river. The State Railways of Thailand offers an all-day trip from Bangkok to the Nakhon Pathom chedi, the bridge and POW cemetery, and the Khao Phang waterfalls.

One fortunate outcome of railway construction was the discovery by a Dutch prisoner – apparently with archeological training – of what he thought to be evidence of a neolithic site. Not until 1961 did a Thai-Danish archaeological research team confirm the find and open a whole new page of Thai prehistory.

A small museum close to the original excavations has many of the finds on exhibition, including a skeleton from one of the burial sites.

Long before it assumed its strategic role in the last war, Kanchanaburi had been a battlefield between the warring Siamese and Burmese; old battlements can still be seen. North of Ban Keo, before the station of Wang Po, are the Khmer ruins of Muang Sing.

Washing clothes in the river Kwai.

SOUTHEAST OF BANGKOK

Bangkok is Thailand's hub for commerce and government, and for tourism. Increasingly, visitors are venturing up-country, but the great majority still do their sightseeing in or around the city. Many of the popular attractions – the Ancient City, the Rose Garden and the Crocodile Farm – are located within easy driving distance of the capital.

The most popular resorts on the East Coast of the Gulf of Thailand are also within convenient reach of Bangkok. Excellent highways now lead out of Bangkok in all directions, and a trip that used to take three or four hours can now be made in just over an hour, assuming the roads are not clogged with traffic.

The **Crocodile Farm** is located in Samut Prakarn Province, near the river-mouth town of Paknam, half an hour's drive (30 kilometers, or 20 miles) south-east of Bangkok on the old Sukhumvit Highway (Route 3). A brochure describes it as "a happy marriage between wildlife conservation and commercial enterprise," and while the crocs that are turned into handbags might argue about the first part, few deny the second.

Started in the 1960s with an initial investment about 10,000 baht (less than US$500), the owner now has three farms (two in the northeast) worth 100 million baht (US$4.5 million). At present, the Samut Prakarn farm has about 30,000 fresh- and saltwater local crocodiles, as well as some South American caimans and Nile River crocodiles. They are hatched in incubation cells and raised in tanks. The young must be protected by netting from mosquitoes, which can blind them by biting their eyes.

The highlight of a visit to the farm is a show in which handlers enter a pond teeming with crocodiles and toss them about rather roughly. While this sounds dangerous in print, the lethargic beasts are more likely to bite less because of innate viciousness than because their noon nap has been interrupted.

Jaw appeal, Crocodile Farm.

After the crocodiles are skinned, incidentally, their meat is sold to restaurants in Samut Prakarn and Bangkok. The farm also has a zoo and amusement park with rides. The irony of all this is that the owners have succeeded in preserving the animal; nearly all the wild Asian species have been hunted to extinction.

Also in Samut Prakarn, a few kilometers from the Crocodile Farm, is the so-called **Ancient City**, which bills itself as the world's largest outdoor museum. The brainchild of a Bangkok millionaire with a passion for Thai art and history, it took around three years to construct. In what used to be 80 hectares (200 acres) of rice fields, designers sketched an area roughly the shape of Thailand and placed the individual attractions as close to their real sites as possible. There are replicas (some full size, most others one-third the size of the originals) of famous monuments and temples from all parts of the kingdom. Some are reconstructions of buildings that no longer exist, like the Grand Palace and Royal Chapel of Ayutthaya,

and some are copies of real places, like the huge temple of Khao Phra Viharn on the Thai-Cambodian border. Experts from the National Museum worked as consultants to ensure historical accuracy of the reproductions. At present, there are more than 60 monuments, covering 15 centuries of Thai history.

In addition to the monuments, the Ancient City also has a model Thai village, in which artisans work on various native handicrafts, such as lacquerware, ceramics and paper umbrellas. It has its own version of the floating market.

For those with time, **Paknam** is a bustling fishing town with an interesting market along its docks. Cross the river by ferry to the famous **Wat Phra Chedi Klang Nam**, which, contrary to its name (the *chedi* in the middle of the river) is now on solid land, the result of the river shifting its course. Thai kings used to stop at this temple on their way in and out of the country on state visits, praying for success in their journeys or thanks on their return.

Chinese
Pagoda,
Ancient City.

AYUTTHAYA: NORTH OF BANGKOK

Were one ignorant of the importance and history of **Ayutthaya**, one would nonetheless be impressed by the beauty and grandeur of this city built by 33 Ayutthayan kings over 400 years.

Ayutthaya was founded around 1350 by a prince of U-thong. Thirty years later, the kingdom of Sukhothai was under Ayutthaya rule, which then spread to Angkor in the east, and to Pegu, in Burma, to the west.

It was one of the richest cities in Asia by the 1600s – exporting rice, animal skins, ivory – and with a population of one million, greater than that of contemporary London. Merchants came from Europe, the Middle East and elsewhere in Asia to trade in its markets. Europeans wrote awed accounts of the fabulous wealth of the courts and of the 2,000 temple spires clad in gilded gold.

As fast as it rose to greatness, it collapsed, suffering a destruction so complete that it was never rebuilt. Burmese armies had been pounding on its doors for centuries before occupying it for a period in the 16th century. Siamese kings then expelled them and reasserted independence. In 1767, however, the Burmese triumphed again. In a rampage, they burned and looted, destroying most of the city's monuments, and enslaving, killing, or scattering the population.

Within a year, Ayutthaya was nearly a ghost town, once with a million people but now fewer than 10,000 inhabitants. Even after the Burmese garrison was defeated, Ayutthaya was beyond repair, a fabled city left to crumble into dust.

From the ruins, it is easy to appreciate the genius of the kings who built this great city. Located 85 kilometers (55 mi) north of Bangkok, Ayutthaya was laid out at the junction of three rivers: Chao Phraya, Pa Sak, and Lop Buri. Engineers had only to cut a canal across the loop of the Chao Phraya to create an island. Canals were also constructed as streets; palaces and temples were erected in addition.

Start close to the junction of the Nam Pa Sak and Chao Phraya rivers, passing by the imposing **Wat Phanan Choeng**. Records suggest that the *wat* was established 26 years prior to Ayutthaya's foundation in 1350. The temple houses a huge seated Buddha, so tightly crowded against the roof that he appears to be holding it up. Wat Phanan Choeng was a favorite with Chinese traders, who prayed there before setting out on long voyages; it still has an unmistakably Chinese atmosphere.

Ayutthaya was at one time surrounded by stout walls, only portions of which remain. One of the best-preserved sections is at **Phom Phet**, across the river from Wat Phanan Choeng. Vendors sell ceramics they claim were dropped overboard by 17th-century sailors, only recently recovered. Given the volume of the wares and length of time they have been on sale, the sailors must have been extremely butterfingered.

Upstream from Wat Phanan Choeng, the restored **Wat Buddhaisawan** (Phutthaisawan) stands serenely on the

Ornate ceiling of a wat.

riverbank. Seldom visited, it is quiet, and the landing is an excellent place to enjoy the river's tranquillity in the evenings. Farther upstream, the restored **Cathedral of St Joseph** is a Catholic reminder of the large European population that lived in the city at its prime.

Where the river bends to the north is one of Ayutthaya's most romantic ruins, **Wat Chai Wattanaram**, erected in 1630. Perched high on a pedestal in front of the ruins, a Buddha keeps solitary watch. The stately *prang* with its surrounding *chedi* and rows of headless Buddhas make a fine contrast to the restored **Queen Suriyothai Chedi** on the city side of the river. Dressed as a man, the valiant Ayutthaya queen rode into battle, her elephant beside that of her husband. When she saw him attacked by a Burmese prince, she moved between them with her elephant and received a lance blow intended for her husband.

Chandrakasem Palace, known as the Palace of the Front, was originally constructed outside the city walls, close to the junction of the rivers and the new canal. King Naresuen built it as a defensive bastion while he was engaged in wars against his northern rivals from Chiang Mai. In 1767, the Burmese destroyed the palace, but King Mongkut later resurrected it in the 19th century as a royal summer retreat for escaping lowland heat. Now housing a small museum, the palace looks out on the noisiest part of the modern town.

The old royal palace, **Wang Luang**, apparently was of substantial size, if the foundations for the stables of 100 elephants are any indication. It was later razed by the Burmese. The bricks were removed to Bangkok to build its defensive walls, so only remnants of the foundations survive to mark the site. Close by stands the three stately chedi of **Wat Phra Sri Sanphet**, a royal temple built in 1491 that honors three 15th-century kings. The identical chedi have been restored and stand in regal contrast to the surrounding ruins.

For two centuries after Ayutthaya's fall, a huge bronze Buddha sat unshel-

tered near Wat Phra Sri Sanphet. Its flame of knowledge and one of his arms had been broken when the roof, set afire by the Burmese, collapsed. Based on the original, a new building, the **Viharn Phra Mongkol Bophit**, was built in 1956 around the restored statue. With a large car park and rows of souvenir stalls facing it, it is often used as a starting point for Ayutthaya tours.

Across the road to the east, **Wat Phra Ram** is one of Ayutthaya's oldest temples. Founded in 1369 by the son of Ayutthaya's founder, its buildings dating from the 1400s have been completely restored twice. Elephant gates punctuate the old walls, and the central terrace is dominated by a crumbling prang to which clings a gallery of stucco *naga*, *garuda* and statues of the Buddha. The reflection of Wat Phra Ram's prang shimmers in the pool that surrounds the complex. Once a marshy swamp, the pool was dug to provide landfill for the temple's foundations.

Two of Ayutthaya's finest temples stand side by side across the lake from Wat Phra Ram. Built in 1424 by the seventh king of Ayutthaya as a memorial to his brothers, the well-known **Wat Ratchaburana** dominates its surroundings. Excavations during its restoration in 1958 revealed a crypt containing gold jewelry, Buddha images and other art objects, among them a charming, intricately-decorated elephant – all probably the property of the interned brothers. These treasures are now kept in the **Chao Sam Phraya Museum**, to the south. In addition, what may be Thailand's finest ancient paintings cover the walls of the crypt.

Across the road, **Wat Phra Mahathat** is one of the most beautiful temple complexes in Ayutthaya, and one of its oldest, dating from the 1380s. Its glory is its huge prang, which originally stood 46 meters (150 ft) high. The prang later collapsed, but it was rebuilt four meters higher than before. Stone Buddha faces, each a meter in height, stand silently around the ruins. Together with the restored chedi that ring the prang, these combine to make this one of the most

Wat Phra Ram, originally founded in 1369.

impressive sites in Ayutthaya. Next door, the government has built a model of how the royal city may have once looked.

Wat Suwan Dararam, constructed near the close of the Ayutthaya period, has been beautifully restored. The foundations of the *bot* dip in the center, in emulation of the graceful deck line of a boat. This typical Ayutthayan decoration is meant to suggest a boat that carries pious Buddhists to salvation. Delicately-carved columns support the roof, and the interior walls are decorated with brilliantly-colored frescoes. Still used as a temple, the wat is magical in the early evening as the monks chant their prayers.

Across the river from the old palace stands another restored temple, **Wat Na Phra Meru**. Here, a large stone Buddha is seated in the "European fashion" on a throne, a sharp contrast to the yoga position of most seated Buddhas. Found in the ruins of Wat Mahathat, the statue is believed to be one of five that originally sat in a recently-unearthed Dvaravati-period complex in Nakhon Pathom.

The bot contains an Ayutthaya-style seated Buddha on the altar. Across a bridge from Wat Na Phra Meru are the ruins of **Wat Konthi Thong**.

East is **Wat Yai Chai Mongkol**, originally established in the mid 1300s. In single-handed combat on elephant-back, King Naresuan slew the crown prince of Burma in 1592. The immense chedi, built to match the Phu Khao Thong Pagoda just north of Ayutthaya, was erected in celebration of the victory.

Beyond Ayutthaya: Just north of Ayutthaya, the **Wat Phu Khao Thong**, better known as the **Golden Mount**, stands with its 80-meter-high (260-ft) chedi alone amidst the rice fields, its upper terraces commanding a panoramic view of the countryside. While the wat dates from 1387, the chedi was built by the Burmese after their earlier and less destructive conquest in 1569. It was later remodeled by the Siamese in their own style. In 1957, to mark 2,500 years of Buddhism, a 2,500 gram (5.5 lb) gold ball was mounted on top of the chedi.

In the opposite direction from the

Canal housing, Ayutthaya.

Golden Mount, the road runs to the only **elephant kraal** left in Thailand. This 16th-century kraal is a reminder of the days when elephants were not only caught and trained to work in the jungles, but were also an essential requisite for a strong army. The last elephant roundup was in 1903. Standing at the edge of the restored stockade with its huge teak columns, one can imagine the thunder of the mighty beasts.

Bang Pa-in, a charming collection of palaces and pavilions once used as a royal summer retreat, lies a short distance downriver from the ruins of Ayutthaya. The rulers of Ayutthaya used Bang Pa-in as long ago as the 17th century, but the buildings one sees today date from the late 19th- and early 20th-century reigns of Rama V and Rama VI, who used to come up from Bangkok.

The attractive palace, a mixture of Italian and Victorian styles built by Rama V, is closed to the public, but visitors can tour an ornate Chinese-style palace in which the king stayed during visits. A Thai-style pavilion called the **Aisawan Tippaya Asna**, in the middle of the adjacent lake as one enters the grounds, is regarded as one of the finest examples of Thai architecture.

Summer palaces: The former summer capital of Siam, **Lop Buri** lies 150 kilometers (100 mi) north of Bangkok, a four-hour drive through the fertile rice bowl of Thailand. Just ten kilometers north of Ayutthaya, the hills of the Korat Plateau appear on the horizon, the first break in the flatness of the Central Plains.

It was not until the mid 1600s that Ayutthaya became a bustling international city with upwards of three dozen nationalities represented. Some French architects even ventured to Lop Buri, where King Narai retreated each summer to escape Ayutthaya's heat.

The grounds of the **Lop Buri Palace** (also called King Narai's Palace, or Narai Ratchaniwet), built between 1665 and 1677, are enclosed by massive walls, which still dominate the center of the modern town. The palace grounds have

One of the last elephant hunts at the kraal of Ayutthaya, 1895.

190

three sections enclosing its governmental, ceremonial and residential buildings. The outer grounds contained the facilities for utilities and maintenance. Moving inward, the middle section enclosed the Dusit Maha Prasat Hall, Chantra Paisan Pavilion, and Phiman Mongkut Pavilion. The inner courtyard was that of the king, where his residence, **Suttha Sawan Pavilion**, was nestled amidst gardens and ponds.

Of King Narai's buildings, the only one that has substantially survived is the **Dusit Maha Prasat Hall**. This was built for the audience granted by the king in 1685 to the ambassador of Louis XIV. It is recorded that the walls of the front structure were paneled with mirrors given by the French king. Holes for the mirrors can still be seen.

Near the Dusit Maha Prasat Hall is the **Phiman Mongkut Pavilion**, a three-story mansion in the colonial style, built in the mid-19th century by King Mongkut. The immensely thick walls and high ceilings show how the summer heat was averted most effectively before air-conditioning arrived. The mansion, small but full of character, displays a mixture of bronze statues, Chinese and Sukhothai porcelain, coins, Buddhist fans, and shadow play puppets. Some of the pieces, particularly the Ayutthaya bronze heads and Bencharong porcelain, are superb.

Another surviving building of the Narai period is the **Chantra Paisan Pavilion**, also in the palace grounds. It was the first structure built by King Narai, and later restored by King Mongkut. The wooden decorations of the roof are not in good proportions, somewhat spoiling the overall effect, but the classic Ayutthaya-period curve of the base is good. The sagging line of the multiple roofs is classic and elegant.

The remains of a grand palace in Lop Buri, said to have belonged to Constantine Phaulkon, rival those of the royal palace. Located just north of Narai's residence, the buildings show traces of European influence, with straight-sided walls and decorations over Western-style windows.

Phaulkon's Palace, Lop Buri.

NORTHEAST OF BANGKOK

Located near enough to Bangkok for a comfortably-paced day trip, the eastern province of **Nakhon Nayok** offers waterfalls and a pretty park. The most scenic route to this province is Route 305, which branches off Route 1 just north of Rangsit, 30 kilometers (20 mi) north of Bangkok. A wide road runs northeast along a lovely canal, passing rice fields and small rivers to reach Nakhon Nayok, about 140 kilometers (90 mi) from the capital.

From the town, Route 33 heads northwest and then, within a few kilometers, another second road leads off to the right towards two waterfalls, including **Salika Falls**.

Near the parking lot are pleasant outdoor restaurants and stalls selling fruits and drinks. The waterfall itself is impressive around the end of the rainy season, from September to November. Nearby is **Wang Takrai Park**. Along the way is the **Temple of Chao Pau Khun Dan**, named after one of King Naresuan's advisers whose spirit is believed to protect the area. Prince Chumbhot (of Suan Pakkad Palace in Bangkok) established the 80-hectare Wang Takrai Park in the 1950s; a statue of him stands on the opposite bank of the small river flowing through the park. His wife, Princess Chumbhot, planted many varieties of flowers and trees, including some imported species.

Cultivated gardens sit among tall trees, which line both banks of the main stream flowing through the two-kilometer-long park. Bungalows are available for rent.

Before returning to Bangkok, dine at the park restaurant. Just outside the park entrance, the road on the left crosses a river and continues five kilometers to **Nang Rong Falls**, an inviting three-tiered cascade situated in a steep valley.

Khao Yai National Park, the nearest hill resort to Bangkok, lies 200 kilometers (125 mi) north of the capital, and covers 2,000 square kilometers (770 sq.mi). Established in 1962, it is the oldest national park in Thailand. With its proximity to Bangkok, its visitors are approaching one million in number annually. This cool retreat boasts bungalows, motels, restaurants, an 18-hole golf course, and many nature trails and roads. It takes about three to four hours to drive to Khao Yai (Big Mountain) from Bangkok, via one of two routes.

The long route leads up Route 1. Just before entering Sara Buri, about 110 kilometers (70 mi) from the capital, a right turn onto the Friendship Highway (Route 2) eventually ends up at the foot of the park. The road climbs and twists among the hills for 15 kilometers until **Nong Khing Village**. Dine at the Khao Yai Restaurant and check out the accommodations.

The second route requires driving to Nakhon Nayok via the roads described above. Just beyond Nakhon Nayok, a road leads to the left for about 50 kilometers along a twisting road to the park headquarters. Accommodations can be booked through the tourism office in Bangkok. If camping in the park, notify officials; take mosquito nets and repellent. The State Railways of Thailand offers a day trip each Saturday at reasonable rates.

Khao Yai's highest peaks lie on the east along a land form known as the **Korat Plateau**. Khao Laem is 1,350 meters (4,430 ft) high and Khao Kaeo, 1,020 meters (3,350 ft). Evergreen and deciduous trees, and palms and bamboo provide ample greenery throughout the park; unlike much of Thailand, patches of indigenous rain forest remain in the park. Monkeys, gibbons and langurs are commonly seen. Wild, but not considered dangerous, are the elephants, bears, gaurs, boars and deer that roam the huge, protected reserve.

After dark, the park conducts "hunts" in large trucks, shining spotlights on night-feeding animals such as deer. At night, winter temperatures may drop to below 15°C (60°F); warm clothes are handy.

Many trails snake through the park, to waterfalls like Haei Sawat and to grassy areas where one may see elephants roaming. In several clearings, there are observation towers to watch animals feed.

Chedi of Wat Phra Ram, Ayutthaya.

UPCOUNTRY

Regardless of which compass heading one follows in escaping the Bangkok area, one is often said to be going "upcountry", even if traveling south. What matters is that one is leaving Bangkok for somewhere, for anywhere – for someplace different and far from the greater Bangkok metropolitan area.

Finding someplace beyond the magnetic pull of Bangkok is exceedingly simple, as diversity and contrast characterize both Thailand's people and its geography. Within an area of 514,000 square kilometers – roughly the size of France – set in the center of the political jigsaw puzzle of Southeast Asia are tropical rain forests, broad rice plains and forest-clad hills – and those ever-seductive beaches and warm waters in the south.

In the Central Plains to the north of Bangkok, several major rivers flow through the fertile land. Most notable of these is the Chao Phraya, which winds down from the north to nurture the rice before slicing through the center of Metropolitan Bangkok and emptying into the Gulf of Thailand. The course of the Chao Phraya is that of Thailand's history: the Angkor-style towers of Lop Buri, where the Khmers once ruled; the spectacular history of Sukhothai, perhaps the finest era in the nation's long history; the sprawling ruins of Ayutthaya farther south and just north of Bangkok; and then Bangkok itself.

Farther to the north still, Chiang Mai nestles at the foot of the highlands, and has become one of Thailand's most popular visitor destinations. Travelers seek both the natural ambience of the northern regions and the diversity of the region's hilltribes.

South along the Gulf of Thailand coast, Pattaya offers expansive beaches, lively nightlife, and superb waters just a few hours from downtown Bangkok. Once the resort gem of Asia, Pattaya has slid into the shadow of Ko Samui and Phuket. But it is undergoing an overhaul in both image and facilities, and may one day regain its dominant resort standing.

Phuket, of course, has become synonomous with both beach laziness and resort nightlife. The island has managed to establish an appeal for just about any type of traveler, whether moneyed aristocrat or frugal backpacker. Neighboring areas such as Ko Phi Phi and Krabi are increasingly pulling visitors from Phuket, although one sometimes wonders if, like Bangkok's traffic, anyone has given the consequences any thought.

On the other side of the isthmus from Phuket is Ko Samui, once the enclave of budget travelers seeking the end of the earth and now, for better or worse, seducing the first-class traveler.

Preceding pages: morning mist in the northern fields; limestone islands near Phuket. Left, tempting waters of Ko Phi Phi.

SUKHOTHAI

The route towards the ancient city of **Sukhothai** (Dawn of Happiness) passes through "new" Sukhothai, a bustling modern town of concrete shophouses. About 10 kilometers (7 mi) farther on, the road enters the limits of old Sukhothai, through the **Kamphaeng-hak (Broken Wall) Gate**; the authorities chose to run the road directly through the ruins, rather than around them.

The Sukhothai Kingdom began in 1240, when King Intradit drove away the Khmers. Sukhothai, which grew to include most of modern-day Thailand and parts of the Malay Peninsula and Burma, is synonymous with some of the finest artistic endeavors in Thai history, including perhaps the most exquisite Buddha images. Unfortunately the golden age was short lived, just two centuries and nine kings long. The upstart Ayutthaya absorbed Sukhothai in 1438. The most notable Sukhothai king was Ramkamhaeng, who, among other accomplishments, developed the Thai script, introduced Theravada Buddhism and solidified links with China.

The remains of ancient Sukhothai's massive walls reveal that the inner city was protected by no fewer than three rows of earthen ramparts and two moats. The city was begun by Khmers, who left behind three buildings and the beginnings of a water system, similar to that of Angkor Wat. After the Angkorian empire began shrinking, the Khmers abandoned the ancient Sukhothai and the Thais moved in, building their own structures. They eschewed the intricate Khmer irrigation system, installing a much less complex one of their own. It is suggested that water, or the lack of it, in part contributed to the city's demise. It is possible that the city was originally served by the Yom River, which later shifted course and deprived Sukhothai of a dependable source of water.

Within the walls of Sukhothai are the ruins of some twenty *wat* and monuments; the greatest of them is **Wat Mahathat**. It is not known with certainty who started this shrine, which Griswold called "the magical and spiritual center of the kingdom," but it is presumed to have been the first king of Sukhothai. Wat Mahathat owes its present form to a remodeling completed by King Lo Thai, around 1345.

Wat Sri Sawai, southwest of Wat Mahathat, was originally a Hindu shrine that contained an image of Siva. Triple towers remain, built in a modified Khmer style; the stucco decoration, added to the towers in the 15th century, shows mythical birds and divinities.

Wat Sra Sri, on the way to the southern gate of the city, has a chedi of the Sri Lankan type. The ordination hall (*bot*) lies on an island to the east of the spire. The ruins of the main shrine consist of six rows of columns, which lead to a well-restored, seated Buddha image. Achille Clarac comments, "The detail, balance and harmony of the proportions and decoration of Wat Sra Sri, and the beauty of the area where it stands, bear witness to the unusual and refined aesthetic sense of the architects of the Suk-

Left, Wat Mahathat. **Right**, temple image of a standing Buddha.

hothai period." Indeed, well stated. **Wat Chana Songkhram** and **Wat Trakuan**, located immediately north of Wat Mahathat, have particularly fine Sri Lankan-style chedi, of which only the lower parts still stand. Wat Trakuan has revealed many bronze images of the Chiang Saen period.

Leaving the walled city by the northern San Luang, or the "Royal Shrine" gate, and traveling about a kilometer, one arrives at the important shrine of **Wat Phra Phai Luang**. It originally consisted of three laterite towers covered with stucco, probably built in the late 12th century, when Sukhothai was still part of the Khmer empire. This shrine might have been the original center of Sukhothai, since Wat Mahathat is of a later period. A fragmentary seated stone Buddha image, accurately dated to 1191 and the reign of the Khmer King Jayavarman VII, was found here and is now in the grounds of the town's Ramkamhaeng Museum.

During restoration in the mid 1960s, a large stucco image of the Buddha in the central tower collapsed, disclosing numerous smaller images inside. Some date these images to the second half of the 13th century.

Beyond Wat Phra Phai Luang is **Wat Si Chum**, which has one of the largest seated Buddha images in the kingdom. The *mondop*, or enclosing shrine, was built in the second half of the 14th century, but the image itself, called *Phra Achana,* or "The Venerable," is believed to be the one mentioned in King Ramkamhaeng's inscription.

There is a stairway within the walls of the mondop that leads to the roof; largish persons should not attempt to ascend the narrow passage. The ceiling of the stairway is made up of more than 50 carved slate slabs illustrating scenes from Buddhist folklore. Their function is to turn the ritual climbing of the stairs into a symbolic ascent to Buddhahood.

There is a story that troops gathered here before an ancient battle were inspired by an ethereal voice that seemed to come from the Buddha itself. Some suggest a brilliant ploy by a general who

Ruins of Wat Chetupon.

hid one of his men on the stairway and instructed him to speak through one of the windows concealed by the body of the image; the effect was magical, however, and the soldiers thoroughly routed the enemy.

South of the walled city is another group of shrines and monasteries. One of the most interesting is **Wat Chetupon**, where the protecting wall of the viharn is made of slate slabs shaped in imitation of wood. The gates are also formed of huge plates of slate mined in the nearby hills. On a small scale, they resemble the megaliths of England's Stonehenge. The bridges across the moat that surround the temple are also made of stone slabs.

On the central tower of Wat Chetupon are Buddha images in the standing, reclining, walking and sitting postures. The walking Buddha here is regarded as one of the finest.

Twin of Sukhothai: About 50 kilometers (35 mi) north of the modern town of Sukhothai, along a concrete highway, lies the old city of **Si Satchanalai**, on the banks of the Yom River. Founded in the middle of the 13th century, as was Sukhothai, it served as the seat of the viceroys of Sukhothai and was always mentioned as the twin city of the capital. Whereas restoration, removal of trees, and the installation of lawns have removed some of the grandeur of Sukhothai, Si Satchanalai's setting gives it an aura few other ancient sites have. It is a pleasure to wander through the wooded complex, rounding a corner and being surprised by a new wat or monument.

The first and most important monument to visit in Si Satchanalai is **Wat Chang Lom**. There can be little doubt that this is the "Elephant-girdled Shrine" described in King Ramkamhaeng's stone inscription.

The great king records that he started to build it in 1285 to house some exceptionally holy relics of the Lord Buddha, and that it was finished six years later. It is the only surviving stupa that can be attributed with virtual certainty to King Ramkamhaeng. Built of laterite and stucco, it is a large bell-shaped spire of the Sri Lankan type standing on a two-

story, square basement. The upper tier contains niches for Buddha images, now mostly empty, while the lower level contains 39 elephant caryatids, built of laterite blocks.

Si Satchanalai is also associated with the famed Sawankhalok ceramics, which were among Thailand's first export products. The brown bowls and their distinctive double-fish design were sent to China aboard junks; remains of them have been found off the coast of Pattaya. It is still possible to buy genuine antique Sawankhalok ceramics in the area; most, however, are copies.

Phitsanulok now has only a few mementos of the past; a fire over three decades ago razed most of the old town. The new city is a rather dull collection of concrete shop houses.

However, nothing can detract from its superb location along the Nan River, with its quays shaded by flowering trees and its houseboats moored beside the steep banks. The great fire spared **Wat Phra Sri Ratana Mahathat**, the principal shrine in Phitsanulok.

Wat Chang Lom in Si Satchanalai, built in 1285.

CHIANG MAI

Time and progress have wrought transformations on the once-remote "Rose of the North", **Chiang Mai**. Concrete lamp standards have replaced trees, concrete houses for teak houses, and noisy, piston-hammering *tuk-tuk* for the silent but rapidly disappearing pedal *samlor*. They have also introduced that bane of modernity – traffic jams – to its once-tranquil streets. A source of popular handicrafts and a useful base for northern treks, Chiang Mai is increasingly attracting industry, too.

Despite its increasingly rapid urbanization, 700-year-old Chiang Mai remains prized as a pleasant dry-season escape from the sticky humidity of Bangkok. Situated 305 meters (1,000 ft) above sea level in a broad valley divided by the picturesque 560-kilometer-long (350-mi) **Ping River**, the city reigned for seven centuries as the capital of the Lanna (Million Rice Fields) Kingdom. The city's northern remoteness kept the region outside the rule of Bangkok well into this century.

In its splendid isolation, Chiang Mai developed a culture quite removed from that of the Central Plains, with wooden temples of exquisite beauty and a host of unique crafts, including lacquerware, silverwork, wood carvings, ceramics and umbrella-making. Its dozen hilltribes only added to its luster as an exotic far-flung realm. Although hospitality of both the hilltribes and the northern Thais is being strained – if not considerably commercialized – by the sheer numbers of visitors, they remain more gracious than in many cities to the south.

But it's not like it used to be, indeed. Chiang Mai, the nation's second-largest city, has caught the fancy of tourist and entrepreneur alike, both eager to flee the high prices, chaos and pollution of Bangkok, 700 kilometers (400 mi) to the south. Land that once nurtured rice now sprouts factories and condominiums, and tall hotels are being erected throughout the downtown area to accommodate the hordes of visitors.

Modern Chiang Mai: Most visitors spend only a few days in Chiang Mai before setting off on hilltribe treks to explore the cool air of the mountains. But there is much to see during those few days.

Despite its size, modern Chiang Mai – anchored by the old city, which is defined by a square moat and defensive wall built in the 19th century – is an easy city to navigate. The town is dominated by the green mass of **Doi Suthep**, a modest mountain 15 kilometers (10 mi) to the northwest. On its crown is a *wat,* which appears with crystalline clarity through the chill December dawn air.

Near the moat, a minibus fills with hardy trekkers setting off for Fang, 150 kilometers (100 mi) to the north, and for jungle trekking. Reflected in the water is a caravan of saffron-robed Buddhist monks on their morning alms walk. Padding silently on bare feet, they pause briefly before houses and shops, people putting rice and curries into their bowls.

The commercial area centers along **Tapae Road**, with a number of hotels, shops and guesthouses. New hotels are

Wat Chiang Mun, built by the founder of Chiang Mai.

also rising along **Huai Kaeo Road**, which leads to Doi Suthep. Buses ply such circuitous routes that a nominal fare buys a complete tour of the city. More expensive, but still extremely cheap, *tuk-tuk* noisily haul passengers to any point around town. Pedal *samlor* provide a more leisurely way of travel. Many travelers hire motorcycles or push bicycles; most guesthouses rent bicycles for a few baht per day.

The city's history began with **Wat Chiang Mun**, which translates as "power of the city". It was the first temple to be built by Mengrai, who resided there during the construction of the city in 1296. Located in the northeast part of the old city, it is the oldest of Chiang Mai's 300-plus wat. Two ancient, venerated Buddha images are kept in the abbot's quarters and can be seen on request. *Phra Sae Tang Tamani* is a small ten-centimeter-high (four-inch) crystal Buddha image taken by Mengrai to Chiang Mai from Lamphun, where it had reputedly resided for 600 years. Apart from a short sojourn to Ayutthaya,

the image has remained in Chiang Mai ever since. On Songkran, every April 13, it is ceremonially paraded through the streets.

The second image, a stone *Phra Sila* Buddha in bas-relief, is believed to have originated in India around the 8th century. Both statues are said to possess the power to bring rain and to protect the city from fire. The only other important structure in Wat Chiang Man is Chang Lom, a 15th-century square *chedi* buttressed by rows of stucco elephants.

Imperiously occupying the head of one of the city's principal streets is **Wat Phra Singh**, possibly Chiang Mai's second-most important temple, after Wat Prathat Doi Suthep, and definitely its largest. Founded in 1345, its thick walls shut out the urban bustle.

Calamity is associated with **Wat Chedi Luang**, built in 1401 to the east of Wat Phra Singh. A century and a half later, a violent earthquake shook its then 90-meter-high (295-ft) pagoda, reducing its height to 42 meters (140 ft). It was never rebuilt, although there are

recent ambitions at restoration. But even in ruins, the colossal monument is impressive. For 84 years the Emerald Buddha was housed in this wat before being moved to Vientiane. King Mengrai was reportedly killed nearby by a bolt of malicious lightning.

Close to the wat's entrance stands an ancient, tall gum tree, whose longevity is tied to that of the city. When it falls, says a legend, so will the city. As if serving as counterbalance, the *lak muang,* or city boundary stone, in which the spirit of the city is said to reside, stands near its base.

Located north of the city walls, **Wat Jet Yod** was completed by King Trailokaraja, in 1455. As its name "Seven Spires" suggests, it is a replica of the Mahabodhi Temple, in India's Bodhgaya, where Buddha gained enlightenment while spending seven weeks in its gardens. The beautiful stucco angels that decorate its walls are said to bear faces of Trailokaraja's own family. Although similar to a temple in Burma's then-capital of Pagan, it did not stop the Burmese from severely damaging it during their invasion of 1566.

One of the most impressive city temple complexes is **Wat Suan Dok**. At its northwest corner are whitewashed chedi that contain the ashes of Chiang Mai's royal family; the huge central chedi is said to hold no fewer than eight relics of Buddha. **Wat Cheta Wan**, near the east gate, has three tiled chedi and mythical animals that seem to come alive in the rays of the morning sun.

Beyond the old city: A road leaves the old city at its northwest corner, passing the north's most important educational institution, **Chiang Mai University**, officially opened in 1965 on a 200-hectare (600-acre) campus. It holds the **Tribal Research Center**, a small ethnographical museum where one can compare the costumes and implements of several Thai hilltribes.

A bit farther is an arboretum with many species of northern Thai trees. Next to it is the **Chiang Mai Zoo**, started as a private collection, and a **botanical garden**. Given the extensive poaching

The chedi of Wat Suan Dok hold the ashes of the royal family of Chiang Mai.

in recent decades, it just may contain more wild animals than the hills.

A steep series of hairpin curves rise 12 kilometers (8 mi) up the flanks of Doi Suthep to Chiang Mai's best-known temple, **Wat Doi Suthep**. The site was selected in the mid 1300s by an elephant that was turned loose with a Buddha relic strapped to its back; where it stopped, it was believed, a temple would be built. It not only climbed the slopes of Doi Suthep to this site, it dropped dead here.

Commercialized hilltribes: From the palace entrance, the road continues through pine forests to the commercialized Meo hilltribe village of **Doi Pui**. The village has been on the tourist track for some time, but recent improvements have brought benefits – perhaps – to its inhabitants, including a paved street hemmed by souvenir stands; with a bit of perseverance, it is possible to wander by the houses to see how the people live.

Once subsistence farmers, the tribespeople have learned that visitors come bearing gifts, and a camera automatically triggers a hand extended for a donation. Meos are nomadic people here, and in Burma and Laos. They once depended upon opium cultivation for their livelihoods; despite government efforts to steer them towards more socially-acceptable crops, many still cultivate patches deep in the hills.

Festivals and fetes: Chiang Mai is best visited during winter, late November through early February, when the "Rose of the North" is abloom with an astounding variety of beautiful flowers. Numerous resorts in nearby Mae Sa Valley carpet the hillsides with flower gardens, and each February the annual **Chiang Mai Flower Festival** fills the streets with floral parades and open areas with flower exhibitions.

Be careful on the streets of Chiang Mai on April 13, and for several days thereafter, for a sudden deluge of water can saturate you despite clear blue skies. **Songkran**, the traditional Thai new year, is when one sprinkles water on friends to bless them. It rapidly degenerates into a deluge of cascading proportions.

Songkran festival in Chiang Mai.

SOUTH TO PATTAYA

The main route along the Eastern Gulf Coast is Sukhumvit Highway, which becomes Route 3 outside of Bangkok. Route 3 officially originates at Bangkok's busy Ratchadamri intersection, at the Erawan Shrine. Eventually it leads to the Cambodian border.

A sprawling and industrious town of about a quarter million merchants, traders and craftsmen, **Chon Buri** is but a lunch break or rest stop for most visitors on the way to Pattaya.

However, Chon Buri has its fair share of attractions. Just outside of town is **Wat Buddhabat Sam Yot**, Buddha's Footprint Mountain of Three Summits. Built amidst green trees by an Ayutthayan king and renovated during the reign of King Chulalongkorn, this hilltop monastery was once used to conduct the water oath of allegiance, when princes and governors drank the waters of fealty, pledging loyalty to the throne.

Near the center of Chon Buri, a colossal gold-mosaic image of Buddha dominates **Wat Dhamma Nimitr**. The largest image in the Eastern Gulf region, and the only one in the country depicting the Buddha in a boat, the 40-meter-high (135-ft) statue recalls the story of the Buddha's journey to the cholera-ridden town of Pai Salee. On the same hill is the local Chinese Buddhist Society, with the burial shrines of prominent Society members.

Most of Thailand's oyster population breeds off the Chon Buri coast, and farther south along the gulf. But the coastal town is better known for its production of animal feed made from tapioca, which is grown in the region. During the 1970s and early 1980s, the area around Chon Buri enjoyed a minor boom as a tapioca center. Within a few years, this crop, formerly cultivated only for local use, became the country's number-one foreign exchange earner. Moreover, Thailand became the world's number one producer, supplying 95 percent of the world's demand.

South of Chon Buri, on the road past Ang Sila, the beach at **Bang Saen** comes alive each weekend as hordes of Thai middle-class tourists descend in buses. A profusion of beach umbrellas, inner tubes and wrinkled watermelon rinds quickly cover the sandy beach, the surf filled with bobbing heads.

At the Bang Saen Reservoir **bird refuge**, with permission it is possible to sit in a blind and observe waterfowl. Up the hill behind the reserve is the **Khao Khieo Open Zoo**. Operated by Bangkok's Dusit Zoo, it presents animals in their natural setting; in one section, visitors can wander among deer, elephants, donkeys and other wild animals. On the hill above are some simple, but comfortable, bungalows that can be reserved by contacting the Dusit Zoo.

Si Racha, south of Chon Buri, descends from the hills and extends into the sea on tentacle-like piers. Its famous hot sauce can be enjoyed at waterfront restaurants, where delicious and fresh shrimp, crab, oyster, mussel or abalone are dipped into the thick, tangy red liquid. An offshore rock supports a

Preceding pages: fisherman on southern island. Left, home of some of the best golf courses.

picturesque wat with Thai and Chinese elements. The footprint of the Buddha, cast in bronze, graces the wat, as do pictures of the goddess of mercy, Kuan Yin, and the Monkey God.

Thai Riviera: For several decades, **Pattaya** long reigned as Thailand's premier beach resort. Few areas in Asia have undergone such a precipitous rise to fame and, some had suggested until recently, a plummet in popularity.

This huge resort was once a quiet beach known only to a handful – just a few clusters of bungalows, a rough clubhouse for a group of sailing enthusiasts, some good seafood restaurants and a small fishing village that gave the place its name. But it had all the ingredients for success: a graceful, four-kilometer-long (three-mile) crescent of golden sand lapped by gentle waves, warm tropical water, balmy breezes, tranquillity.

By the 1970s, others were beginning to discover its charms. A new road cut travel time to two hours, bringing the resort within easy reach of Bangkok. Big hotels began to rise along the beach.

By the 1980s, Europeans flocked to its beaches, and those of Jomtien, the neighboring beach four kilometers south. In the capitals of Asia, a beach vacation anywhere but in Pattaya was unheard of. It fell on shady times, but Pattaya is attempting to change its reputation from a party town to a family resort. Indeed, with 20,000 hotel rooms and nearly three million visitors annually, Pattaya may soon again be a world-class beach resort for all persuasions.

Pattaya's two busiest main roads run parallel to the four-kilometer-long bay. The northern portion of Beach Road is dominated by first-class hotels, restaurants and open-air bars. Second Road also has many hotels and restaurants interspersed with bars, discotheques, shows and other night spots. Numerous *soi* connecting the Beach Road and Second Road hold small hotels, restaurants and a number of bars.

More to the south: Pattaya's hill separates the main resort area from an area of luxury hotels and private beaches. Farther south is the resort of **Jomtien**, with

beaches only marginally better than Pattaya's. Here are bungalow complexes, some fine hotels and a host of good seafood and other restaurants.

Pattaya and Jomtien are a paradise for watersports lovers, with equipment for windsurfing, sailing, snorkeling and diving available for rent, along with jetskis, water scooters and waterskiing equipment. The brave may try parasailing, strapped into a parachute harness and towed aloft by a speedboat.

Off shore, **Ko Larn** – identified in brochures as Coral Island but whose name translates as Bald Island – used to be known for its coral reefs. These have long since been destroyed by fishermen using dynamite to stun the fish. Yet glass-bottomed boats still ferry visitors from the trawlers to the shore, their passengers peering in vain at the dead gray coral in hopes of seeing something alive and moving.

Ko Larn has the wide, soft sand beaches that Pattaya lacks and it is a wonderful place to spend a leisurely day. The shore is filled with good sea-food restaurants, and there are water sports facilities for those who want to stir from their beach chairs. The island also has a golf course.

Year by year, visitors have been exploring farther and farther south of Pattaya, discovering new resort areas with perhaps less noise and crowds. One popular resort is **Nong Nooch Village**, a complex of bungalows situated in parkland around a lake, offering a wide variety of activities, including an elephant show, an orchid nursery and a cactus garden.

Overlooking a scenic bay sprinkled with small islands, the small fishing town of **Sattahip**, about 20 kilometers (15 mi) south of Pattaya, blossomed overnight to become an attractive, busy deep-water port. It now acts as a headquarters for the Thai navy. In the heart of town, a large and modern temple rests on turquoise pedestals, while in the commercial center, a boisterous market teems with fish, fruit and vegetables.

Sattahip is a place to decompress, offering little more to do than stroll past the shops or sit in an open-front coffee shop sipping an *oliang* (the great local version of sweet iced coffee that came from French Cambodia). Enjoy a spicy curry near the market, or browse over teak elephants in the shops.

Situated 220 kilometers (140 mi) from Bangkok, **Rayong** is divided by an estuary that cuts through the commercial district of sundries stores, coffee shops and a forest of tall TV antennas. Rayong is famed for its *nam plaa*, or fish sauce, the source of salt in Thai diets and the *sine qua non* of Thai condiments. Producing the sauce is a cottage industry in Rayong, and many homes have backyard factories. Nam plaa is made from a small silver fish that abounds in the Gulf; it is decomposed for about seven months to produce a ruddy liquid, which is filtered and bottled on the spot. Mmm. And mixed with chili, it becomes *nam plaa prik*, even more interesting. The resorts associated with Rayong occupy a strip of beach to the southeast of Rayong.

Idyllic isle no more: This scenic fishing port is sheltered on the west by a rocky **After a day's fishing.**

outcrop, and by the six-kilometer-long island of **Ko Samet** to the south. The island is remembered by students of Thai literature as the place where Sunthorn Phu, a flamboyantly romantic court poet, retired to compose some of his works. Born in nearby Klaeng, Sunthorn called the island Ko Kaeo Phisadan, or "island with sand like crushed crystal".

Sunthorn's assessment was as practical as it was poetic; the island and the beaches of the mainland produce some of the finest sand in the world, a fact appreciated by glass makers.

From a quiet poetic retreat, the island has gained popularity as a superb resort, but not without controversy. Cheap bungalow complexes are quickly being razed to build small hotels, and while the loss of budget lodging is to be regretted, the increasing garbage will not.

Most of the resort and bungalow development is, in fact, illegal. The island is part of a national park, and development along the coast has progressed despite the law. The government has virtually closed down the island several times, banning overnight stays. Locals claim it is their right to do what they want with the island. There is no question, however, that the island has lost its pristine appeal.

Further south, mystery prevails at **Khao Chamao National Park**. Villagers claim photographs shot from the mystic jagged peaks invariably turn out blank when processed. Nothing in the gray-streaked outcrop suggests magical power; it dominates a valley of red dust and farmlands.

Khao Wong is filled with caverns. In Tam Plak, a hollow near the wat, water drips on the brow of a stalagmite image of Lord Buddha. Worshippers visit the cave to offer prayers and light yellow candles. One old woman, her face powdered white to cool her skin after bathing, has lived there since childhood, but claims she has not yet seen all the caves. Perhaps with good reason: Villagers claim that crocodiles live in underground streams, despite cave walls said to gleam with diamonds.

Jomtien Beach.

SOUTHERN ISLANDS

For decades, Phuket was known to only a few. The long road south from Bangkok to reach it, the lack of a bridge across the causeway, bad roads on the island itself and a seeming disinterest in developing it for recreation meant that it languished in isolation – but a rich one with its tin deposits, rubber and coconuts – for decades.

In the 1970s, it began appearing on the maps of budget backpackers. Word spread, and eventually its airport was expanded to handle jets from Europe, Australia and elsewhere in Asia. Phuket's wealth, traditionally drawn from tin and rubber, comes today almost exclusively from tourism.

Unlike many provincial towns, **Phuket Town** has an identity of its own. The style is set by the beautiful colonial-style houses built by tin and rubber barons at the end of the 19th century, following a disastrous fire that destroyed the downtown area. Tours of these beautiful old buildings are available from several local agents. Three stories high, the rowhouses were built by middle-income Chinese to house their extended families. The ground floor normally serves as a shop and reception hall; the upper floors are the living quarters.

Phuket's glory, however, lies in its many beautiful beaches, and it has a wealth of them. All are located on the western side of the island; the eastern shore is primarily of rocky shoals.

The most developed beach is **Patong**. In the early 1970s, Patong was little more than a huge banana plantation wedged between the mountains and a wide crescent of sand.

It has, however, made up for lost time, and with a vengeance. The banana plantation has been replaced by hotels, supermarkets, arcades, entertainment centers and a range of amenities.

Unlike most other Phuket beaches, Patong has a wide range of water sports facilities, including scuba diving, windsurfing, waterskiing, parasailing, jetskis, sailing and boogie boards. Dive shops offer trips into the bay or west to the **Similan Islands National Marine Reserve**, considered one of the best diving areas in Asia, with crystal-clear water and a multitude of marine life. One can also snorkel at Kata Noi, two beaches to the south, or at Phi Phi island, four hours east of Phuket.

Patong has many restaurants specializing in Thai seafood. The prize item on the menu is the giant Phuket Lobster, weighing up to three kilograms (6 lb) and enough to feed two hungry diners.

The long **Bang Thao** beach is dominated by the immense Laguna Resort, housing five resorts within a combined 1,300 guest rooms. Most unique is **The Banyan Tree**, with quite private and decidedly romantic bungalows, many with private swimming pools. **Nai Yang** beach, just south of the airport and set in the heart of Nai Yang National Park, is cooled by a forest of casaurina trees.

Beyond Nai Yang is Phuket's longest beach, **Mai Khao**. The nine-kilometer-long beach is as yet undeveloped, despite attempts by entrepreneurs wishing

to cover it in resorts. The thwarting concern is environmental. Here, each December through February night, giant sea turtles still lay their eggs in deep holes they laboriously dig in the sand with their powerful flippers.

South of Patong is **Relax Bay**, with its single hotel, Le Meridien Phuket. Beyond is **Karon Beach** and past a small ridge running a finger into the sea, **Kata Beach**. Karon has several large- and medium-sized hotels, but is otherwise occupied by a myriad of bungalows. Not as developed as Patong, Karon and Kata both have clean, wide beaches. Karon even has enough wave action for surfing.

Kata is the site of Asia's second **Club Med**, a tribute to its beauty. There are other bungalow complexes, as well as some good restaurants, including **The Boathouse**, a small boutique bungalow retreat anchored by a renowned restaurant offering the island's best wine list. Water sports facilities are limited to windsurf boards, jetskis and sailboats.

The coastal road continues along a ridge to **Nai Harn**, providing spectacular views for several kilometers along the coast. At the southwestern edge of Phuket, Nai Harn is one of the island's prettiest beaches. Nestled between two tall hills, fronted by a calm sea and backed by a lagoon, it is an ideal idyllic setting. Its only resort is Mandarin Oriental's **Phuket Yacht Club**, boasting rooms with truly a view. Nai Harn is renowned for its sunsets.

Ra Wai holds one of the island's two *chao lay,* or sea gypsy, villages. The sea gypsies were once nomadic fishing families, roaming from island to island. They are skilled fishermen both above and below the water. From a young age, they used to dive to great depths in search of giant lobsters, staying below for up to three minutes. However, recent environmental and tourism concerns have robbed the sea gypsies of their traditional fishing grounds, and now they live primarily on public assistance and handouts from tourists.

Phuket is the departure point for journeys to Ko Phi Phi, a few hours east by

One of Phuket's typically fine beaches.

boat, and Phang Nga Bay to the north.

Phi Phi and Phang Nga: Turquoise waves caress a beach so dazzlingly white, it is almost painful to the eye. Colorful fishing boats seem suspended in midair, so crystalline is the water. With palm-fringed beaches and lofty limestone mountains as a backdrop, **Ko Phi Phi** rivals Phuket as one of the most beautiful islands in Asia. At least, it used to be.

Phi Phi lies equidistant, about three kilometers, from both Phuket and Krabi. Phi Phi comprises two islands: the smaller Phi Phi Ley, a craggy limestone monolith similar to the other barren peaks of Phang Nga Bay, and Phi Phi Don, which, unlike its sister, is fringed with bays and beaches. Its small population, which once lived in quaint little fishing villages, has in the last decade sold the entire island to developers, and now the beaches are lined with tacky resorts and Spartan bungalow complexes. The pristine white sand is covered with lounging tourists, and the surf is often fouled with their garbage.

The only advantage in visiting Phi Phi lies offshore. While the reefs of Phuket were destroyed by tin mining before World War I, the reefs that surround Ko Phi Phi are still thriving. For the interested diver or snorkeler who prefers swimming from the beach rather than off a boat, Phi Phi provides several days' worth of stunning underwater beauty. It is questionable, though, how long the reefs will survive.

The nearby Phi Phi Ley is renowned as a site for swallows who build their nests on the ceilings of rocky caverns. Men climb up precarious ladders to collect the nests, which are sold as delicacies to Chinese gourmets. Tours may be booked to view this gathering, although travelers should be aware that no demonstration is made in any cave that still hosts swallows.

One of the wonders of the world is **Phang Nga Bay** – a collection of enormous limestone mountains that rise straight out of the sea. The boat winds among these on its way to the outer islands, leaving the traveler's imagination to drift and imagine animals and

Cave of Phang Nga Bay.

mythical beasts that the contorted shapes suggest. Just before the mouth of Phang Nga River, the boat approaches the base of **Khao Kien mountain**, where a cavern contains primitive paintings depicting human and animal forms. To the right lies a large rock island called **Ko Pannyi**, where an entire Muslim fishing village stands on stilts over the water.

On what seems a collision course with a huge limestone outcrop, the boat slips into a barely discernible, overgrown entrance of **Tham Lod cave**. For more than 50 meters, the boat slides under giant stalactites. Rocks protruding from the water appear to have been sliced by a sword-wielding god. In Tham Nak cave, a twisted stalagmite at the entrance resembles a *naga* serpent, giving this cave its name. Green stalactites burst from the ceiling like a frozen waterfall. The whole mountain-island seems, from the outside, to drip with streaked limestone.

Ko Talu receives its name from *talu,* meaning to pass from one side to the other – in this case, not over the mountain, but under it. The boat squeezes through a cave filled with stalactites. **Ko Khao Ping Gun** is perhaps the most spectacular of Phang Nga's islands. Behind the beach, the mountain seems to have split in two, the halves leaning against each other. Locals say they are two lovers.

A small staircase leads to a cavern above the water; limestone formations look like large mounds of spilled glue. Well, maybe.

This area was the setting of part of the James Bond movie, *The Man with the Golden Gun*. A small beach overlooks another island, Ko Tapoo, or Nail Island, which looks like a thorny spike driven into the sea.

Ko Samui: In the last few years, the Ko Samui archipelago of over 80 islands has captured the imagination of travelers seeking perhaps the definitive tropical island. The 250-square-kilometer (100-sq-mi) island, Thailand's third-largest and about the same size as Penang, has a unique ambience that is very different from that of Phuket.

While Phuket has rubber plantations and high-rise resorts, Samui has coconut groves and wooden bungalows. A well-maintained and driveable road encircles the island.

The island has a definite feel to it and tends to appeal to younger travelers. With an occasional glance over its shoulder to Balinese resort designs, Samui isn't ten years behind Phuket, as often claimed, but ten years different. Mainland dwellers say Samui folk are a breed apart – *chaow Samui*.

The charm of Samui is in its idyllic yet understated beaches, hills, forest waterfalls, and rocky coves that support a relatively unchanged way of life.

When the island's airport opened in 1989, Samui's rapid transition to more comfortable and expensive lodgings was accelerated. Regulations, however, forbid construction of buildings higher than the tree tops. Only half a given plot of land can be built upon by resort owners; the rest must remain green.

Around the island's dozen or so minor beaches, there is an informal mix of affordable and affluent resorts, often

Islands amidst Phang Nga Bay.

side-by-side. Accommodation in Samui now ranges from elegantly-deluxe to rustic-hammock.

The water is warm but not quite as clear as Phuket and Phi Phi. In Samui, there is adequate sunshine for a beach holiday in all months except October and November, when rain prevails.

Visitors will find a crowded selection of landscaped resorts and a vibrant nightlife scene centred around **Chaweng Beach**, on the island's east side. Ever-popular Chaweng has the biggest choice of accommodation, mostly in the mid-range. Gently-curving bays with fine white sand and crystal-clear water follow each other in succession over a distance of six kilometers.

South of Chaweng is **Lamai Beach**, with its small plots of family owned land. The sand and beaches are not quite as good as at Chaweng. In the center of the bay, almost directly on the beach, is an entertainment strip filled with discos, pubs and a few less salubrious beer bars. At both ends of the lovely bay are a number of moderately-priced hotels.

Almost the entire northern coast of Ko Samui is occupied by three lovely bays. On a cliff to the northeast sits the island's true landmark, a huge **Buddha statue**. Bangrak Beach, which ends by the cliff, was subsequently rechristened **Big Buddha Beach**.

Mummified smile: Most of Samui's sacred sites are in the southeast part of the island: the jade Buddha image at **Wat Sumret**; the Buddha footprint; the Coral Buddha image. Perhaps the most interesting, if not curious, place to visit is **Wat Khunaraam**, not so much for the *wat* as for the so-called **mummified monk**. A revered teacher of meditation during his life, the monk meditated his way into the next world here in 1973; he left his body is such a dehydrated condition that decomposition did not occur. The body now sits in a glass coffin.

A mere 12 kilometers (8 mi) north of Samui, **Ko Pha Ngan** – a slightly smaller island with the same inviting topography and fine sandy beaches – has been colonized by international budget travelers living in simple beach huts.

Quiet beach, Ko Samui.

INSIGHT GUIDES
Travel Tips

...AND THE LOCAL TIME AT YOUR DESTINATION IS

A MEMBER IN STAR ALLIANCE

S | M | O | O | T | H |

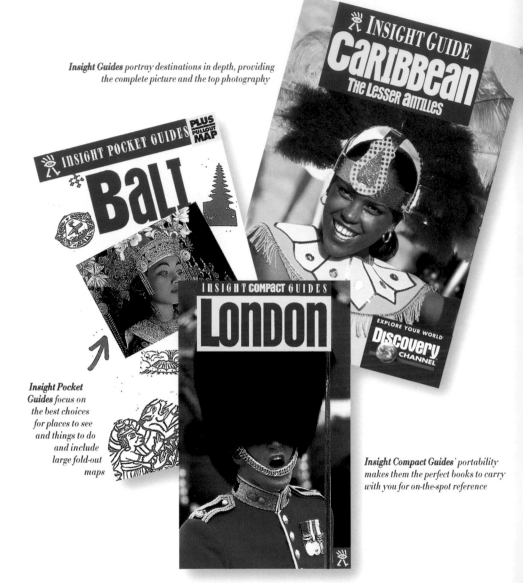

Insight Guides portray destinations in depth, providing the complete picture and the top photography

Insight Pocket Guides *focus on the best choices for places to see and things to do and include large fold-out maps*

Insight Compact Guides' portability makes them the perfect books to carry with you for on-the-spot reference

Three types of guide for all types of travel

INSIGHT GUIDES Different people need different kinds of information. Some want *background information* to help them prepare for the trip. Others seek *personal recommendations* from someone who knows the destination well. And others look for *compactly presented data* for on-the-spot reference. With three carefully designed series, Insight Guides offer readers the perfect choice. Insight Guides will turn your visit into an experience.

The world's largest collection of visual travel guides

Getting Acquainted

The Place 222
Time Zones 222
Climate 222
The Population 222
The People 222

Planning the Trip

What to Bring 224
What to Wear 224
Entry Regulations 224
Health 224
Hygiene 225
Currency 225
Public Holidays 226
Getting There 226
Special Facilities 227
Useful Addresses 227

Practical Tips

Emergencies 228
Weights and Measures 230
Business Hours 230
Tipping 230
Religious Services 231
Media 231
Postal Services 231
Telecoms 232
Tourists Offices 233
Embassies 234

Getting Around

On Arrival 234
Domestic Travel 235
Public Transport 236
Private Transport 237

Where to Stay

Hotels 237
Guesthouses 239

Eating Out

What to Eat 240
Where to Eat 240
Drinking Notes 243

Attractions

Sightseeing Tours 243
Culture 244
Nightlife 245
Festivals and Fairs 246

Shopping

Shopping Hours 249
Export 249
Complaints 249
Shopping Areas 249
What to Buy 249

Sports & Leisure

Participant Sports 251
Spectator Sports 251

Language

Origins and Intonation 252
Thai Names 252
Phonology 253
Useful Phrases 253

Further Reading

General 253
History 254
People 254
Religion 254
Art and Culture 254
Thai Writers 254
Other Insight Guides 254

Art/Photo Credits 255
Index 256

Getting Acquainted

The Place

Lying between 7 degrees and 21 degrees latitude, Thailand has a total land area of 514,000 sq km (198,000 sq mi), nearly the size of France or twice as large as England. The country is said to resemble an elephant's head with its trunk forming the southern peninsula. Bangkok, its capital, is sited at its geographic center, approximately at the elephant's mouth. The country is bordered by Malaysia on the south, Burma on the west, Laos across the Mekong River to the northeast and Cambodia to the east.

The north is marked by low hills and contains the country's tallest peak, Doi Inthanon, standing 2,590 metres (8,500ft) tall. A range of hills divides Thailand from Burma and forms the western boundary of the broad alluvial Central Plains, the country's principal rice-growing area. To the east, the Plains rise to the Korat Plateau, which covers much of the Northeast. The spine of the southern peninsula is the same range of hills that separate Thailand from Burma, sloping down to the Andaman Sea on the west and the Gulf of Thailand on the east. Thailand has a total of 2,600km (1,600 mi) of coastline.

Bangkok is situated at 14 degrees north latitude. Bangkok is a city divided into halves by a river, the Chao Phraya, which separates central Bangkok and Thonburi. The city covers a total area of 1,565 sq km (602 sq mi) of delta land, of which no natural area is more than 2 metres (7 ft) above any other.

Time Zones

Thailand Standard Time is 7 hours ahead of Greenwich Mean Time.

Climate

There are three seasons in Thailand – hot, rainy and cool. But to the tourist winging in from anywhere north or south of the 30th parallel, Thailand has only one temperature: hot. To make things worse, the temperature drops only a few degrees during the night and is accompanied 24 hours by humidity above 70 percent. Only air-conditioning makes Bangkok and other major towns tolerable during the hot season. The countryside is somewhat cooler, but, surprisingly, the northern regions can be hotter in March and April than Bangkok.

Adding together the yearly daytime highs and the night time lows for major world cities, the World Meteorological Organization has declared Bangkok to be the world's hottest city. When the monsoon rains fall, the country swelters.

The following temperature ranges give a reliable guide to the degree of heat to be expected:
- Hot season (March to mid-June): 27°–35°C (80°–95°F)
- Rainy season (June to October): 24°–32°C (75°–90°F)
- Cool season (November to February): 18°–32°C (65°–90°F), but with less humidity.

The Population

Thailand's population is around 60 million. Most people (95 percent) are Theravada Buddhists. About 75 percent of the population are ethnic Thai. There is a small percentage of Thai Malay living in the south who are Muslim and speak Malay. The 2 percent of the population who are Confucianist are mainly in the Chinatown area of Bangkok. Some 10 to 15 percent of Thailand's total population are of Chinese descent. Hilltribe people living in the north and west total about half a million and most of the tiny group of Christians in Thailand are concentrated among them.

Bangkok's population is around 10 million, although a semi-permanent migrant population has, in recent years, swelled that number. The city functions as the epicenter of the country's political, business and religious life, a city some 35 times larger than Thailand's second- and third-larges cities of Chiang Mai and Korat.

The People

Culture and Customs

Thais are remarkably tolerant and for giving of foreigners' foibles, but there are a few things that will rouse them to anger.

For one, they regard the royal family with a reverence unmatched in other countries; they react strongly if they consider any member of royalty ha been insulted. Ill-considered remark or refusing to stand for the royal an them before the start of a movie wi earn some very hard stares.

A similar degree of respect is ac corded the second pillar of society Buddhism. Disrespect towards Bud dha images, temples or monks is no taken lightly. Monks observe vows o chastity that prohibit their bein touched by women, even their mothe When in the vicinity of a monk, woman should try to stay clear to avoi accidentally brushing against hirr When visiting a temple, it is accep able for both sexes to wear long pant but not shorts. Unkempt persons are frequently turned away from majc temples.

From the Hindu religion has com the belief that the head is the fount wisdom and the feet are unclean. Fc this reason, it is insulting to touch at other person on the head, point one" feet at or step over another persor Kicking in anger is worse than spittin

When wishing to pass someor who is seated on the floor, bow slight while walking and point an arm dow to indicate the path to be taken. It also believed that spirits dwell in th raised doorsills of temples and trac tional Thai houses, and that when or steps on them, the spirits becom angry and curse the building with ba luck.

Greetings

The Thai greeting and farewell Sawasdee, spoken while raising th hands in a prayer-like gesture, the fi gertips touching the nose, and bowir the head slightly. It is an easy greetir to master and one which will w smiles.

Dress and Hygiene

Thais believe in personal cleanliness. Even the poorest among them bathe daily and dress cleanly and neatly. They frown on those who do not share this concern for hygiene.

Public Behavior

Twenty years ago, Thai couples showed no intimacy in public. That has changed due to Western influence on the young, but intimacy still does not extend beyond holding hands. As in many traditional societies, displaying open affection in public is a sign of bad manners.

Terms of Address

Thais are addressed by their first rather than their last names. The name is usually preceded by the word khun, a term of honor. Thus Silpachai Krishnamra would be addressed as Khun Silpachai when someone speaks to him.

You will find some Thais referred to in newspapers with the letters M.C., M.R. or M.L. preceding their names. These are royal titles normally translated as "prince" or "princess". The five-tier system reserves the highest two titles for the immediate royal family. After that comes the nobility, remnants of the noble houses of old. The highest of these three ranks is Mom Chao (M.C.), followed by Mom Rachawong (M.R.) and Mom Luang (M.L.).

The title is not hereditary, thanks to a unique system that guarantees Thailand will never become top-heavy with princes and princesses. Each succeeding generation is born into the next rank down. Thus, the son or daughter of a Mom Chao is a Mom Rachawong. Soon, Thailand will be a nation of Nai, or Mr, and Nang, or Miss or Mrs – a truly democratic realm.

Concepts

A few Thai concepts will give not only an indication of how Thais think but will smooth a visitor's social interaction with them. Thais strive to maintain equanimity in their lives and go to great lengths to avoid confrontation. The concept is called kriangjai and suggests an unwillingness to burden someone older or superior with one's problems. In many cases, it means not giving someone bad news until too late for fear it may upset the recipient.

Jai yen, or "cool heart", an attitude of remaining calm in stressful situations, is a trait admired by Thais. Getting angry or exhibiting a jai ron (hot heart) is a sign of immaturity and lack of self-control. Reacting to adversity or disappointment with a shrug of the shoulders and saying mai pen rai ("never mind") is the accepted response to most situations.

Sanuk means "fun" or "enjoyment" and is the yardstick by which life's activities are measured. If it is not sanuk, it is probably not worth doing.

Thais converse readily with any stranger who shows the least sign of willingness. They may be shy about their language ability but will struggle nonetheless; speak a few words of Thai and they respond even more eagerly. Be prepared, however, for questions considered rude in Western societies such as: How old are you? How much money do you earn? How much does that watch (camera, etc.) cost? Thais regard these questions as part of ordinary conversation and will not understand a reluctance to answer them. If, however, one is reticent about divulging personal information, a joking answer delivered with a smile will usually suffice; for example, to the above question of "How old are you?", answer with "How old do you think?" (Out of politeness, they will usually guess a lower age and one can agree with them.)

The Economy

Nearly 70 percent of Thailand's 60 million people are farmers who till alluvial land so rich that Thailand is a world leader in the export of tapioca (No. 1), rice (No. 2), rubber (No. 2), canned pineapple (No. 3), and is a top-ranked exporter of sugar, maize and tin. Increasingly, Thailand is turning to manufacturing, especially in clothing, machinery, and electronics.

The Government

Thailand is a constitutional monarchy headed by His Majesty, King Bhumibol. The royalty's power has been reduced considerably from the period before the 1932 revolution. However, the present king can, by the force of his personality and moral authority, influence the direction of important decisions merely by a word or two.

Although he no longer rules as an absolute monarch of previous centuries, he is still regarded as one of the three pillars of the society – monarchy, religion and the nation. This concept is represented in the five-banded **national flag**: the outer red bands symbolizing the nation; the inner white bands the purity of the Buddhist religion; and the thick blue band at the center representing the monarchy.

The decades he has spent working with farmers to improve their lands and yields has influenced others to follow his example in serving the people. Her Majesty, Queen Sirikit, and other members of the royal family have also been active in promoting the interests of Thais in the lower economic strata. Thus, the photographs of the king and queen hang in nearly every home, shop and office, placed there, not out of blind devotion, but out of genuine respect for the royal family.

The structure of the government is defined by the 1932 constitution. Despite the many revisions, the constitution has remained true to the spirit of the original aim of placing power in the hands of the people, although the exercising of it has favored certain groups over others, especially the military, which has often abused its power.

Modeled loosely on the British system, the Thai government consists of three branches: legislative, executive and judiciary, each acting independently of the others in a system of checks and balances. The legislative branch is composed of a senate and a house of representatives. The senate consists 262 leading members of society, including business people, educators and a heavy preponderance of high-ranking military officers. They must be over 35 years of age and must not be members of political parties. Members are selected by the prime minister and approved by the king. The house of representatives comprises 391 members elected by popular vote from each of the 76 provinces of Thailand.

The executive branch is represented by a prime minister, who must be an elected member of parliament. He is selected by a single party or coalition of parties and rules through a cabinet of ministers, the exact number dependent on his own needs. They, in turn, implement their programs through the very powerful civil service.

The judiciary consists of a supreme court, an appellate court, and a pyramid of provincial and lower courts. It acts independently to interpret points of law and counsels the other two branches on the appropriateness of actions.

Planning the Trip

What to Bring

Bangkok, Chiang Mai, Pattaya, and Phuket are modern destinations with most of the modern amenities found in similar places in Europe or North America.

Lip balm and moisturizers are needed in the north during the cool season. Sunglasses and hats are useful items to protect eyes and sensitive skin from tropical glare.

Electricity

Electrical outlets are rated at 220 volts, 50 cycles and accept flat-pronged or round-pronged plugs.

What to Wear

Clothes should be light and loose; natural blends that breathe are preferable to synthetics. Open shoes (sandals during the height of the rainy season, when some Bangkok streets get flooded) and sleeveless dresses for women, short-sleeved shirts for men, are appropriate. Suits are worn for business and in many large hotels but, in general, Thailand lacks the formal dress code of Hong Kong or Tokyo. Casual but neat and clean clothes are suitable for most occasions. Some formality is needed for business appointments.

The cool season in the north can be chilly. A sweater or sweatshirt will be welcome, especially when traveling in the hills.

One exception is the clothing code for Buddhist temples and Muslim mosques. Shorts are taboo for women and for men wanting to enter some of the important temples. Those wearing sleeveless dresses may also be barred from certain temples. Improperly dressed and unkempt visitors will be turned away from large temples like the Wat Phra Kaeo (Temple of the Emerald Buddha) and from the Grand Palace. Dress properly in deference to the religion and to Thai sensitivities.

Entry Regulations

Visas and Passports

Travelers should check visa regulations at a Thai embassy or consulate before starting their journey. All foreign nationals entering Thailand must have valid passports. At the airport, nationals from most countries will be granted a free transit visa valid up to 15 days, provided that they have a fully-paid ticket out of Thailand. A 30-day transit visa may also be issued to some visitors.

Tourist visas, obtained from Thai embassy prior to arrival, allow for a 60-day stay from the date of entry into the kingdom.

People who are waiting for a work permit to be issued can apply for a non-immigrant visa which is good for 90 days. A letter of guarantee is needed from the Thai company you intend to work for and this visa can be obtained from a Thai embassy or consulate at home.

Visas can be extended before they expire by applying at the Immigration Department on Soi Suan Plu, Sathorn Thai Road, tel: 286 4231. (Monday–Friday 8.30am–4pm.)

Visitors wishing to leave Thailand and return before their visas have expired can apply for a re-entry permit prior to their departure at immigration offices in Bangkok, Chiang Mai, Pattaya, Phuket and Hat Yai. An exit visa, however, is not required.

Visa Extensions

If planning a longer stay, a transit visa valid for 30 days or a tourist visa valid for 60 days must be obtained from a Thai embassy or consulate abroad by filing an application, supplying three passport-sized photographs and paying a fee. Visas can be extended before the visa's expiration date. There is a fee.

Passport Division
(Ministry of Foreign Affairs)
Sri Ayutthya Side Building
Sri Ayutthya Road
General telephone: 245-5342, 246-1997, 247-0102, 247-2244
Alien Section: 245-5342
Complaint Section: 245-9166

Immigration Office (Visa extensions)
Soi Suan Phlu (off Sathorn Tai Road)
Tel: 286-9176

Customs

The Thai government prohibits the import of drugs, dangerous chemicals, pornography, firearms and ammunition. Attempting to smuggle heroin or other hard drugs may be punishable by death. Scores of foreigners are serving long prison terms for this offence.

Foreign tourists may freely bring in foreign banknotes or other types of foreign exchange. For travelers leaving Thailand, the maximum amount permitted to be taken out in Thai currency without prior authorisation is 50,000 baht.

Foreign guests are allowed to import without tax, one camera with five rolls of film, 200 cigarettes, and one litre of wine or spirits.

Customs Department
(Ministry of Finance)
Sunthornkasa Road
General telephone: 240-2617/8, 249-0431, 249-4121
Customs Tariff Division: 249-4162, 249-4199
Director of Customs Division: 249-4351
Export Inspection Division: 249-0441, 249-0446
Inspection Division: 249-5238
Technical and Foreign Division: 249 2525

Health

Visitors entering the kingdom are no longer required to show evidence of vaccination for smallpox or cholera. But before you leave home, check that tetanus boosters are up-to-date. Immunization against cholera is a good idea if traveling extensively in rural areas. Malaria and dengue fever persist in the rural areas. When in the hills – especially in the monsoon season – apply mosquito repellent on exposed skin when the sun begins to set.

Most first-time visitors experience a degree of heat exhaustion and dehydration that can be avoided by drinking lots of bottled water and slightly increasing the amount of salt in the diet. Sunblock is essential.

AIDS is not confined to "high risk" sections of the population in Thailand and visitors are at risk from casual sex if they do not use condoms. It is estimated that almost the entire population of prostitutes in the country are HIV positive.

Hygiene

Thais place high value on personal hygiene and are aware of the dangers of germs and infections. They do not, however, place such a high priority on keeping the environment clean. Establishments catering to foreigners are generally careful with food and drink preparation.

Bangkok water is clean when it leaves the modern filtration plant; the pipes that carry it into the city are somewhat less than new and visitors are advised to drink bottled water or soft drinks. Both are produced under strict supervision, as is the ice used in large hotels and restaurants. Most streetside restaurants are clean; a quick glance should tell you which are and which are not.

Precautions

With its thriving nightlife and transient population, Bangkok is a magnet for sexual diseases. The women (and men) in these service industries are aware of the consequences of carelessness and of not insisting that their partners take precautions, but economic necessity, coupled with a Thai reluctance to offend anyone, means that there is a great risk of taking home a souvenir one would rather not share with friends and loved ones.

Assume that there is a good chance of picking something up and take appropriate measures. Some massage parlors, mindful of the dangers, now bar foreign patrons and cater only to Thais in the belief that they reduce their risks.

Malaria is still highly-dangerous in some regions of Thailand. The best protection is to avoid being bitten. Mosquitoes are most active at night,

between the hours of sundown and sunrise. After dark you should wear long trousers, long-sleeved shirts, shoes and socks or stockings. Hands and neck should be protected with an insect repellent and you should sleep in rooms with adequate mosquito screens on the windows and under a mosquito net. If you decide to protect yourself with anti-malarial tablets, remember that mosquitoes in many areas are resistant to many of the proprietary brands of medication. Seek advice from a tropical institute before your departure. Should you nonetheless contract malaria, there is a network of malaria centres and hospitals throughout Thailand. It is important to remember that the most dangerous form of malaria often appears disguised as a heavy cold. If you contract what appears to be influenza you should consult a doctor immediately. This also applies during the weeks after your return from the tropics.

Currency

The baht is the principal Thai monetary unit. It is divided into 100 units called satangs. Banknote denominations include 1,000 (gray), 500 (purple), 100 (red), 50 (blue) and 20 (green).

While the banknotes are easy to decipher, the coinage is a confusing matter with a variety of sizes and types for each denomination. There are 10-baht coins (brass center with a silver rim), two different 5-baht coins (silver pieces with copper rims), three varieties of 1 baht coin (silver; usually only the small-size will fit in a public telephone), and two small coins of 50 and 25 satang (both are brass-colored).

Exchange Rates

There is no currency black market, but there are legal money changers.

Banking System

Thailand has a sophisticated banking system with representation by the major banks of most foreign countries. Money can be imported in cash or traveler's checks and converted into baht. It is also possible to arrange telex bank drafts from one's hometown bank. There is no minimum requirement on the amount of money that must be converted. Both cash

and traveler's checks can be changed in hundreds of bank branches throughout the city; rates are more favorable for traveler's checks than for cash. Banking hours are 10am–4.30pm, Monday–Friday, but nearly every bank maintains money-changing kiosks. These kiosks may be found in Bangkok as well as Thailand's other major cities. Hotels generally give poor rates in comparison with banks.

Banks in Bangkok include Thai institutions and branches of foreign banks. Most are equipped to handle telegraph and telex money transfers and a wide range of money services. Banking hours are 8.30am–3.30pm. Upcountry, the services are much more restricted. If you have overseas business to conduct with a bank, it is better to do it in Bangkok.

THAI BANKS

Bank of Asia, 191 Sathorn Thai Road. Tel: 287 2111/3

Bank of Ayutthya, 550 Ploenchit Road. Tel: 255 0022, 255 0033.

Bangkok Bank, 333 Silom Road. Tel: 231 4333.

Bangkok Bank of Commerce, 99 Surasak. Tel: 234 2930.

Bangkok Metropolitan Bank, 2 Chalermkhet 4. Tel: 223 0561/89

First Bangkok City Bank, 20 Yukoi 2. Tel: 223 0501.

Krung Thai Bank, 35 Sukhumvit Road. Tel: 255 2222.

Nakornthon Bank, 90 Sathorn Nua Road. Tel: 233 2111/9.

Siam City Bank, 1101 New Petchaburi Road. Tel: 253 0200-9.

Siam Commercial Bank, 1060 New Phetchaburi Road. Tel: 256 1234.

Thai Danu Bank, 393 Silom Road. Tel: 230 5000.

Thai Farmers Bank, 400 Phaholyothin Road. Tel: 273 1191, 270 1122.

Thai Military Bank, 34 Phahonyothin Road. Tel: 299 1111.

Union Bank of Bangkok, 1600 New Phetchburi Road. Tel: 253 0488.

OVERSEAS BANKS

Bank of America, 2/2 Wireless Road. Tel: 251 6333.

Bank of Tokyo, Thaniya Bldg, 62 Silom Road. Tel: 236 0119, 236 9103

Banque Indosuez, 142 Wireless Road. Tel: 352 3616/7, 253 0106.

Banque Nationale de Paris, 5th Dusit Thani Bldg, 946 Rama IV Road. Tel:

233 4310, 238 1655.
Chase Manhattan Bank, North Sarthorn Road. Tel: 235 7978.
Citibank, 127 Sathorn Thai Road. Tel: 213 2441.
Deutsche Bank, 205 Wireless Road. Tel: 651 5000.
Hongkong Bank, Hongkong Bank Bldg, 64 Silom Road. Tel: 233 5995.
Sakura Bank, Boonmitr Bldg, 138 Silom Road. Tel: 234 3841/2.
Standard Chartered Bank, 946 Rama IV Road. Tel: 266 0200.

Credit Cards

American Express, Diners Club, MasterCard and Visa are widely accepted throughout Bangkok. In up-country destinations, it is better to check that plastic is accepted, and not to count on using cards. Credit cards can be used to draw emergency cash at most banks.

Credit Card Warning: Credit card fraud is a major problem in Thailand. Don't leave your credit card in safe-deposit boxes. When making a purchase, make sure that you obtain the carbons, rip them up and throw them away elsewhere.

Notification of loss of credit cards can be made at the following offices in Bangkok.

American Express, 388 Phaholyothin Road. Tel: 273 0033. Open 8.30am–5.30pm Monday–Friday.
Diners Club, 191 Silom Road. Tel: 234 5715. Open 8.30am–5pm Monday–Friday.
Visa and **MasterCard**, Thai Farmers Bank, 400 Phaholyothin Road. Tel: 273 1199. Open 8.30am–3pm, Monday–Friday.

Public Holidays

The following dates are observed as official public holidays:
New Year's Day January 1
Magha Puja February (full moon)
Chakri Day April 6
Songkran (Thai New Year) April 13–15
Labor Day May 1
Coronation Day May 5
Plowing Ceremony May (variable)
Visakha Puja May (full moon)
Asalha Puja July (full moon)
Khao Pansa July
Queen's Birthday August 12
Chulalongkorn Day October 23

King's Birthday December 5
Constitution Day December 10
New Year's Eve December 31

Chinese New Year in February is not an official public holiday, but many businesses are closed for several days.

Getting There
By Air

Bangkok is a gateway between east and west and a transportation hub for Southeast Asia. Served by more than 50 regularly-scheduled airlines, Thailand has four international airports: Chiang Mai, Phuket, Hat Yai and Bangkok. For example, it is possible to fly Thai Airways directly from Phuket to Hat Yai to Tokyo, Seoul, Perth, Kuala Lumpur, Penang, Singapore, Bandar Seri Bengawan.

The flying time from the UK is about 12 hours, from the west coast of America, about 21 hours. Flights from Australia and New Zealand take about 9 hours.

Thai Airways serves more than 50 cities on four continents. Its domestic arm operates a network of daily flights to 21 of Thailand's major towns aboard a fleet of 737s and Airbuses. Thai offers a visitor's ticket which allows for four flights for about US$250. Extra coupon flights can be added.

AIRLINE OFFICES

Air France, ground floor, 942/51 Rama IV Road (Charn Issara Bldg). Tel: 233 9477, 234 1333; airport: 523 7302, 523 7303.
Air India, Convent Road. Tel: 235 0557/8; airport: 535 2122.
Air Lanka, 942/34–35 Rama IV Road (Charn Issara Bldg). Tel: 236 0159, 236 0292; airport: 535 2330/1.
Air New Zealand, World Travel Service, 1053 New Road. Tel: 237 1560.
Bangkok Airways, Queen Sirikit National Convention Center, New Ratchadapisek Road. Tel: 229 3456, 229 3434.
British Airways, 2nd floor, 942/8 Rama IV Road (Charn Issara Bldg). Tel: 236 8655/6; airport: 535 2143/6.
Cambodian Air, 57/16 Wireless Road. Tel: 251 2498.
Canadian Airlines, 6th floor, Maneeya Building, 518/2 Ploenchit Road. Tel: 251 4521; airport: 535 2227/8.

Cathay Pacific, 5th Ploenchit Tower, Ploenchit Road. Tel: 263 0606; airport: 535 2155.
China Airlines, 4th floor, Peninsula Plaza, 153 Ratchadamri Road. Tel: 253 4241; airport: 535 2160.
Delta Airlines, Patpong Building, Suriwong Road. Tel: 237 6838; airport: 535 2991.
Dragonair, Montri Road, Phuket. Tel/fax: (076) 215 734.
Garuda Indonesia, Lumpini Tower, Rama IV Road. Tel: 288 6470; airport: 523 8865.
Japan Airlines, JAL Building, Ratchadapisek Road. Tel: 274 1411/25; airport: 535 2135.
KLM, Maneeya Centre, Ploenchit Road. Tel: 254 8325/7; airport: 523 7276.
Korean Air, 699 Silom Road. Tel: 235 9220; airport: 523 7320.
Lufthansa, Soi 21, Sukhumvit Road. Tel: 264 2400/8; airport: 535 2211.
Malaysian Airlines, Ploenchit Tower, Ploenchit Road. Tel: 263 0565; airport: 535 2288.
Myanmar Airways, Charn Issara Tower, Rama IV Road. Tel: 267 5078; airport: 523 7420.
Pakistan International, Tai Lai Thong Bldg, 52 Suriwongse Road. Tel: 233 5215; airport: 535 2127.
Philippine Airlines, Chongkolnee Building, 56 Suriwongse Road. Tel: 233 2350/1; airport: 523 9086, 523 6928.
Qantas, 11th floor Charn Issara Bldg, 942/51 Rama IV Road. Tel: 267 5188/99; airport: 535 2149.
Royal Brunei, 20th floor, Charn Issara Bldg, 942/52 Rama IV Road. Tel: 233 0056; airport: 535 2152.
SAS, Soi 25 Sukhumvit Road. Tel: 260 0444; airport: 523 8853.
Singapore Airlines, 12th floor, Silom Center Building, 2 Silom Road. Tel: 236 0440, 236 0303; airport: 523 2260.
Thai Airways, head office: 89 Vibhavadi Rangsit Road, tel: 513 0121; Silom office: 485 Silom Road, tel: 233 3810; Rajawong office: 45 Anuwong Road, tel: 224 9602/3; Asia Hotel office, 296 Phyathai Road, tel: 215 0787/8; airport: 535 2846/7.
United Airlines, 9th floor, Regent House, 183 Ratchadamri Road. Tel: 231 0300; airport: 535 2621/2.
Vietnam Airlines, 584 Ploenchit Road. Tel: 251 4242.

By Rail

Trains operated by the State Railways of Thailand are clean, cheap and reliable, albeit a little slow. There are only two railroad entry points into Thailand, both from Malaysia on the southern Thai border. The trip north to Bangkok serves as a scenic introduction to Thailand.

The Malay Mail leaves Kuala Lumpur every day at 7.30am and 8.15am, and 3pm, 8.30pm and 10pm, arriving 7 to 9 hours later at Butterworth, the port opposite Malaysia's Penang Island at 1.35pm, 5.50pm, and 9.10pm and 5.30 am and 6.40am respectively. A daily train leaves Butterworth at 1.40pm, crossing the border into Thailand and arriving in Bangkok at 9.30 the next morning. There are second-class cars with seats which are made into upper and lower sleeping berths at night. There are also air-conditioned first-class sleepers and dining cars serving Thai food. Prices from Butterworth to Bangkok are US$50 or less, depending upon class of service.

Trains leave Bangkok's Hualampong Station daily at 3.15pm for the return journey to Malaysia.

A second, somewhat less convenient but more entertaining, train travels from Kuala Lumpur up Malaysia's east coast to the northeastern town of Kota Bahru. Take a taxi across the border to catch the srt train from the southern Thai town of Sungai Kolok. Trains leave Sungai Kolok at 12 noon and 3pm, arriving in Bangkok at 8.35am and 10.35am the following day.

If you like to travel in style and prefer not to fly, the Eastern & Oriental Express (Tel: 251 4862) is Asia's most exclusive travel experience. Traveling several times a month between Singapore, Kuala Lumpur and Bangkok, the 22-carriage train with its distinctive green-and-cream livery passes through spectacular scenery. It's very expensive, but elegantly classic.

By Road

Malaysia provides the main road access into Thailand, with crossings near Betong and Sungai Kolok. It is possible to cross to and from Laos from Nong Khai by using the Friendship Bridge across the Mekong River. Visitors need visas. Drivers will find that most Thai roads are modern and well maintained. The Malaysian border closes at 6pm but that may one day be extended.

Special Facilities
Left Luggage

There are two left luggage facilities at Don Muang International Airport. One is on the 1st floor on the northern end of the arrival hall after passing through customs. The second is in the departure hall on the 3rd floor near the currency exchange counter. The fee is 20 baht per bag per day.

Porter Services

There are no porters as such, but luggage carts are available free for both arriving and departing passengers. Upon request, the airport can also provide wheelchairs and other assistance for disabled persons.

Reservations

Hotel reservations can be made in the airport arrival lounge once you have passed through customs. It is recommended that you book a room in advance during the Christmas–New Year and Chinese New Year holidays and outside of Bangkok for Songkran in mid-April.

Children

Children enjoy the unusual animals of Dusit Zoo, or paddling boats in its lake or in Lumpini or Chatuchak Park. Magic Land at 72 Paholyothin Road, near the Hyatt Hotel, is an amusement park with a ghost house, bumper cars and carnival rides. On weekdays, the ticket covers an unlimited number of rides. On weekends, it is limited to 2 hours. Open 10am–5.30pm Monday to Friday; 9.30am–7pm Saturday and Sunday.

East of town at 101 Sukhapiban 2 Road, Siam Park City is a theme park with water slides and flumes. It is open 10am–6pm, Monday to Friday; and 9am–7pm, Saturday and Sunday. A word of warning: The park prohibits the wearing of T-shirts in the swimming areas so take plenty of suntan oil for tender young skins.

Safari World is an amusement park about 10 km from the center of town. A minibus service is available to the park.

Gays

Gays quickly discover that Thailand is one of the most tolerant countries in the world. In Bangkok, most of the gay bars are on Patpong 3 or the upper end of Silom Road. Transvestites and transvestite shows are common in Bangkok, and also in Phuket and Pattaya.

Disabled

The facilities for the handicapped are underdeveloped. Sidewalks are uneven, studded with obstructions and there are no ramps. Few buildings in Bangkok have wheelchair ramps.

Useful Addresses
Doing Business

Most hotels have business centers with communications and secretarial services in several languages. Elsewhere in Bangkok, it is possible to lease small offices with clerical staff.

GOVERNMENT OFFICES

Board of Investment
(Office of Prime Minister)
555 Vibhavadi Rangsit Road
Tel: 537-8101-70
Fax: 537-8177
The BOI is authorised to grant tax holidays and other incentives to promote certain industries. It is fruitless to phone, write or fax this agency. Potential investors must visit in person.

Ministry of Commerce
Department of Commercial Registration
73 Krungthonburi Road
General Telephone: 438-5957, 438-6005
Fax: 225-8493
Commercial Registration: 221-4853
Public Relations: 221-9872, 221-6105
Patent and Trade Mark Division: 222-6918, 221-1882, 222-3595
Trade Mark Registration Section: 221-2851, 222-2872

Department of Commercial Relations
Rachadaphisek-Ladprao Road
General telephone: 551-5058-71
Exhibition Division: 513-1908-18
Foreign Marketing Division: 511-5066-77, 513-1909-18
Information Division: 513-1907

Trade Information Division: 511-5066-77, 511-4263

Department of Foreign Trade
Sananchai Road
General telephone: 223-1481-5,225-1315-29, 222-0738-9
Export-Import Control Division: 222-0501, 222-1866
Goods Analyses: 223-3414, 225-2926
Foreign Trade Policy Division: 223-3513
Inspection Services Section: 282-8182-3
Overseas Commercial Office: 224-8009

Customs Department
(Ministry of Finance)
Sunthornkasa Road
General telephone: 240-2617/8, 249-0431, 249-4121
Customs Tariff Division: 249-4162, 249-4199
Director of Customs Division: 249-4351
Export Inspection Division: 249-0441, 249-0446
Inspection Division: 249-5238
Technical and Foreign Division: 249-2525

BUSINESS ORGANIZATIONS

American Chamber of Commerce, 140 Wireless Road. Tel: 251 1605, 251 9266. Open 8.30am–noon, 1–4.30pm Monday–Friday.
British Chamber of Commerce, 54 Soi 21 Sukhumvit Road. Tel: 260 7288, 234 1169. Open 8am–noon, 1–4.30pm Monday–Friday.
British Council, 428 Soi 2 Siam Square, Rama I Road. Tel: 252 6136, 252 6111. Open 8.30am–4pm Monday–Friday. In Chiang Mai: 198 Bamrungrat Road. Tel: 242 103.
Franco-Thai Chamber of Commerce, 104 Wireless Road. Tel: 251 9385. Open 8.30am–noon, 2–5pm Monday–Friday.
German-Thai Chamber, 699 Klongboonma Bldg, Silom Road. Tel: 266 4924/5. Open 9am–noon Monday–Friday.
Goethe Institute, 18/1 Soi Ngamduplee, Rama 4 Road. Tel: 286 9002/3. Open 8am–5pm Monday–Friday; and from 8am–noon on Saturday.
Japanese Chamber of Commerce, 4th floor, Panunee Bldg, 518/3 Ploenchit Road. Tel: 251 7418. Open 9am–5pm

Monday–Friday; and 9am–noon Saturday.

GOVERMENT OFFICES

Tourist Authority of Thailand
(state enterprise)
372 Bamruangmuang Road
General telephone: 225-0058-76, 226-0078-87
Fax: 280-1744
Public Relations: 282-9524, 282-5264
Tourist Assistance: 281-5051, 281-0372
Tourist Police: 282-8129

THAI LAW FIRMS

These Bangkok law firms employ foreign, native English-speaking lawyers and/or Thai lawyers who speak and write very fluent English.

Baker and McKenzie, 92/54-7 N. Sathorn Road. Tel: 234-8621-9, Fax: 236-6071-3. A franchise of the mega-multinational US firm.
Domnern, Somgiat and Boonma, 719 Siphya Road, Bangrak 10500. Tel: 237-1882, Fax: 236-3479. Specialises in international property law.
Internet Law Consultants, 191 Silom Complex, 22F, Silom Road, Bangrak 10500. Tel: 231-3391-4, Fax: 231-3395
Rilleke and Gibbins, 64/1 Soi Tonson, Ploenchit Road 10330. Tel: 254-2640-59, Fax: 254-4304. US-affiliated.

SPECIAL CLUBS

Alliance Francaise, 29 S. Sathorn Road. Tel: 213 2122/3. Open Monday–Friday, 8am–7.30pm; Saturday, 9–7pm. In Chiang Mai: 138 Charoenprathet Road. Tel: 235 277.
American University Alumni (AUA), 179 Ratchadamri Road. Tel: 252 8170/3. In Chiang Mai: 24 Ratchadamnern Ave. Tel: 211 377.
Foreign Correspondents Club of Thailand, Thai Jewellery Centre, Silom Road. Open Monday–Saturday, 9am–midnight.
Lions Chaophaya (Bangkok) Association, 10 Soi Soomvijai, New Petchburi Road. Tel: 258 9037. Meetings on the last Thursday of the month. Foreign members are welcomed.
Rotary Club, Bangkok Rotary, Grand Hyatt Erawan Hotel. Tel: 254 1234. Foreign members welcome; English is the medium.

Practical Tips

Emergencies

Medical Services

HOSPITALS

Bamrungrad and Samitivej hospital bear the closest resemblance to Western hospitals, but so do their fees. For those with comprehensive medical insurance, these are the places to go. Otherwise, the other hospitals listed below have reasonable standards, accept credit cards and employ English-speaking staff.

Thai physicians are often too eager to order tests that employ "high techonology" and they tend to over-prescribe both antibiotics and painkillers. Use your prerogative as a foreigner and find out precisely what is being prescribed. If you are in pain, insist that you do not need painkillers. Every physician and genuine pharmacists will have a pharmaceutical reference book in English. It is interesting to see that many drugs banned in Western countries are quite common in Thailand.

Most of these hospitals also have dental clinics that provide emergency services. Note that for both medical and dental services, Bangkok Adventist hospital provides only emergencies on Friday afternoon and Saturday but operates full services on Sunday and the rest of the week. This hospital is popular with foreign resident missionaries of all faiths.

Bangkok Adventist Hospital, 430 Phitsanuloke Road. Tel: 281 1422, 282 1100.
Bangkok Christian Hospital, 124 Silom Road. Tel: 233 6981/9.
Bangkok General Hospital, 2 Soi Soonvijai, New Petchaburi Road. Tel: 318 0066.
Bamrungrad Hospital, 33 Soi 3, Sukhumvit Road. Tel: 253 0250/69.
Deja General Hospital, 346 Sri Ayutthaya. Tel: 246 0137.

St. Louis Hospital, 215 Sathorn Thai Road. Tel: 212 0033.
Samitivej Hospital, 133 Soi 49, Sukhumvit Road. Tel: 392 0010.
Siam General Hospital, 15/10 Soi Chokchai 4, Lardprao. Tel: 514 2157/9.
Sukhumvit Hospital, 1411 Sukhumvit Road. Tel: 391 0011.

Medical Clinics

For minor problems, there are numerous clinics in all the major towns and cities. The British Dispensary, located at 109 Sukhumvit Road (between Soi 3 and 5), tel: 252 8056, has British doctors on its staff. In Chiang Mai, go to Chuang Pak Polyclinic at 52/2 Chang Puak Road, tel: 210 213. Most international hotels also have an on-premises clinic, or a physician on call.

Dental Clinics

Dental clinics are almost as numerous as medical clinics.

In Bangkok, one clinic with a long-standing reputation is the Dental Polyclinic, at 211-3 New Petchburi Road, tel: 314 5070. The Dental Hospital, 88/88 Soi 49, Sukhumvit Road, tel: 260 5000/15 looks more like a hotel than a dental hospital and has the latest imported dental equipment.

Other Services

Community Services of Bangkok, 15/1 Sukhumvit Soi 3. Telephone 258-4998. This nonprofit organization offers classes and services for foreign ers living in Bangkok. Counselling services are provided by Western-trained professionals. While English is the usual language, the friendly volunteer staffers can probably recommend professionals who speak other languages. They also have contacts with self-help and support groups.

AIDS. Red Cross (Snake Farm), 1871 Rama IV Road. Provides anonymous testing and counseling. This is also a good place to get inoculations, including the popular Japanese encephalitis series.
Alcohol Anonymous, Holy Redeemer Church, 123 Soi Ruam Rudi 5, off Ploenchit Road. Tel: 256-6305 or 235-6157.
The Samaritans of Bangkok. Tel: 249-9977 or 7530. Anonymous counseling service, in English, 24 hours daily.

In theory, pharmaceuticals are subject to three levels of control. In practice, just about everything is sold just about everywhere. With a bit of caution, Thailand is a great place to stock up. A staffer in a white coat is not necessarily a pharmacist and outside of Bangkok, it is unlikely that she or he is. A genuine pharmacist will speak a little English and will have a pharmaceutical reference book in English.

More so than physicians, these pharmacists or clerks often recklessly recommend powerful drugs, including drugs banned in Western countries, for minor ailments. They also always initially offer the highest dosage of a drug. Ask for a smaller one (*lek kwaa*). It's always possible to purchase one tablet, one capsule or one bandage.

The quality of drugs is acceptable, although one should check expiration dates and be aware that exposure to heat may mean that a drug expires even earlier. For this reason, it may be wise to buy drugs in an air-conditioned venue, such as a supermarket. Brand-name Western drugs – usually British or German – are much cheaper than at home. Even cheaper are the thousands of drugs (no one knows how many) manufactured by about 100 Thai firms. Their speciality is "off patent" drugs, that is, copies of old Western drugs whose patents has expired.

Amphetamines are the Thai drug of choice, but Thais also like strong combinations of caffeine, cough medicines, painkillers and anti-fever medications. The knock-out potion favoured by prostitutes is the potentially fatal Halcion, which is banned in some Western countries.

Although they are most easily found in Chinatown, Chinese herbal medicine shops are all over Bangkok. Often they sell both Western and Chinese medications.

Tampons: Tampons are not easy to find and only one brand is available, O.B. In fact, "O.B." is the Thai term to request them. Look in the shops of big hotels and in the drug stores in the vicinity. In department stores, check both the supermarket and the pharmacy counter. Outside of tourist meccas, it's fruitless to search. However, sanitary napkins come in countless varieties and can be found in the smallest hamlets.

Security and Crime

When in Thailand, avoid the following:
- Touts posing as Boy Scouts soliciting donations on Bangkok's sidewalks. The real Boy Scouts obtain funds from other sources.
- Touts on Patpong offering upstairs live sex shows. Once inside, one is handed an exorbitant bill and threatened with mayhem if he or she protests. Pay, take the receipt, and go immediately to the Tourist Police to gain restitution, which may or may not be forthcoming.
- Persons offering free or very cheap boat rides into the canals. Once you are well into the canal, you are given the choice of paying a high fee or being stranded.
- Persons offering to take you to a gem factory for a "special deal". The gems are usually flawed and there is no way to get your money back.
- Persons on buses or trains offering sweets, fruits or soft drinks. The items may be drugged and the passenger is robbed while unconscious. This is unfortunate because Thais are generous people and it is normal for them to offer food to strangers. Use discretion.

If you do run into trouble in Bangkok, the **police emergency number is 191**. There are also Tourist Police assigned specially to assist travelers. They are located at the Tourist Assistance Center at the Tourism Authority of Thailand headquarters at No. 4 Ratchadamnern Nok Avenue. They also maintain a booth on the Lumpini Park, corner of the Rama 4 and Silom roads intersection. Most members of the force speak English.

Thais are generally helpful in emergencies, but they do have an infamous idiosyncracy. If you become unconscious or disorientated following a criminal attack, traffic accident or a plane crash, it's virtually guaranteed that by the time you reach the hospital, you will be relieved of your money, credit cards, jewelry and possibly passport. If you temporarily vacate a hotel room because of a fire, it may be pilfered by your return.

It's impossible to prepare for every contingency, of course. It's always wiser to keep credit cards on your person than in a hotel safe. It may be a good idea, though, to hide copies of account numbers and photocopies of your passport in several places.

Particularly in cases of criminal attacks, victims are supposed to be taken to a Police Hospital. Usually, it's the one across from the Erawan Shrine. Thais probably won't know if this rule applies to foreigners and, by all means, foreigners should take advantage of this misunderstanding. Insist on being taken to one of the hospitals listed in the previous section, making it clear that you have no wish to avoid police questioning. The sight of the dirt and grime in a police hospital could induce cardiac arrest in a sensitive Westerner.

Tourist Assistance: 281-5051, 281-0372
Tourist Police: 282-8129

All tourists seem to know that if a taxi driver or tour bus brings them to a store, there are no bargains to be had. The driver, guide or whoever earns a commission for bringing in tourists or a 30 percent cut from the sale price, or both. Beyond this sphere, tourists too readily drop their guard in Thailand.

The costliest scams revolve around gems and jewelry. A person with a bit of expertise can find good deals on Thai sapphires and Burmese jade and rubies. For novice buyers, though, the risk is very high. Certificates of authenticity are meaningless. If you discover that you have been cheated, even one day after a purchase, there is no recourse. No shop owners, including repeated offenders, have ever been prosecuted. The policemen who frequently loiter inside jewelry shops certainly won't lend the complaining tourist any support.

Some of the most clever con artists work the area around Erawan Shrine (across from the police station) and near the intersection of Surawong and Rama IV roads (next to the traffic police stand). They are dressed in safari suits, claim they are students or professors, and speak excellent English (many are Filipinos). One strikes up a conversation, treats you to coffee, exclaims that his daughter/sister is planning to study in your country and invites you home to meet his wife and family, where a card game ensues.

Less sophisticated, but highly successful, are the touts and tuk-tuk drivers that hang around the lanes and entrances leading to popular tourist sites, notably Jim Thompson's House. These people will inform you that the site is "close today!" Ignore them and check for yourself. The site is usually open; the ruse is intended to divert you into taking a shopping tour.

On trains and long-haul buses, never accept food or drinks offered by the friendliest of strangers. Even foil-wrapped chocolate may be drugged. Some tourists warn against the food served on the privately-run tourist buses. While they may be over-cautious, it is most definitely true that overnight buses, including the top-line Songserm VIP buses, employ shady employees. During the night, a cohort of the driver, seemingly sleeping in the central aisle, inches his way along, rifling or razoring through bags at the feet of sleeping passengers. By the time passengers wake up, the thief has long ago been let off the bus.

Probably because it's unavoidable, tourists complain that the biggest scam in Thailand is "foreigners' pricing" (*rakhaa farang*). At an official level, most government-run sites levy entrance fees for foreigners that are two, three, even five times the rate for Thais.

The price of clothing, watches and other trinkets sold at street stalls is subject to an individual's bargaining skills. Food, however, has a set price, whether it is sliced fruit vended from a cart or a full-course meal. If you know the price that Thais pay, you can usually succeed in paying the same (this is much less likely outside of Bangkok). The moral: ascertain the price before you sit or consume. If it sounds exorbitant, bargain fiercely or walk away. Don't show anger.

For many of the mom-and-pop shops and for any shop close to a big hotel, a foreign face cranks up the price. A 100-percent mark-up for a can of Coke or a bottle of water is common. The solution is to seek out big shops, department stores and convenience stores, such as 7-11, where prices are marked. For Thai customers, these places are more expensive than the small shops; for farang, they are cheaper.

Thailand uses the metric system of meters, grams and liters.

Government offices are open from 8.30am–4.30pm on Monday–Friday. Business hours are from 8am or 8.30am–5.30pm on Monday–Friday. Some businesses are open half days from 8.30am–noon on Saturdays. Banks are open from 8.30am–3.30pm, five days a week but operate money-changing kiosks throughout the city, which are open until 8pm, seven days a week.

The Central Post Office in Bangkok is located on New Road between Suriwongse and Siphya roads. It opens at 8.30am and closes at 4.30pm on Monday–Friday, and from 8.30am–12.30pm on Saturdays, Sundays and holidays.

Branch post offices are located throughout the city and many of these usually stay open until 6pm. Kiosks along some of the city's busier streets sell stamps and aerograms and ship small parcels. Hotel reception counters will send letters for their guests at no extra charge.

Most department stores are open from 10am–9pm seven days a week. Ordinary shops open at 8.30am or 9am and close between 6pm and 8pm, depending on the location and type of business. Some pharmacies in the major cities remain open all night.

Small open-air coffee shops and restaurants open at 7am and close at 8.30pm, though some stay open past midnight. Large restaurants generally close at 10pm. Most coffee shops close at midnight; some stay open 24 hours.

Tipping is not a custom in Thailand, although it is becoming more prevalent. A service charge of 10 percent is generally included in restaurant bills and is divided among the staff. A bit extra for the waitress would not go unappreciated. Do not tip non-metered taxi or tuk-tuk drivers unless the traffic has been particularly bad and he has been especially patient; 10 baht would suffice for a long journey over 60 baht.

230

Hotel room boys and porters are becoming used to being tipped but will not hover with hand extended.

Religious Services

Interdenominational

International Church of Bangkok, 67 Soi 19, Sukhumvit Road. Tel: 260 8187. Services: 8am.
International Christian Assembly, 196 Soi Yasoop 1, Ekamai Road. Tel: 391 4387. Services: 10.30am, 6pm.

Anglican

Christ Church, 11 Convent Road. Tel: 234 3634. Services: 8am, 10am.

Baptist

Calvary Baptist Church, 88 Soi 2, Sukhumvit Road. Tel: 251 8278. Service: 10.45am.

Catholic

Holy Redeemer Church, 123/19 Soi Ruam Rudi, Wireless Road. Tel: 256 6305. Sunday Mass: 8.30am, 9.45am, 11am, 5.30pm.
Assumption Cathedral, 23 Oriental Lane, New Road. Tel: 234 8556. Sunday Mass: 10am.
St Louis Church, 215/2 South Sathorn Road. Tel: 211 0220. Mass: 6am, 8am, 10am, 5.30pm.

Hindu

Thamsapha Association, 50 Soi Wat Prok, New Road. Tel: 211 3840. Services: 7am 10pm.

Jewish

Jewish Association of Thailand (Ashkenazi), 121 Soi Sainam Thip 2, Soi 22, Sukhumvit Road. Tel: 258 2195. Service: 6.30pm on Friday. Please contact Rabbi Kantor.
Even Chen Synagogue (Sephardic), The Bossotel, 55/12-14 Charoen Krung Road, (near Shangri-La Hotel). Tel: 234 9409. Services: 9.30am on Saturday.

Muslim

Sha-Roh-Tal Islam Mosque, 133 Soi I Sukhapiban Road. Tel: 328 8950. Services: 12.30pm–2pm.

Sikh

Wat Sirikurusing Saha, 565 Chuckrapetch Road. Tel: 221 1011. Services: 6am, 5pm.

Media

Press

Thailand has two long-standing English-language dailies, *The Bangkok Post* and *The Nation*. If you are familiar with newspapers in any of the neighboring countries, you will be pleasantly surprised by the free-wheeling coverage. Many big hotels will supply one or both of these papers at no charge. Relative newcomers are the tabloid-ish *Thailand Times* and the conservative *Business Day*, partially owned by the Singapore *Straits Times*.

The *International Herald Tribune* and the *Asian Wall Street Journal* are sold in Bangkok, Chiang Mai, Pattaya and Phuket, although at relatively few newsstands. It's most fruitful to look in hotel shops and outlets of Asia Books, DK and Bookazine. In Bangkok, such vendors often also sell the *Financial Times* and Belgian, French, German, Italian, Japanese and Spanish dailies. Outside of the four big tourist centers, you will be lucky to find even the domestic English papers.

At any one time, probably about a dozen English-language magazines are being published in Thailand. For foreign visitors, the most useful and interesting is the monthly *Bangkok Metro*. In addition to basic survival advice, the listings include recommended restaurants and music venues. The English-language "business" magazines, mostly monthly, have a broad interpretation of the term. The slickest is *Manager*.

The most curious of the English-language periodicals are called "hi-so" by Thais and "suck-up" rags by expats. Among them are *Living in Thailand*, *Thailand Tatler* and sporadic glossy hotel productions. Each issue consists of photos and profiles of Thai millionaires and many jewelry ads. Every interviewee, whether a drop-out from New Secretarial Institute or the proud progeny of an ex-director, is treated with the same swooning flattery. No slightly unpleasant fact about Thailand ever intrudes. Foreigners find these rags hilarious or appalling, but they do convey much about how the Thai elite still wish to be regarded.

Radio

AM radio is devoted entirely to Thai-language programs. FM frequencies include several English language stations with the latest pop hits. Radio Thailand offers 4 hours of English-language broadcasts each day at 97 MHz. Of value to visitors is an English-language program of travel tips broadcast regularly throughout the day.

Television

Bangkok has five Thai language television channels. In addition, there are now two cable television networks in Bangkok. I.B.C. has five channels, four of which covering news, entertainment, sports and movies are broadcast in English. Sky TV has three channels, all in English. As well as the two cable television networks, all the major hotels and many of the smaller ones also receive satellite television from around the world.

Bookshops

English-language books are sold at the many outlets of Asia Books and DK. Below are listed their flagship stores. DK also operates small French and German shops at Alliance Française and Goethe Institute. On Kaosan Road, a half-dozen shops and stalls sell and buy used foreign-language books. Besides English, French, German and Japanese titles are common. The bookstores sell foreign-language magazines (at daunting prices), as do branches of Central and Robinson department stores.

Asia Books, 221 Sukhumvit Road (between Sois 15 & 17). Tel: 252 7277
DK Book House, 2F Seacon Square, Srinakarin Road (off Bangna-Trad Highway). Tel: 393-8040. This is the largest bookstore in Southeast Asia, but reaching it may consume an entire day.
Elite Used Books, 593/5 Sukhumvit Road (near Soi 33/1). Tel: 258-0221. Also at 1/12 Sukhumvit Soi 3. Tel: 258-0221. More than English titles.

Postal Services

The Thai postal service is not very reliable. As you can tell from the letters in the local newspapers, foreigners' complaints don't focus on speed so much as lost mail. The odds for domestic mail can be improved by registering or sending items "EMS". EMS costs 15 baht (60 US cents) for a business-sized letter. EMS is supposed to guarantee that a letter reaches a domestic destination in two days.

If you wish to send valuable parcels, bulky documents or irreplaceable film overseas, turn to DHL, Federal Express, TNT Skypak, UPS or other private international courier service. Unfortunately, such services are only offered from Bangkok. Never send or attempt to receive credit cards or blank checks through the Thai postal service. Ask your international correspondents to use boring stamps or a postal meter; a plausible theory holds that Thai postal staff pilfer foreign mail in order to obtain the colorful stamps.

The General Post Office in Bangkok is located on the riverside between Suriwongse and Siphya roads on Charoen Krung Road ("New Road"). It is open from 7.30am to 4.30pm, Monday to Friday; and from 9am to noon on weekends and holidays. The Banglampoo post office, close to Kaosan Road, is open Saturday mornings from 9am to noon. Offices elsewhere in Bangkok and throughout the country are usually open around 8am and close at 4 or 4.30pm on weekdays. They are closed on Saturday, Sunday and holidays. The GPO and many larger offices sell packing boxes and materials.

Mini post offices – little more than windows, actually – pop up in Bangkok in unexpected places, such as office buildings and hotels. A red sign in English will confirm suspicions; outdoors, there may be no indication of a post office within. These outlets offer basic mail services and accept small packages, but, unlike full-scale post offices, have no telecommunications services. Mail boxes have one or two slots. In the latter case, one is for destination Bangkok and the other is for everywhere else in the world. In Bangkok, although not elsewhere, usually this is indicated in English.

Post and Telegraph Department
Chaengwatana Road
International Service Division: 271-3515
International Post Section: 279-6196
International Telecommunications Section: 271-3512

Thailand is rehabilitating and overhauling its communications system, not that it always works; the lines have a way of getting jammed, like the traffic, especially after a heavy rain. Most hotels have telephones, telegrams, telexes and fax facilities.

Directory Assistance: 13 (in English)

Area Codes

Thailand area code: 66
Bangkok: 02
Chiang Mai: 053
Chiang Rai: 053
Chiang Saen: 053
Chumphon: 077
Hat Yai: 074
Hua Hin: 032
Kanchanaburi: 034
Ko Samui: 077
Krabi: 075
Mae Hong Son: 053
Mae Sai: 053
Mae Salong: 053
Nakhon Ratchasima (Korat): 044
Pattaya/Jomtien: 038
Phang Nga Bay/Ao Nang: 076
Phi Phi: 075
Phuket: 076
Songkhla: 074
Sukhothai: 055
Surat Thani: 077

Telephone

Thailand has a Third World telecommunications system. Service is improving slowly, at least in Bangkok. Top-notch hotels will have IDD service, which enables callers to directly connect with an operator in North America, Western Europe and the more developed countries of Asia (not counting Malaysia). Without IDD, and in most other hotels in the country, a hotel operator and/or an "international" Thai operator will intervene. Thai operators are good-natured but have trouble pronouncing foreign names. IDD or no, hotels will still levy a service charge for each international call. In addition, the basic service is very expensive, costing at least one-third more than US rates. Calling collect (reverse charges) is therefore advisable. "Callback" services, which employ US lines to call elsewhere in the world, are very popular (but technically illegal) in Thailand.

Despite the drawbacks of hotel tel-

ephoning, there are few alternatives. Seek out the main post office. On the grounds of the Bangkok GPO, on Charoen Krung Road (New Road) and near the Oriental Hotel, is an annex with the country's most advanced telecommunications equipment. It is open 24 hours per day. (Women should be aware that the air-conditioned premises are a round-the-clock gathering place for the city's immigrant men; they are harmless if resolutely ignored.) Most notable are self-service IDD phones that allow direct connections with MCI, Sprint and AT&T operators. This is also the cheapest place to make calls to non-IDD – that is, less developed – countries. International fax rates (though not domestic) are the best here. Ask to use the self-service fax machines; this service is not promoted. Do not believe signs at the city's myriad small shops advertising international services at "GPO rates".

For long-distance calls within Thailand, the advice for international calls generally applies. More "long distance" public phones are cropping up in Bangkok. They will be identified as such in English and should not be mistaken for international phones. They require telephone cards that can be purchased in post offices and chain convenience stores.

That leaves the confusing mess of local public service. You will notice red, pink and aqua telephones with coin slots on the counters of many open-fronted shops. (Rarely are they found in hotels.) These require small one-baht coins; insert the money, dial the number and then, only after your party answers, press the small button that deposits the coin. Free-standing booths are also appearing; they accept one-baht or five-baht coins. Since one baht pays for only a very short time (about one minute), the call may be cut off abruptly. Keep feeding in coins.

Even when enclosed in booths, public phones are daunting for foreigners because they are virtually always located within a foot of the noisiest thoroughfares and sidewalk construction. These are also the only type of local phones available at post offices. In Bangkok, shopping malls are always good places to hunt for relatively quiet telephone environs.

Whatever the location, it is highly likely that a public telephone will be out of order. You may well try a half-dozen phones before finding one that works. If you are desperate, seek out a travel agency, photo shop or very Western-ish office, assume a forlorn look and request to use the phone. Emphasize that you wish to make a local call (that is, "Bangkok"). Since the cost is 3 baht, offer to pay 5 baht or 10 baht.

Mastering the mechanics of Thai telephones is only half the battle. Even if the call goes through, there is a very good chance that you won't reach the party you seek. One reason is that Thai telephone numbers change frequently. If you are fairly certain of the number, try to leave a message – that is, your name and telephone number. Only in a very Westernized office will a secretary (or whoever) ask to convey a message. You certainly can bring up the suggestion yourself.

But the fact remains very few such messages are passed on. At any rate, seldom do Thais in a business capacity return telephone calls, even if the caller is an acquaintance. Bureaucrats never seem to return phone calls. The only option is to keep up a barrage of calls. Do not hesitate to call three, four or five times per day. Send simultaneous faxes. Befriend the secretary.

Once you reach your party, don't ask him if he received any of your 27 messages. Behave as if this is the first attempt.

The telephone caller usually encounters the ambiguous phrase, "X no come today". This may mean that X will come later today. It may mean that X moved to another building a year ago. It may well mean that he/she has never heard of X. In any case, much perseverance is required. Ask to speak to a better English speaker (say phasaa ankrit, which means "English language"). Get a Thai speaker to intervene for you.

If you are told that no such X exists, try calling at different times during the day. If X is known, ask if he can be reached at other numbers; this information will never be volunteered. As a matter of fact, whenever people give you their telephone number or a business card, or if they suggest someone you should contact, ask for additional numbers, home numbers, fax numbers and so on. Never, never assume you can find a number through directory

assistance or the instantly-obsolete telephone directories.

Note: There is a serious shortage of telephone lines in Bangkok, which is being addressed by the installation of an additional 2 million telephones. The modernisation has meant that some existing telephone numbers have changed, often upon short notice, so if you have a problem getting through, try telephoning 13 to verify the number. The operators speak English.

Tourist Offices

TAT Offices

Planning a trip to Thailand can be made easier if you contact a travel agent or an office of the Tourism Authority of Thailand. These offices offer promotional brochures, maps and videotapes of the country's many attractions.

The Tourism Authority of Thailand is the Thai government's official tourism promotion organization. The head office at 372 Bamrung Muang Road (Tel: 226 0060, 226 0072, 226 0085) will provide you with essential tourist information, for a more complete service, the information office, at 4 Ratchadamnern Nok Avenue (Tel: 280 1305), has a wealth of brochures on various attractions and personnel to answer questions.

TAT has its own travel information site, on the World Wide Web: http://www.cs.ait.ac.th/tat/. The TAT's e-mail address for sending inquiries is tat@cs.ait.ac.th.

Listed below are some of the offices of the Tourism Authority of Thailand.

THAILAND

Bangkok: 372 Bamrung Muang Road 10100. Tel: 226 0072, fax: 224 6221.
Chiang Mai: 105/1 Chiang Mai-Lamphun Road. Tel: (053) 248 604, 248 607, fax: (053) 248 605.
Kanchanaburi: Saeng Chuto Road. Tel: (034) 511 200, fax: (034) 511 200.
Lop Buri: H.M. The Queen's Celebration Building, c/o Lop Buri Provincial Hall, Narai Mahart Road. Tel: (036) 422 768, 422 769, fax: (036) 422 769.
Nakhon Si Thammarat: Sanam Na Muang, Ratchadamnoen Road. Tel: (075) 346 515-6, fax: (075) 346 517.

Pattaya: 382/1 Chaihat Road, Pattaya City. Tel: (038) 428 750, 427 667, fax: (038) 429 113.
Phra Nakhon Si Ayutthaya: Si Sanphet Road. Tel: (035) 246 076/7, fax: (035) 246 078.
Phuket: 73-75 Phuket Road. Tel: (076) 212 213, 211 036, fax: (076) 213 582.
Udon Thani: c/o Provincial Education Office, Phosi Road. Tel: (042) 241 968, fax: (042) 241 968.

ASIA PACIFIC

Australia: 7th floor, Royal Exchange Bldg, 56 Pitt St, Sydney 2000. Tel: (02) 247 7549, fax: (02) 251 2465.
Hong Kong: Room 401, Fairmont House, 8 Cotton Tree Drive, Central. Tel: (852) 868 0732, (852) 868 0854, fax: (852) 868 4585.
Japan: Hibiya Mitsui Bldg, 1-2, Yurakucho 1-chome, Chiyoda-ku, Tokyo 100, tel: (03) 358 06776/7, fax: (03) 388 07000, Hirana machi Yachiyo Bldg, 5th floor, 1-8-13 Hiranomachi Chuo-ku, Osaka 541, tel: (06) 231 4434, fax: (06) 231 4337; Hakata Pal Bldg, 2nd Floor, 2-63 Gokushu-machi, Hakata-ku, Fukuoka 812, tel: (092) 262 3031, fax: (092) 262 3032.
Malaysia: c/o Royal Thai Embassy, 206 Jalan Ampang, Kuala Lumpur. Tel: (093) 242 601, fax: (093) 248 918.
Singapore: c/o Royal Thai Embassy, 370 Orchard Road, Singapore 0923. Tel: 737 3060, fax: 732 2458.
South Korea: Room 2003, 20th Floor, Coryo Daeyungak Center Building, 25-5, 1-ka. Chungmu ro, Chung-ku, Seoul. Tel: (02) 779 5417, 779 5418, fax: (02) 770 5419.
Taiwan: Thailand Trade and Economic Office, 2B Central Commercial Building, 16-18 Nanking East Road, Section 4, Taipei. Tel: (02) 579 6111, fax: (02) 577 9914.

EUROPE

France: 90 Avenue des Champs-Elysees, 75008 Paris. Tel: 45 62 86 50, fax: 01 45 63 78 88
Italy: Ente Nazionale per il Turismo Thailandese, Via Barberini 50 00187, Rome. Tel: (06) 487 3479, fax: 487 3500.
England: 49 Albemarle St, London W1X 3FE. Tel: (171) 499 7670/9, fax: (171) 629 5519.
Germany: Bethmannstr, 58/IV., D-6000, Frankfurt/M.I. Tel: (069) 295

704, (069) 295 804, fax: (69) 281 468.

USA

New York: 5 World Trade Center, Suite 2449, New York, NY 10048. Tel: (212) 432 0433, fax: (212) 912 0920.
Los Angeles: 3440 Wilshire Blvd, Suite 1101, Los Angeles, CA 90010. Tel: (213) 382 2353, 382 2354, fax: (213) 380 6476.

Embassies

Australia, 37 Sathorn Tai Road. Tel: 287 2680. Visas: 8.15am–12.15pm.
Austria, 14 Soi Nantha, Sathorn Tai Road. Tel: 287 3970/2. Visas: 9am–noon.
Belgium, 44 Soi Pipat, off Silom Road. Tel: 236 7876, 236 0150. Visas: 8.30am–1pm.
Brunei, 19 Soi 26, Sukhumvit Road. Tel: 260 5884/7, 261 1877/9. Visas: 8.30am–noon and 1–4pm.
Burma, 132 Sathorn Nua Road. Tel: 233 2237, 234 4698. Visas: 8.30am–noon.
Canada, 138 Boonmitr Bldg, 11 & 12th floors, Silom Road. Tel: 237 4126. Visas: 8–11am.
China, 57 Ratchadaphisek Road, Dindaeng. Tel: 245 7032. Visas: 9am–noon.
Denmark, 10 Soi Atthakan Prasit, Sathorn Tai Road. Tel: 213 2021/5. Visas: 9am–3pm (Friday: 9am–noon).
France, 35 Soi 36 (Soi Rong Phasi Kao), Charoen Krung Road. Tel: 234 0950/4. Visas: 8.30am–noon issued by Consular Section, 29 Sathorn Tai Road. Tel: 213 2181/4.
Germany, 9 Sathorn Tai Road. Tel: 213 2331/6. Visas: 8.30–11.30am.
India, 46 Sukhumvit Soi 23 (Soi Prasanmit) Sukhumvit Road. Tel: 258 0300-6. Visas: 9am–noon.
Indonesia, 600-602 Phetchaburi Road. Tel: 252 3135/40. Visas: 8.30am–noon and 1.30–3.30pm.
Israel, 31 Soi Lang Suan, Ploenchit Road. Tel: 252 3131/4. Visas: 8am–noon.
Italy, 399 Nang Linchi Road, Tung Mahamek. Tel: 287 2054/7. Visas: 9.30–11.30am.
Japan, 1674/4 New Phetchaburi Road. Tel: 252 6151/9. Visas: 8.30am–noon at Asoke Tower, Sukhumvit 21. Tel: 259 0234/7.
Korea, 23 Thiam-Ruammit Road, Huay

Kwang, Samsaennork. Tel: 247 7537/9. Visas: 8.30am–noon and 1.30–4.30pm.
Laos, 193 Sathorn Tai Road. Tel: 213 2573/4, 213 1203, 287 3963. Visas: 8am–noon.
Malaysia, 35 Sathorn Tai Road. Tel: 286 1390/2. Visas: 8.30–11.30am.
Nepal, 189 Soi 71, Sukhumvit Road. Tel: 391 7240. Visas: 8.30am–noon.
Netherlands, 106 Witthayu Road. Tel: 254 7701/5. Visas: 9am–noon.
New Zealand, 93 Witthayu Road. Tel: 251 8165. Visas: 8.30–11.30am.
Pakistan, 31 Soi 3 (Soi Nana Nua), Sukhumvit Road. Tel: 253 0288/90. Visas: 9am–noon.
Philippines, 760 Sukhumvit Road. Tel: 259 0139/40. Visas: 8.30am–noon and 1.30–4pm.
Singapore, 129 Sathorn Tai Road. Tel: 286 2111, 286 1434. Visas: 8.30am–noon.
Sri Lanka, 48/3 Soi 1, Sukhumvit Road. Tel: 251 2788/9. Visas: 8.30am–noon and 1–3.45pm.
Switzerland, 35 Witthayu Road. Tel: 253 0156/60. Visas: 9am–noon.
United Kingdom, 1031 Ploenchit Road. Tel: 253 0191/9. Visas: 8–11am, (Friday: 8am–noon)
United States, 95 Witthayu Road. Tel 252 5040/9, 252 5171/9. Visas: 7.30–10am.
Vietnam, 83/1 Witthayu Road. Tel: 251 5835/8. Visas: 8.30–11.30am and 1.30–4pm.

Getting Around

On Arrival

From Bangkok Airport

The journey from Don Muang Airport into the central city can take from 45 minutes to four hours, depending on traffic conditions. The worst period is between 4 and 9pm.

Negotiating an exit from the airport is daunting. If you are on a business trip, you will quickly understand why it is the norm for Bangkok hosts to deploy a personal greeter and escort. Emerging in the arrival hall, you may

be harangued by touts and pimps both inside and outside the barriers. Never volunteer your name or destination to these people. However, they may have already obtained your name (How? Who knows?) These creeps must somehow be distinguished from the legitimate hotel representatives. If you already have a reservation at a big hotel, they will be waving your name on a sign and be ready to take you via air conditioned mini-bus to the hotel.

Both Thai Airways and a private company, Phraphirun, hire out cars that bring you directly to your destination. A typical central city fare is 600 baht this could easily be two or three times the fare of a metered taxi, but this choice may be considerably less nerve-wracking.

Taxis

All taxis officially serving the airport are air-conditioned and metered. At a counter in the arrival hall and close to the exit, a clerk hands out a numbered slip. If you are going to a difficult destination (such as a private home), ask the clerk to write it in Thai. You give the slip to a taxi driver right outside the door. If the taxi already has a passenger, refuse to get in. Make sure the driver turns on the meter. Now the fun begins.

Once on the road, the driver may attempt to wrest an extra few hundred baht. Of course, one never admits to a Bangkok taxi driver that this is a first visit. In fact, it's your tenth. Or better you live here. A hearty laugh may then dissuade him from the extortion bid. If not, you could passively agree. Then once you have arrived at your hotel and removed your bags, only pay what is indicated on the meter. Try not to express anger. An angry driver may immediately stop and dump you. This isn't as disastrous as it sounds. Another taxi or tuk-tuk will come along soon enough.

Another option is to take a taxi that hasn't paid the airport concession fee. Go upstairs to the departure area where taxis are dropping passengers on their way to flights. These drivers are not supposed to pick up new fares but they are on the lookout and will take a long time to pull away from the curb.

Another alternative is to take the pedestrian overpass in front of the ai port. When you reach the other side of the highway, there are usually a half-dozen air-conditioned metered taxis waiting. In both these "alternative" taxis, the drivers will also try to wangle an extra 100 baht or so. But they seem to be less persistent, perhaps because they aren't attempting to re-coup the concession fees as the official cabs are.

You may come across two types of unmetered taxis. For an experienced haggler, it's okay to take one of the nearly extinct non-metered marked taxis, but don't take an unmarked "black cab".

Buses

Buses into the city stop in front of the airport. The number 29, in both the air-conditioned and regular varieties, ends up at Hualampong train station. The air-con number 10 goes to Victory Monument. Many new air-con routes have been added; the clerks at the Tourist Authority desk in the arrival hall may be able to assist you. Since it's unlikely that a bus will go directly to your final destination, Victory Monument is a good target. From there, you can catch another bus or a taxi.

Air-con buses stop running around 10pm. All buses are intended for basic commuting and are not designed to take bulky luggage. Even if you have a small pack, it's not advisable to mount a bus between 4 and 8pm. During this rush period, buses may be packed to the gills. Thais probably won't say any-thing to you, but will disapprove.

Train

The fastest and cheapest way into the city is to take the train. The station is across the street from the airport. In about 15 minutes and for 5 baht, you can be at the main Hualampong sta-tion, not far from Chinatown. There are trains at least every hour during the daytime; ask at the Tourist Authority counter. Some visitors decide to skip Bangkok altogether and take the train in the other direction; Ayutthaya is a good start. One drawback: if you have heavy luggage, humping it over the pedestrian bridge and onto the train may not be easy. Another is that you should not count on an air-conditioned car or even a seat.

Up-Country Destinations

Arriving on an overseas flight, many people immediately transfer by small bus to the domestic terminal in the same airport and thus avoid battling Bangkok altogether. The privately-owned Bangkok Airways provides serv-ice to Ko Samui, Phuket, Hua Hin, Trang, Mae Hong Son, U Taphao and Loei.

Airport helicopter service

You can skip over some of Bangkok's justly notorious traffic by taking a heli-copter "taxi" between the international airport and the Shangri-La Hotel. A one-way trip on either direction costs 3,500 baht (US$140) per person and a minimum of three passengers is re-quired. Flights can only be made be-tween 7am and 5.30pm, so it's impos-sible to fly over the heaviest traffic evening gridlock. Bookings should be made at least 24 hours in advance. If you are staying at the Shangri-La, you can request the helicopter at the same time that you book a room. Even if you are not staying at the hotel, you can still use the service by booking through the concierge via the hotel's general number (Tel: 236-7777). Some nearby riverside hotels are also accustomed to arranging the service. Or you can contact the helicopter com-pany itself, Sichang Flying Service, at 655 0186-9.

For the **return trip to the airport**, the Authorized Transportation Service has in-town offices at 485 Silom Road (Tel: 235 4365, 235 4366), Montien Hotel (Tel: 233 7060), and Asia Hotel (Tel: 215 0780). Most major hotels have air-conditioned limousines. Non-metered taxis make the trip for 150–250 baht depending on traffic condi-tions. Metered taxis will be less expen-sive if there are no traffic jams on the way. The river express shuttle is also worthy of relaxing consideration; you can be at the airport check-in counter in an hour, as traffic concerns are not an issue.

By Air

Thai Airways operates a domestic net-work serving nearly two dozen towns, offering seven daily services to some of them, such as Chiang Mai and Phuket. Bangkok Airways operates daily services from Bangkok to Ko Samui and between Samui and several provincial towns.

Bangkok Airways is Thailand's first privately-owned domestic airline and provides a highly efficient, first-class service to most of the major resort destinations in Thailand, as well as Phnom Penh in Cambodia.

If you are planning a trip to the tropi-cal island of Ko Samui from Bangkok, you will save much traveling time by air, which by road and boat may amount to a 14-hour journey.

By Rail

The State Railways of Thailand oper-ates three principal routes from Hualampong Railway Station. The northern route passes through Ayutthaya, Phitsanuloke, Lampang and terminates at Chiang Mai. The north-eastern route passes through Ayut-thaya, Sara Buri, Nakhon Ratchasima, Khon Kaen, Udon Thani and termi-nates at Nong Khai. The southern route crosses the Rama 6 bridge and calls at Nakhon Pathom, Petchburi, Hua Hin and Chumphon. It branches at Hat Yai, one branch running southwest through Betong and on down the west-ern coast of Malaysia to Singapore. The southeastern branch goes via Pattani and Yala to the Thai border opposite the Malaysian town of Kota Bharu.

In addition, there is a line from Makkasan to Aranyaprathet on the Cambodian border. Another leaves Bangkok Noi Railway Station for Kanchanaburi and other destinations beyond along the old Death Railway. There is also a short route leaving Wongwian Yai station in Thonburi that travels west along the rim of the Gulf of Thailand to Samut Sakhon and then to Samut Songkram.

Express and rapid services on the main lines offer first-class air-condi-tioned or second-class fan-cooled cars with sleeping cabins or berths and din-ing cars. There are also special air-con-ditioned express day coaches that travel to key towns along the main lines. 20-day rail passes are available. In Bangkok, details from:

Hualampong Station: Rama 4 Road. Tel: 233 7010, 233 7020.
Bangkok Noi Station: Tel: 411 3102.

By Road

Air-conditioned bus service is available to most destinations in Thailand. vip coaches with extra leg room are the best for overnight journeys to Phuket and Chiang Mai. Air-conditioned coaches also leave half-hourly from the eastern bus terminal on Sukhumvit Road (opposite Soi 63) for Pattaya and other points beyond. For the very adventurous, there are fan-cooled buses filled with passengers and chickens and tons of luggage that are used by poorer Thais for their journeys across the country.

To reach a small town from a large one, there are smaller buses or baht buses – pick-up trucks with a passenger compartment on the backs.

Public Transport
Taxis and tuk-tuks

The introduction of metered taxis a few years ago has virtually wiped out non-metered taxis. It seems that Thais don't like to bargain either. There's no need to settle for a non-metered taxi; a metered taxi will soon show up. All are air-conditioned. Drivers don't speak much English, but they know the locations of all major hotels.

Foreigners frequently mangle Thai pronunciation, so it's a good idea to have a destination printed on a piece of paper. Thai drivers can usually understand street addresses printed in capital Roman letters, but few can read maps. Try to get someone to write the destination in Thai.

Taxi drivers will ask for expressway tolls, but they are not supposed to exact extra fees for luggage or additional passengers. Nonetheless, it's good form to add a little in such cases.

If you know Bangkok well, you might be able to negotiate a price below that which you would pay for a metered taxi, but taxi drivers are experts at outwitting their less knowledgeable passengers, so if just a casual tourist, stick to the metered taxis. The minimum basic fare is 35 baht.

If the English fluency of taxi drivers is limited, that of tuk-tuk (also called samlor) drivers is even less. Tuk-tuk are the brightly-colored three-wheeled taxis whose name comes from the noise their two-cycle engines make.

Since the introduction of metered taxis, there's little reason why foreigners continue to take tuk-tuks, unless they wish to say they have tried one. Except for the most experienced hagglers, few tourists will be able to bargain a tuk-tuk fare that is lower than that of a metered taxi.

Some tuk-tuk drivers loitering around hotels will offer as 10-baht fare "anywhere". The hitch is that you must stop at a tourist shop where the driver will get gas coupons in exchange for bringing you in. If you don't mind pretending to examine jewelry for 10 minutes, this isn't a bad deal.

Motorcycle Taxis

The side roads leading off the major roads are called soi. Motorcycle taxi stands are clustered at the most hazardous spots near soi intersections with main roads and the exits of shopping centers (Isn't this illegal? Actually, motorcycle taxis are illegal). You don't have to search for them. These are the young men in fluorescent jackets who pester you with shouts of "Moto-sigh! Moto-sigh!"

It is, of course, extremely dangerous to climb on the back of one of these things, but the drivers are experts at weaving through Bangkok's heavy traffic and may cut travel time in half. Only hire a driver who provides a passenger helmet. Motorcycle drivers must be bargained with. Because they know you are desperate, don't count on a figure that is any lower than a taxi fare.

Some motorcycle taxis only ply up and down a soi (lane) off a major thoroughfare, such as Sukhumvit Road. The fare is usually a flat five baht. You probably won't find passenger helmets on offer along these routes.

Buses and Mini-buses

Public buses come in three varieties: microbus, air-conditioned and non-air-conditioned "ordinary". The privately-owned red-and-gray microbuses constitute the city's premium service. Air-conditioned and equipped with squalling music videos, they don't accept more passengers once all 20 or so seats are filled. The fare is 25 baht and no change is given. The problem is that these bus routes are not listed on any map and even Thais find the routes baffling.

Fares on the blue air-conditioned buses start at six baht and increase with distance. The ordinary buses are either red and (dirty) white or blue and (dirty) white. A subset are the privately run green mini-buses which have the same numbers as ordinary buses and follow the same routes. The drivers of these ramshackle buses are quite reckless. The usual fare on ordinary buses is 3 baht, 50 satang, but it goes up to 4 or 5 baht after 10pm. On both the air-conditioned and ordinary buses, a conductor provides change and a small receipt. Hold onto the receipt; an inspector may come aboard.

In theory, the routes of both air-conditioned and ordinary buses appear on standard bus maps. Note that despite the same numbers, air-con buses seldom follow the same routes as ordinary ones. In practice, routes change and many air-con routes have been added in recent years. No map is up-to-date.

In addition, sometimes routes are truncated or buses may take "short cuts" via the expressway. These deviations are indicated – in Thai – on a removable sign close to the door. If a conductor on an air-con bus persistently asks your destination, she is probably attempting to discover whether you are aware that you are on an expressway bus. She or fellow passengers will understand if you ask "Expret-way?"

The conductors on air-con buses may understand a modicum of English or, more accurately, they are accustomed to the way that foreigners distort the pronunciation of roads and places. A tourist can't expect more than that and should expect less on the ordinary buses. It is likely, though that few passengers on microbuses and air-con buses will speak a little English.

It is always a good idea to have a destination written in Thai or Roman capital letters. Your memory may be good, but your pronunciation probably isn't. Thais often don't know the names of small roads and lanes, even if they live close by. They will respond better to the name of a landmark, temple, big hotel or big market.

Except for those who have already conquered the public buses of India and China, it's advisable to avoid taking buses during the peak periods that is, roughly between 7 and 9am nd between 4 and 9pm. At the best of imes, it's difficult to predict whether a us will stop to pick up passengers. During peak periods, the odds decline. Both air-con and ordinary buses are acked, with passengers hanging from he doors. Female Westerners some-imes faint (in which case, Thai women re very helpful). Don't even consider orcing a Western child under the age f 6 onto one of these buses.

BUS STATIONS

or bus and coach journeys to destina-ions outside of Bangkok, the major erminals are:

astern: Opposite Soi 63 (Ekamai), ukhumvit Road. Tel: 391 2504, 392 521.

Northern and Northeastern: Moh Chit, haholyothin Road. Tel: 271 0101/5, 79 4484/7.

outhern: Boromrat Chonnani Road. el: 435 0511, 434 5558.

Boats

White express boats with red trim run egular routes at 20–30 minute inter-als up and down the Chao Phraya iver, going all the way to Nonthaburi, 0 km (6 mi) north of the city. The ervice begins at 6am and ceases at .30pm. Fares are less than 10 baht or short distances.

Ferries, often red, cross the river at ozens of points and cost just a cou-le of baht per journey. They begin op-rating at 6am and stop at midnight.

A basic mode of city transport are he longboats plying the canal that tarts at Wat Saket, near Democracy Monument, and runs along New etchburi Road and beyond. Glance at he map and you'll deduce that the tops include Jim Thompson's House, he World Trade Center and Asoke ane. Fares start at 5 baht. Make sure ou tell the boatman where you wish to ight; the boat won't necessarily stop herwise. This canal "taxi" runs only uring daylight, roughly between 6am nd 6.15pm.

The trip provides an interesting view f the backside of Bangkok, but the anal water is inky black and smells te a sewer. many people would prefer pay this price rather than endure ad traffic. As is the case with all ngboats, ferries and "river taxis", ese sometimes capsize. If you can't vim, don't take them.

Private Transport

Limousines

Most major hotels operate air-condi-tioned limousine services. Although the prices are at least twice those of ordinary taxis, they offer the conven-ience of English-speaking drivers and door-to-door service.

Rental Cars

Thailand has a good road system with over 50,000 km (31,000 mi) of paved highways and more are being built every year. Road signs are in both Thai and English and you should have no difficulty following a map. An interna-tional driver's license is required.

Driving on a narrow but busy road can be a terrifying experience with right-of-way determined by size. It is not unusual for a bus to overtake a truck despite the fact that the oncom-ing lane is filled with vehicles. It is lit-tle wonder that when collisions occur, several dozen lives are lost. Add to that, many of the long-distance drivers consume pep pills and have the throt-tle to the floor because they are get-ting paid for beating schedules. One is strongly advised to avoid driving at night for this reason. When dusk comes, pull in at a hotel and get an early start the next morning.

Avis, Hertz and numerous local agencies offer late-model cars with and without drivers and with insurance coverage for Bangkok and upcountry trips. A deposit is required.

Upcountry, agencies can be found in major towns like Chiang Mai and Phuket. These also rent four-wheel-drive jeeps and mini-vans. When rent-ing a jeep, read the fine print carefully and be aware that you are liable for all damages to the vehicle. Ask for first class insurance, which covers both you and the other vehicle involved in a col-lision.

There are no car rental desks at the international airport. Contacted by tel-ephone, agencies will deliver the car to your hotel and you can fill out the rental forms there.

Avis, 2/12 Wireless Road. Tel: 255 5300/4.

Hertz, Soi 71, Sukhumvit Road. Tel: 711 0574/8.

Grand Car Rent, 233-5 Soi Asoke. Tel: 248 2991/2.

Klong Toey Car Rent, 1921 Rama IV Road. Tel: 251 9856.

SMT Rent-a-Car, 931/11 Rama 1 Road, (opp. National Stadium). Tel: 216 4436, 216 8020.

Both these private companies rent taxis or vans for day trips in Bangkok or beyond. The fees probably won't be more than 1,500 baht ($60) per day. The drivers will speak some English. Call:

Taxi-Meter, VMS Communication, tel: 319-9911-3.

J &J Car Rent, tel: 531-2262.

Where to Stay

Hotels

The hotel accommodation in all the major tourist destinations in Thailand is equal to the very best anywhere in the world. The facilities in the first-class hotels may have as many as 10 or more different restaurants serving Western and Asian cuisine, coffee shops, swimming pools, exercise rooms, business centers, banqueting halls, shopping arcades, and cable & satellite television. The service is sec-ond to none. Indeed, most of the mod-erately-priced hotels rival what in Eu-rope would be considered a first-class hotel. Even the budget and inexpen-sive hotels will invariably have a swim-ming pool and more than one food outlet.

If on a limited budget, there are numerous guesthouses offering clean, economical accommodation. Once of primary interest only to backpackers because of their sparse facilities, many have now been upgraded to in-clude fans, air-conditioning and bath-rooms in the rooms rather than down the hall. As such, they afford a viable alternative to more up-market trav-elers. Prices range from 80 to 250 baht. Generally possessing no more than a dozen rooms, they are more like pensions than hotels and appeal to travelers who like personalised serv-ice, friendly staff and a more relaxed pace. Their numbers are legion and to list them would fill several books. In Bangkok they are to be found along Khaosarn Road and Soi Ngam Duphli off Rama IV Road.

Expensive (3,000 baht up)

Amari Airport, 333 Choet Wutthakat Road. Tel: 566 1020/1, 566 2060/9, fax: 566 1941. Closest hotel to international airport and therefore popular with travelers arriving late and departing early. Connected to airport with footbridge and shuttle bus.

Amari Boulevard, Soi 7, Sukhumvit Road. Tel: 255 2930, 255 2940, fax: 255 2950. Small but luxurious. An oasis in a raucous tourist area filled with street markets, noodle shops and bars.

Amari Watergate, 847 Petchaburi Road. Tel: 653 9000/19, fax: 653 9044. New highrise hotel in old market area. The roaring expressway in front of it can be a problem for guests.

Arnoma Swissotel, 99 Ratchadamri Road. Tel: 255 3410, fax: 255 3456/7. Good location for business visitors and tourists. Good restaurants and service.

Asia, 296 Phaya Thai Road. Tel: 215 0808, fax: 215 4360. Offers many extra facilities possibly to offset the noisy, non-stop traffic at its doors.

Bel-Aire Princess, 16 Soi 5, Sukhumvit Road. Tel: 253 4300/30, fax: 255 8850. One of the small "boutique" hotels offering personalized service. Close to many big business organizations.

Central Plaza, 1695 Phahonyothin Road. Tel: 541 1234, fax: 541 1087. Midway between the airport and city, but a long way from anywhere except the popular weekend market at Catuchak Park.

Dusit Thani, 946 Rama IV Road. Tel: 236 0450/9, fax: 236 6400. Bangkok's first highrise hotel. Adjacent to major banks and business headquarters on Silom Road. Close to nightlife on Patpong.

Emerald, 99/1 Ratchadapisek Road. Tel: 276 4567, fax: 276 4555. A big, new establishment in a growing business, shopping and recreation quarter but a long journey from the center at peak traffic periods.

Evergreen Laurel, 88 North Sathorn Road (intersection with Soi Pipat). Tel: 266 7223, fax: 266 7222. Smallish but elegant, European atmosphere. On

a busy thoroughfare but close to big business and foreign embassies.

Grand Hyatt Erawan, 494 Ratchadamri Road. Tel: 254 1234, fax: 253 5856. On a major intersection and home to the famous Erawan Shrine, one of the best known religious symbols in Bangkok. Adjacent to shopping malls and horse-racing and golf courses.

Hilton International, 2 Witthayu Road. Tel: 253 0123, fax: 253 6509. Set in beautiful garden with pool. Close to embassies. Good access to and from the airport.

Holiday Inn Crown Plaza, 981 Silom Road. Tel: 238 4300, fax: 238 5289. Between business center and river. A choice location with small shops nearby.

Imperial Queen's Park, 36 Soi 22, Sukhumvit Road. Tel: 261 9000, fax: 261 9530. With 1,400 rooms it is Bangkok's biggest hotel. A cavernous place where guests must walk long distances. Interesting shops, bars and restaurants in the vicinity.

Imperial, 6 Witthayu Road. Tel: 254 0023/100, fax: 253 3190. Sprawling hotel with extensive sports facilities and choice of restaurants. Close to several foreign embassies.

Indra Regent, 120/126 Ratchaprarop Road. Tel: 252 1111, fax: 253 3849. Surrounded by old markets and eating places which are gradually making way for Thailand's largest wholesale center for garments.

Landmark, The, 138 Sukhumvit Road. Tel: 254 0404, fax: 253 4259. Central location, and near airport road. Well-equipped for business travelers. Good shopping in and outside the hotel.

Le Meridien President, 135/26 Gaysorn Road. Tel: 253 0444, fax: 253 7565. Central location. The hotel has a French flavor and the best hotel coffee shop in town. Elegant shops and restaurants nearby.

Mansion Kempinski, 75/23 Soi 11, Sukhumvit Road. Tel: 253 2655, fax: 253 2329. In the big tourist district, this hotel offers discreet luxury and a hint of central Europe.

Marriot Royal Garden Riverside, 257/1-3 Charoen Nakhon Road. Tel: 476 0022, fax: 476 1120. A resort hotel with the conveniences of nearby downtown. On the western side of the river, a bit to the south, but there are fine views of the riverside life from the ho-

tel terraces. Nearby street offer tourists offbeat glimpses of Bangkok. Free river shuttle to Oriental Pier.

Monarch Lee Gardens, 188 Silom Road. Tel: 238 1991, fax: 238 1999. In the heart of the banking and insurance district but conveniently placed for good shops and restaurants. Night life is also close.

Novotel Bangkok, Soi 6, Siam Square. Tel: 255 6888, fax: 236 1937. French management. This is a busy quarter of small shops, movie theaters, eating places and traffic chaos.

Oriental, The, 48 Oriental Ave. Tel 236 0400/20, fax: 236 1937. A visit is a must, even if it is only to have a drink on the river terrace. The Oriental is part of the history of East meeting West. Repeatedly voted one of the world's best hotels, mainly because of its riverside location and its superb service.

Regent Bangkok, The, 155 Ratchadamri Road. Tel: 251 6127, fax: 25 9195. High luxury in the heart of the city. With music and tea in the lobby lounge, there are echoes of the old Orient. The best hotel swimming pool in Bangkok.

Royal Orchid Sheraton, 2 Captain Bush Lane, Si Phraya Road. Tel: 23 5599, fax: 236 8320. One of the big three riverside hotels with high level of services and exceptional facilities. All have road access difficulties at peak traffic times but guests may travel by river and see little-known areas of Bangkok.

Shangri-La, 89 Soi Wat Suan Plu, Charoen Krung Road. Tel: 236 7777, fax: 236 8570. Every room has a river view. The evening buffet on the riverside terrace is famous. The biggest hotel on the river.

Siam City, 477 Si Ayutthaya Road. Tel: 247 0120, fax: 247 0178. A new hotel with good facilities near government offices and army headquarters. A good place to hobnob and people watch.

Siam Intercontinental, 967 Rama Road. Tel: 253 0355, fax: 253 227. With 10 acres of gardens, tennis courts, jogging paths, swimming pools, golf greens and driving range, this is a cool retreat from the roar of the city. Big and small shops, movie houses and restaurants are just beyond the front gates.

Sukothai Bangkok, 13/3 Sathorn T

Road. Tel: 287 0222, fax: 287 4980. Quiet, luxurious, a cool, green hotel favored by diplomats. Near the city's center on a busy thoroughfare but set well back amid tropical gardens.

Moderate (2,000 baht up)

Ambassador, 171 Soi 11-13, Sukhumvit Road. Tel: 254 0444, fax: 253 4123.

Bangkok Palace, 1091/336 New Phetchaburi Road. Tel: 255 0305, 253 0510-50, fax: 253 3359.

First, 2 Phetchaburi Road. Tel: 255 0111, fax: 255 0121.

Impala, 9 Soi 24, Sukhumvit Road. Tel: 258 8612/6, fax: 258 8747.

Maruay Garden, 1 Soi 40, Phahon-yothin Road. Tel: 561 0510/29, fax: 579 1182.

New Peninsula, 293/3 Surawongse Road. Tel: 234 3910/7, fax: 236 5526.

Plaza, 178 Surawongse Road. Tel: 235 1760/79, fax: 237 0746.

Royal Princess, 269 Lan Luang Road. Tel: 281 3088, fax: 280 1314.

Silom Plaza, 320 Silom Road. Tel: 236 3441/84, fax: 236 7566/7.

Somerset, 10 Soi 15, Sukhumvit Road. Tel: 254 8500/24, fax: 254 8534.

Swissotel, Convent Road. Tel: 233 5345, fax: 236 9425.

Tai-Pan, 25 Soi 23, Sukhumvit Road. Tel: 260 9898, fax: 259 7908.

Tantawan Place, 119/5-10 Sura-wongse Road. Tel: 238 262 0/39, fax: 238 3228.

Winsor, 8-10 Soi 20, Sukhumvit Road. Tel: 258 0160/5, 258 1524/6, fax: 258 1491.

Inexpensive (1,000 baht up)

Ariston, 19 Soi 24, Sukhumvit Road. Tel: 259 0960/9, fax: 259 0970.

Bangkok Centre, 328 Rama IV Road. Tel: 238 4848/57, fax: 236 1862.

Continental, 971/16 Phahon-yothin Road. Tel: 278 1385, 279 7567, fax: 271 3547.

Euro Inn, 249 Soi 31, Sukhumvit Road. Tel: 259 9480/7, fax: 259 9490.

Golden Dragon, 20/21 Ngam Wong Wan Road. Tel: 589 0130/41, fax: 589 8305.

Golden Horse, 5/1-2 Damrongrak Road. Tel: 280 1920, fax: 280 3404.

Grand De Ville, 903 Mahachai Road. Tel: 225 7554/92, fax: 225 7593.

Grand Inn, 2/7-8 Soi 3, Sukhumvit

Road. Tel: 254 9021/7, fax: 254 9020. 24 rooms.

Jasmin, 2082 New Phetchaburi Road. Tel: 319 2421/8, fax: 319 2430.

Jim's Lodge, 125/7 Soi Ruam Rudi, Ploenchit Road. Tel: 255 3100, 255 0190/9, fax: 253 8492.

Majestic Palace, 97 Ratchadamnoen Klang Road. Tel: 281 5000, 280 5610/22, fax: 280 0965.

Morakot, 2802 New Phetchaburi Road. Tel: 314 0761/3, fax: 319 1465.

New Fuji, 299-310 Surawongse Road. Tel: 234 5364/6, 233 8270/2, fax: 236 5526.

New Trocadero, 343 Surawongse Road. Tel: 234 8920/9, fax: 236 5526.

Park, 6 Soi 7, Sukhumvit Road. Tel: 255 4300/8, fax: 255 4309.

President Inn, 155/14-16 Soi 11, Sukhumvit Road. Tel: 255 4230/4, fax: 255 4235.

Rajah, 18 Soi 4, Sukhumvit Road. Tel: 255 0040/83, fax: 255 7160.

Ramada, 1169 Charoen Krung Road. Tel: 234 8971/5, fax: 237 1225. 60 rooms.

River Side Plaza, 753/45 Ratchawithi Road. Tel: 434 0090/3, fax: 435 1642.

Royal Garden Home, 63/1-4 Soi 3, Sukhumvit Road. Tel: 253 5458/61, fax: 253 3612.

Ruamchit Travel Lodge, 11/1 Soi 10, Sukhumvit Road. Tel: 252 6403, 251 0284, fax: 255 1372.

Silom Street Inn, 284/11-13 Silom Road. Tel: 238 4680, fax: 238 4689.

Suriwongse Tower Inn, 410/3-4, Suriwongse Road. Tel: 235 1206/9, fax: 237 1482.

Thai, 78 Prachathipatai Road. Tel: 282 2831/3, fax: 280 1299.

Tower Inn, 533 Silom Road. Tel: 234 4051, 234 4053, fax: 234 4051. 140 rooms.

Viangtai, 42 Tani Road, Banglampu. Tel: 280 5392/9, fax: 281 8153.

White Orchid, 409-421 Yaowarat Road. Tel: 226 0026, fax: 255 6403.

YWCA, 13 Sathorn Tai Road. Tel: 286 1900, fax: 287 1996.

Budget (less than 1,000 baht)

A One Inn, 13-15 Soi Kasemsan 1. Tel: 216 4770, fax: 216 4771.

Burapa, 160/14 Charoen Krung Road. Tel: 221 3545/9, fax: 226 1723.

Business Inn, 155/4-5 Soi 11,

Sukhumvit Road. Tel: 254 7981/4, 255 7155/8, fax: 255 7159.

China Inn, 19/27-28 Soi 19, Sukhumvit Road. Tel: 255 7571/3, 253 3439, fax: 254 1333.

Classic Inn, 120/51-54 Ratchaprarop Road. Tel: 255 3988, fax: 255 3886.

Comfort Inn, 153/11 Soi 11, Sukhumvit Road. Tel: 251 9250, 254 3559/60, fax: 254 3562.

Crown, 503 Soi 29, Sukhumvit Road. Tel: 258 0318/9.

Dynasty Inn, 5/4-5 Soi 4, Sukhumvit Road. Tel: 250 1397, 252 1386, 252 4522, fax: 255 4111.

Embassy, 21 Pradipat Road. Tel: 279 8441, fax: 271 0945.

Florida, 43 Phayathai Road. Tel: 247 0990, 247 0103, fax: 247 7419.

Fortuna, 19 Soi 5, Sukhumvit Road. Tel: 251 5121/6, 253 2593, fax: 253 6282.

Siam, 1777 New Phetchaburi Road. Tel: 252 4967/8, 252 5081, fax: 255 1370.

Super, 49 Soi Ruamsirimit, Phahon-yothin Road. Tel: 272 3496/7, fax: 272 3491.

Swan, 31 Custom House Lane, Charoen Krung Road. Tel: 233 8444, 234 8594, 213 5198.

World, 1996 New Phetchaburi Road Tel: 314 4340/6, fax: 314 6930.

Guesthouses

Apple Guest House, 10 Phra Athit Road. Tel: 281 6838. Restaurant.

Bangkok Christian Guest House, 123 Soi Saladaeng 2, Silom Road. Tel: 233 2206, fax: 237 1742. Dining room. Centrally located. 380 baht.

Bangkok Youth Hostel, 25/2 Phitsanuloke Road. Tel: 282 0950, 281 0361, fax: 281 6834.

Boston Inn, 4 Soi Si Bamphen, Rama IV Road. Tel: 286 1680, 286 0726.

Chart Guest House, 61 Khao-San Road. Tel: 280 3785.

K.T. Guest House, 14 Suthisarn Road. Tel: 277 4035. 20 rooms. 200–250 baht.

Lee Guest House, 21/38-39 Soi Ngam du Plii, Rama IV Road. Tel: 286 2069. 80–100 baht.

Narai Guest House, 5/7 Soi 53, Sukhumvit Road. Tel: 258 7173, 258 0601, fax: 259 7244.

P. Guest House, 151-157 Trok Sa-Ke, Tanao Road. Tel: 224 1967.

Peachy Guest House, 10 Phra Athit

Road. Tel: 281 6471, 281 6659.
Ruamchit Mansion, 1-15 Soi 15, Sukhumvit Road. Tel: 251 6441/2.
Santi Lodge, 37 Sri Ayutthaya Road. Tel: 281 2497.
Sri Guest House, 1 Soi 38, Sukhumvit Road. Tel: 391 9057, 381 1309.
T.T. Guest House, 138 Soi Wat Mahaphutharam. Tel: 236 3053/4.
Tavee Guest House, 83 Sri Ayutthaya Road. Tel: 280 1447.
YWCA and **YMCA**, 27 S. Sathorn Road. Tel: 286 5134. 50 rooms, some cottages, sports facilities, European, Chinese and Thai restaurant. Quiet. 350–900 baht.

Eating Out

What to Eat

The dramatic rise in the number of Thai restaurants around the world says something about the popularity of one of the world's supreme cuisines. It is no surprise that when gourmets arrive on these shores fresh from Thai dining experiences at home, they fall into a feeding frenzy that lasts their entire stay.

The base for most Thai dishes is coconut milk. Ginger, garlic, lemon grass and fiery chilies give Thai dishes a piquancy that can set tender palates aflame. While many of the chilies are mild, their potency is in obverse proportion to their size; the smallest, the *prik kii no* or "rat dropping chilies", are guaranteed to dissolve your sinuses and cloud your vision with tears. For those averse to spicy food, chefs can bland the curries or serve one of the dozens of non-spicy curries.

Where to Eat

In Europe, the very best restaurants are not usually to be found in hotels. In Thailand, the reverse is true. There are, of course, exceptions to both these generalities. All the following restaurants contribute to making Thailand a gourmet's paradise.

Thai Dinner and Cultural Shows

Baan Thai, 7 Sukhumvit Soi 32. Tel: 258 5403. Pleasant atmosphere in a group of old Thai houses in a tropical garden. Open daily 7.30pm with Thai dancing starting at 9pm.
Maneeya Lotus Room, 518/4 Ploenchit Road. Tel: 251 0382. Open daily. Lunch 10am–2pm. Nightly 7pm with Thai classical dance performance at 8.15pm.
Sala Rim Nam, Oriental Hotel. Tel: 437 6211. Located in a beautiful, temple-like building across the river from the Oriental – particularly good Thai dancing. Free boat service from Oriental Hotel landing.
Sala Thai, Indra Hotel, 120-126 Ratchaprarop Road. Tel: 2080022. Attractive reproduction of a classic building on an upper floor of the hotel. Silom Village Trade Center, 286 Silom Road. Tel: 235 8760. Open-air and indoor restaurants, traditional food stalls, Thai cultural show presented every Saturday & Sunday from 12.45am and Thai classical dance shows daily at 8pm. Informal atmosphere.

Hotel Buffets

Many hotels in Bangkok vie with each other to prove that their lunch and dinner buffets surpass that of their competitors both in quality and value for money. The result is an overwhelming choice of prices. You will not be disappointed wherever you choose to go, and even the least-expensive buffets still offer a bewildering variety of dishes. All are highly recommended.

Thai Cuisine

All Gaengs, 173/8-9 Suriwongse Road. Tel: 233 3301. Elegant, modern decor and delicious Thai cuisine.
Benjarong, Dusit Thani Hotel, 946 Rama IV Road. Tel: 236 0450/9. Superlative Royal Thai cuisine served on exquisite benjarong ware.
Bon Vivant, Tawana Ramada Hotel, 80 Surawongse Road. Tel: 236 0361. Splendid cuisine with a host of traditional Thai dishes, all beautifully prepared and presented.
Bussaracum, 35 Soi Pipat 2, Convent Road. Tel: 235 8915. Extremely popular with local connoisseurs of classical Thai cuisine; pleasant, informal atmos-

phere.
Cabbages and Condoms, 8 Soi 12, Sukhumvit Road. Tel: 252 7349, 251 5552. Value for money and first-class cuisine. If you are not familiar with Thai food, this should be among one of your first choices. The profits support various family planning and hiv awareness programs and other charitable projects.
Celadon, Sukhothai Bangkok, 13/3 South Sathorn Road. Tel: 287 0222 Exceptional cuisine in the setting of an exotic water garden.
Chilli House, Patpong 4, (near the Rome Club), Silom Road. Tel: 237 2777. You can enter either via Silom Road or through the Patpong Car Park Building on Patpong 2. Everything expertly prepared and presented by a top Thai chef, especially the seafood dishes; reasonable prices.
D'Jit Pochana, 62 Soi 20 Sukhumvit Tel: 258 1597 with branches at 1082 Paholyothin Road. Tel: 279 5000/2 and New Paholyothin Road. Tel: 531 1644. A long established Thai restaurant with moderate prices.
Laicram, 120/1-2 Soi 23, Sukhumvit Road. Tel: 259 9604. Variety of Thai dishes at moderate prices.
Laguna Fondue, Soi 38 Sukhumvit Road. Tel: 391 1720. Fondue and Thai food.
Lemongrass, 5/1 Soi 24, Sukhumvit Road. Tel: 258 8637. Well known for its excellent cuisine at medium prices
Nipa Thai, Landmark Hotel, 138 Sukhumvit Road. Tel: 254 0404. As with all the many restaurants in this hotel, its Thai restaurant is of the highest standard.
Pan Kitchen, Tai-Pan Hotel, 25 Soi 23 Sukhumvit Road. Tel: 260 9888. Tasty Thai cuisine at reasonable prices. Worth going out of your way to try the inexpensive buffet set lunch which also includes some European dishes.
Salathip, Shangri-la Hotel, 89 Soi Wat Suan Phlu. Tel: 236 7777. Superb Thai dining on the river's edge.
Sara Jane's Larb Lang Suan, 36/2 Soi Lang Suan. Tel: 252 6572. Traditional spicy Northeastern dishes.
Sidewalk, 855/2 Silom Road. Tel: 233 4496. The owner is French born Pierre Chaslin, the author of the best selling "Discover Thai Cooking". Superb cuisine, ordinary decor, reasonable prices.
Sorn Dang (at the Democracy Monument), 78/2 Ratchadamnern Road

Tel: 224 3088. One of the oldest restaurants in town, known for good Thai food.

Spice Market, The Regent Hotel, 155 Rachadamri Road. Tel: 251 6127. Beautifully-decorated restaurant, with dishes that the chef can adapt to suit Western palates.

Thai Pavilion, Holiday Inn Crowne Plaza. Tel: 238 4300. Traditional Thai cuisine in a traditional setting.

Thai Room, 37/20-5 Patpong 2 Road. Tel: 233 7920. Serving Thai, Mexican, Chinese and European food. One of the oldest restaurants in the city.

Thanying, 10 Pramuan Road, Silom. Tel: 236 4361. Serves excellent Thai food. Set in very pleasant surroundings.

The Glass, 22/3-5 Soi 11, Sukhumvit Road. Tel: 254 3566. As well known for its food as its live music in the evenings.

Whole Earth Cafe, 93/3 Soi Lang Suan. Tel: 258 4900. Branch at 71 Soi 26, Sukhumvit Road. Tel: 258 4900. Bangkok's best known Thai vegetarian restaurant; comfortable and friendly. There is also a tasty menu of non-vegetarian fare with excellent Indian dishes.

Seafood

Dusit Rimtarn Seafood Restaurant, Supakarn Shopping Center, Sathorn Bridge. Tel: 437 9671. A view of the river. Seafood and other Thai and Chinese cuisine superbly prepared under the supervision of the Dusit Thani Hotel.

Lord Jim's, Oriental Hotel, 48 Oriental Avenue. Tel: 236 0400. Top-quality restaurant noted for its good atmosphere, excellent food and service; expensive prices.

Sammuk Seafood, 2140-4 Lardprao, Soi 90. Tel: 539 2466/9. One of many inexpensive Thai seafood restaurants in Bangkok. This particular one has won many accolades for the quality of its food.

Sea Food Market, 388 Sukhumvit Road, (opp. Soi Asoke). Tel: 258 0218. Pick out the seafood of your choice from a vast variety on ice and have it cooked to suit your taste; informal and can be expensive if you succumb to the temptation of ordering too much.

Sea Food Restaurant, 1980 New Petchburi Road. Tel: 314 4312. Under the same management as Sea Food Market.

Talay Thong, Siam Inter-Continental Hotel, 967 Rama I Road. Tel: 253 0355. High quality dining, decor and service.

Wit's Oyster Bar, 20/10-11 Soi Ruam Rudi, Ploenchit Road. Tel: 252 1820. A plush English style oyster bar.

Outdoor Thai Restaurants

When giving instructions to the taxi driver, tell him "Suan Aahaan" (garden restaurant) before giving him the name of one of the restaurants below.

Baanbung, 32/10 Soi Intramara 45, Ratchadapisek. Tel: 277 8609, 277 7563.

Buatong, 30 Ratchadapisek Road. Tel: 245 5545.

Tum Nak Thai, 131 Ratchadapisek Road. Tel: 277 8833. This restaurant has merited an entry in the Guinness Book of Records as the largest in the world. Waitresses on roller skates serve food from all regions of Thailand; very popular with tourists.

Riverside Restaurants

Baan Khun Luang, 131/4 Khaw Road. Tel: 241 0928. Thai, Chinese and Japanese cuisine in a riverside setting.

Sala Rim Nam, Oriental Hotel, 48 Oriental Avenue, New Road. Tel: 236 0400.

Savoey Seafood Restaurant, River City Complex, 23 Yotha Road. Tel: 237 7557/8. Excellent Thai and Chinese seafood dishes.

Chinese

Canton Palace, Evergreen Laurel Hotel, 88 North Sathorn Road. Tel: 234 9829. A new restaurant in an elegant new hotel that has already received many acolades for the high standard of its Cantonese cuisine.

Chinatown, Dusit Thani Hotel, 946 Rama IV Road. Tel: 236 0450. Less expensive than the Mayflower also within the hotel, but just as delicious.

Chiu Chau, Ambassador Hotel, 171 Soi 11-13, Sukhumvit Road. Tel: 254 0444. Delicacies from the Southern Chinese province of Chiu Chau (Guangchao).

Coca Noodles, 8 Soi Tantawan, Suriwong Road. Tel: 236 9323, branches at Siam Square, 416/3-8 Henry Dunant Road. Tel: 251 6337, The Mall 4, 1911 Ramkhamhaeng Road. Tel: 318 0097, 1/1 Soi 39, Sukhumvit

Road. Tel: 259 8188. Cantonese hot pot, sukiyaki and noodle dishes.

Dynasty, Central Plaza Hotel, 1695 Phaholyothin Road. Tel: 541 1234. Traditional cuisine with Peking duck, shark's fin and abalone all featured in the extensive menu.

Great Wall, Asia Hotel, 296 Phaya Thai Road. Tel: 215 0808. The heart of any good hotel is in the kitchen and at the Asia Hotel, there are several different kinds of restaurants of which this is one of the best.

Hoi Tien Lao, 762 Laadya Road, (Thonburi bank of river, opp. Royal Orchid Sheraton Hotel). Tel: 437 1121. Cantonese food; one of Bangkok's oldest and most popular Chinese restaurants.

Hong Teh, Ambassador Hotel, 171 Soi 11-13, Sukhumvit Road. Tel: 254 0444. A favorite with local gourmets for banquet entertaining.

Jade Garden, Montien Hotel, 54 Suriwongse Road. Tel: 234 8060. Southern Chinese dishes prepared by Hong Kong chefs in an elegant setting.

Lin-Fa, Siam City Hotel, 477 Sri Ayutthaya Road. Tel: 247 0130. An elegant Chinese restaurant in one of Bangkok's most stylish hotels.

Lok Wah Hin, Novotel, Siam Square. Tel: 255 6888. Cantonese and Szechuan cuisine at its best.

Mayflower, Dusit Thani Hotel, 946 Rama IV Road. Tel: 236 0450. Without doubt, one of Thailand's best hotel Chinese restaurants.

Ming Palace, Indra Regent Hotel, 120/126 Ratchaprarop Road. Tel: 208 0022. Southern Chinese dishes.

Nguan Lee, 101/25-26 Soi Lang Suan, Ploenchit Road. Tel: 251 8366, 252 3614. Covered market; real atmosphere. One of the few restaurants where you can eat the famous Mekong giant catfish.

Rice Mill, Marriott Royal Garden Riverside, 257/1-3 Charoen Nakhon Road. Tel: 476 0022. Built on the site of an old rice mill, this new, luxury riverside hotel has a splendid Chinese restaurant.

Royal Kitchen, 46/1 North Sathorn Road. Tel: 234 3063/5. More elegant and expensive than others.

Scala Restaurant, 218-218/1 Soi 1, Siam Square, (near Scala Theater). Tel: 254 2891. One of the house specialities is Peking Duck. The adjoining restaurant specialises in shark's fin.

Shang Palace, Shangri-La Hotel, 89 Soi Wat Suan Phlu. Tel: 236 7777, ext. 1350 & 1358. Superb Cantonese and Szechuan specialities. The lunchtime dim sum is a real treat.

Shangarila, 58/4-9 Thaniya Road. Tel: 234 0861, branches at 154/4-5 Silom Road. Tel: 234 9147, 306 Yawarat. Tel: 2245933. Northern Chinese cuisine.

Silom Restaurant, 793 Silom Road. Tel: 236 4442. One of the oldest Chinese restaurants in town; northern Chinese dishes.

Silver Palace Restaurant, 5 Soi Pipat, Silom Road. Tel: 235 5118/9. Well known for the variety of its delicious dim sum menu. Cantonese cuisine in opulent surroundings.

Sui Sian, Landmark Hotel, 138 Sukhumvit Road. Tel: 254 0404. Cantonese and other regional delicacies to the highest standards.

Tai-Pan, Imperial Hotel, 6 Wireless Road. Tel: 254 0111, ext. 1473. Cantonese fare in elegant surroundings.

The Chinese Restaurant, Grand Hyatt Erawan, 494 Ratchadamri Road. Tel: 254 1234. Sophisticated Cantonese specialities prepared by Hong Kong chefs.

The Empress, Royal Princess Hotel, 269 Lan Luang Ropad. Tel: 281 3088. Delicious lunchtime dim sum.

Ti Jing, Monarch Lee Gardens Hotel, 188 Silom Road. Tel: 238 1999. A dazzling array of dim sum and other Cantonese delicacies.

Tien Tien Restaurant, 105 Patpong I Road, Bangrak. Tel: 234 8717, 234 6006. Located in the middle of busy, bustling Patpong. Moderate prices. The decor takes second place to the food.

Indian/Arabic/Muslim

Akbar Restaurant, 1/4 Soi 3, Sukhumvit Road. Tel: 253 3479. Northern Indian food at very reasonable prices. Try the prawn korma.

Bangkok Brindawan, 44/1 Soi 19, Silom Road. Tel: 233 4791. Simple decor and some excellent vegetarian dishes. Daily buffet lunch. Inexpensive.

Bukhara, Royal Orchid Sheraton Hotel, 2 Captain Bush Lane. Tel: 234 5599. Superb Indian cuisine with impeccable service.

Cafe India, 460/8 Surawong Road. Tel: 233 0419. Northern Indian cooking in handsomely-decorated surround-ings.

Cedar, 4/1 Soi 49/1, Sukhumvit Road. Tel: 391 4482. Lebanese and Greek cuisine.

Himali Cha Cha, 1229/11 New Road. Tel: 235 1569. Northern cuisine by a master chef named Cha Cha; ask him what he recommends from the daily menu.

Maharajah's, 19/1 Soi 8, Sukhumvit Road. Tel: 254 8876. Some tasty tandoor dishes. Inexpensive.

Moghul Room, 1/16 Sukhumvit Soi 11. Tel: 253 4465. Popular, but more expensive than some.

Mrs. Balbir's, 155/18 Soi 11, Sukhumvit Road. Tel: 253 2281. Excellent cuisine with medium prices.

Rang Mahal, Rembrandt Hotel, 19 Soi 18, Sukhumvit Road. Tel: 261 7100. First-class cuisine and impeccable service.

Tandoor, Holiday Inn Crowne Plaza, 981 Silom Road. Tel: 238 4300. North Indian cuisine of exceptional quality. Moderate prices.

Indonesian

Bali, 15/3 Soi Ruam Rudee, Ploenchit Road. Tel: 254 3581. Customers can savor the best of Javanese cuisine at very reasonable prices.

Japanese

Benihana, Marriott Royal Garden Riverside, 257/1-3 Charoen Nakhon Road. Tel: 476 0022. The preparation of the dishes is a combination of knife-wielding and juggling. The end result is always a superb meal.

Benkay, Royal Orchid Sheraton Hotel, 2 Captain Bush Lane. Tel: 234 5599. The restaurant is noted for its exquisite Japanese cuisine served in an ambience of quiet elegance; a place for refined tastes.

Endogin, Shangri-La Hotel, 89 Soi Wat Suan Phlu. Tel: 236 7777. All that you would expect from one of Bangkok's top hotels.

Genji, Hilton International Hotel, Wireless Road. Tel: 253 0123, ext. 8141. Expensive.

Hagi, Central Plaza Hotel, 1695 Phaholyothin Road. Tel: 541 1234. Popular and with reasonable prices.

Hanaya, 683 Siphya Road. Tel: 234 8095. Clean and unpretentious.

Kagetsu, Asia Hotel, 296 Phaya Thai Road. Tel: 215 0808. Traditional cuisine and setting. Popular and reason-

able prices.

Kiku-No-Hana, The Landmark Hotel, 138 Sukhumvit Road. Tel: 254 0404. First-class Japanese cuisine in a first-class hotel.

Miraku, Imperial Hotel, 6 Wireless Road. Tel: 254 0023. Traditional Japanese dishes in a traditional Japanese setting.

Mizu's, 32 Patpong Road. Tel: 233 6447. One of the oldest Japanese restaurants in the city. The house speciality is sizzling steak. Reasonable prices.

Nishimura, Siam City Hotel, 477 Sri Ayutthaya Road. Tel: 247 0130. First-class dining in style.

Shogun, Dusit Thani Hotel, 946 Rama IV Road. Tel: 236 0450. Sashimi and other Japanese delicacies; elegant decor.

Teikoku, Imperial Hotel, 6 Wireless Road. Tel: 254 0111, ext. 1496. Superb Japanese dishes, traditional decor and surroundings.

Teio, Monarch Lee Gardens Hotel, 188 Silom Road. Tel: 238 1999. Sophisticated Japanese dining. Special family buffet lunches on Saturday and Sunday.

Tokugawa, Ambassador Hotel, 171 Soi 11-13, Sukhumvit Road. Tel: 254 0444, ext. 1569. The teppanyaki is delicious and fun to watch the chef displaying his skill.

Pacific

Trader Vic's, Marriott Royal Garden Riverside, 257/1-3 Charoen Nakhon Road. Tel: 476 0022. The unique style of oven gives a different flavour to the dishes. A delightfully different dining experience.

Vietnamese/Burmese

Cherie Kitchen, 593/13 Soi 33/1 Sukhumvit. Tel: 258 5058. Medium prices.

Le Dalat, 47/1 Soi 23, Sukhumvit Road. Tel: 258 4192 and on 2nd floor, Patpong Building, Surawong Road. Tel: 234 0290. Two of the best in town in the medium price range.

Le Danang, Central Plaza Hotel, 1695 Phaholyothin Road. Tel: 541 1234. A long established Vietnamese restaurant renowned for its authentic cuisine.

Mandalay, 23/17 Soi Ruamrudee. Tel: 255 2893.

Saigon, Asia Hotel, 296 Phaya Thai

Road. Tel: 215 0808. Luxury dining in an elegant setting under the supervision of a Vietnamese chef.

Saigon Bakery, 313 Silom Road. Tel: 231 0434. A Vietnamese restaurant and bakery; inexpensive.

Saigon-Rimsai, 413/9 Soi 55, Sukhumvit Road. Tel: 381 1797. Small, beautifully decorated and the Vietnamese chef produces a variety of inexpensive dishes.

Vietnam, 82-4 Silom Road, (opp. Convent Road). Tel: 234 6174. Southern-style Vietnamese cuisine.

Tea Rooms

Afternoon tea is an English custom that is followed in several of the major hotels. The most famous is in the Author's Lounge at the prestigious Oriental Hotel. The buffet style afternoon teas in some of the hotels are so lavish and the choice so varied that they may easily be mistaken for a full gourmet dinner.

Drinking Notes

Many restaurants catering to western tastes whip up a delicious shake made of pureed fruit, crushed ice and a light syrup. Chilled young coconuts are delicious; drink the juice, then scrape out and eat the tender young flesh. Soft drinks are found everywhere. Try Vitamilk, a health drink made from soya bean milk. For a refreshing cooler, order a bottle of soda, a glass of ice and a sliced lime. Squeeze the lime into the glass, add the soda and instantly, thirst is slaked.

Sip the very strong Thai coffee flavored with chicory. The odd orange Thai tea is sticky sweet but delicious. On a hot day, Chinese prefer to drink a hot, very thin tea, believing that ice is bad for the stomach. Try all three over ice anyway.

Beers include Kloster, Carlsberg, Amarit, Singha and Singha Gold. Carlsberg and Heineken are now brewed in Thailand. Of the many Thai cane whiskeys, mekhong is the most popular. It is drunk on the rocks, with soda and lime or with a bit of honey added to it.

Attractions

Sightseeing Tours

After touring the famous attractions like the Grand Palace, Wat Phra Kaeo, Wat Po, and Wat Arun, visit these lesser-known sites:

See Buddhist monks on their morning alms round by visiting Wat Benjamabophit at about 6.30am. Here, in contrast to the normal practice, Buddhists take food to monks waiting silently outside the gates of the temple.

Tour Vimarn Mek, the world's largest golden teak palace, and its superb collection of crystal, gold and silver art objects. Open Wednesday–Sunday, 9.45am–3pm. Admission is 50 baht or free with an entrance ticket to the Grand Palace.

Early in the morning, wander through Bangkok's largest wet market, Phak Klong Talad, near the foot of the Memorial Bridge. Then visit the flower market on nearby Chakkapet Road.

Enjoy a traditional Thai massage in the sala (pavilion) near the eastern wall of the Wat Po compound.

Board an express boat from the Oriental Hotel or Tha Chang near the Grand Palace and ride 45 minutes upriver to Nonthaburi with its bustling market. Have a drink or a meal at the floating restaurant next to the beautiful old provincial office. Alternatively, take the boat downstream to the last stop near the Krung Thep Bridge.

Take a free guided tour of the National Museum, Tuesday–Thursday at 9.30am.

Enjoy the educational snake show (where cobras are milked) at the Snake Farm (Pasteur Institute) on Rama 4 Road at 11am and 2pm.

On Saturdays and Sundays, explore the Weekend Market at Chatuchak Park. Start early to avoid the midday heat.

Walk down Sampeng Lane in the heart of Chinatown. Explore all the side alleys.

Stroll through a former century of gracious living at the Jim Thompson House. Or visit the complex of old houses at Suan Pakkad Palace.

Visit the Ancient City with its miniature replicas of the kingdom's chief architectural masterpieces.

Rent a private boat at the Oriental Hotel and cruise through Khlong Bangkok Noi, stopping at the Royal Barge Museum. Take the long route home, through the smaller canals to Khlong Bangkok Yai and back to the Oriental.

Attend a Thai boxing match at Ratchadamnern or Lumpini Stadium.

Have your fortune told by an astrologer at the Montien Hotel.

Watch a free likay performance at Lak Muang.

Make a wish and an offering at the Erawan Shrine at Ratchaprasong.

Central Plains

Take the train to the Bridge on the River Kwai. The State Railways of Thailand offers a day trip each Saturday. If you have several days, stay on one of the rafthouses farther up the river.

Ride the Oriental Queen up the Chao Phraya River to Ayutthaya, visiting Bang Pa-in along the way.

Enjoy the water sports in Jomtien or the nightlife in Pattaya.

Take a bus to Petchburi to explore King Mongkut's palace and observatory on top of the hill.

Drive to Ratchaburi to look at the beautiful ceramics crafted and sold there.

Visit King Narai's old palace at Lop Buri.

The Northeast

Drive to the Northeast to see Khmer temples at Phimai, Phanom Wan, Phanom Rung and Muang Tham.

Take a day trip to Khao Yai National Park. The State Railways of Thailand conducts a one-day trip on Saturdays.

Travel the road from Ubon along the Mekong River to Nong Khai. View the Friendship Bridge at Nong Khai, linking Thailand and Laos.

The North

Take the train to Phitsanuloke to see the Phra Buddha Jinnarat image in Wat Mahathat. Continue to Sukhothai to see Thailand's first capital city. Then to Si Satchanalai for some quiet beauty. Complete the journey by dropping south to the walled city of Kampaeng-phet before returning to Phitsanuloke.

Visit the hilltop temple of Doi Suthep at sunset for a panoramic view of Chiang Mai Valley.

Explore the crafts studios along the road to Borsang.

Drive the tree-lined road to Lamphun to visit Wat Phra That Haripunchai and Wat Chamathewi.

Take a trek to visit hilltribes outside of Chiang Mai or Chiang Rai.

Attend the demonstration of elephant's skills in moving teak logs at the Young Elephant's Training School at Lampang or the Chiang Dao Elephant Camp.

Ride a longboat 3½ hours down the Kok River from Tha Ton to Chiang Rai.

Visit Mae Sai on the Burmese border and then drive to the Golden Triangle where the borders of Laos, Thailand and Burma meet in the middle of the Mekong River.

The South

Visit the islands of Phang Nga Bay.

Ride the train from Bangkok to Penang in Malaysia.

Roam the farm areas and coastal roads of Phuket in a rented jeep.

Rent a motorcycle and visit all the beaches of Ko Samui.

Cruise around Phuket on a Chinese junk.

Find a beach anywhere and vegetate.

Trekking

It's called trekking, but a two- to seven-day hike in the northern Thai hills shouldn't conjure up daunting visions of the Nepali version. Thailand's highest mountain, Doi Inthanon, is less than 2,000 meters. While you should be fit, you need not be excessively so. Retirees trek and so do children as young as ten.

Seeing tribal people living and working in their natural settings is the primary reason most people take treks. For those who have been struck in Bangkok, total immersion in clean air and green things may feel like a physical and mental necessity. Trekkers also tend to have interests in birdwatching, botany, agriculture, opium, herbal medicine or New Age ideas. For wildlife enthusiasts, there's a chance to spot small game, such as antelope, wild pigs, bats and, yes, large snakes.

Most of the walking is on level ground and well-worn paths. The going becomes tough only during the height of the hot season, from March to May. Even then, the nights are cool enough to require a blanket. The best season is from November to March. Second best may be in June and July, before the full onslaught of the rainy season.

No special equipment is required. You carry a change of clothing, toilet articles, a flashlight and mosquito repellent. The guide takes care of the rest, including food, water bottles and transportation. You pay for the optional toke of opium. Water purification tablets should be brought from home, but an adequate substitute, iodine, can be bought in Thailand (one drop to a liter). You can sleep on the hardwood floor of a villager's thatched house while pigs root in the open space below. It's spartan, but no hardship for anyone accustomed to camping.

Culture

Modern pop culture seems to have gained ascendancy over traditional Thai arts, despite government support for Thai arts and performers. Foreign culture is promoted by the respective country cultural organizations, but little is done to attract foreign performers in the manner of, say, Hong Kong's Art Center and the annual Hong Kong Arts Festival.

The many museums in Bangkok and in major towns around the country are devoted to preserving the past and contain some superb specimens. Exhibitions of modern art are arranged by private gallery owners, foreign cultural centers, or by corporate patrons, usually banks.

Museums

The National Museum at 4 Phra Athit Road, tel: 226 1600, next to Sanam Luang in the heart of the old royal city, is a repository of archaeological finds, Buddha images, old royal regalia, ceramics and art objects (usually Buddhist) from neighboring countries. The walls of the Buddhaisawan Chapel in the museum grounds are covered in some of the finest Buddhist murals in Thailand. The museum is open from 9am–4pm, Wednesday to Sunday. Last ticket sold at 3.30pm.

The National Museum offers free guided tours of Buddhist and other art and conducts them in a number of languages. The schedule is:

English: Thai art and culture (Tuesday, Thursday); Buddhism (Wednesday).
French: Thai art (Wednesday).
German: Thai art and culture (Tuesday, Thursday).
Japanese: Thai culture and pottery (first two Tuesdays of the month); Buddhaisawan Chapel (third Tuesday of the month); Thai art (fourth and fifth Tuesday of the month).
Mandarin and Spanish: On request (groups only). Tel: 224 1402.

Tours last about 2 hours and start at 9.30am. For information call 224 1333. Whatever tour you take, be sure to visit the Buddhaisawan Chapel and the Cremation Chariot Hall (Hall 17) afterwards.

Almost every urban center in Thailand has a branch of the National Museum.

Art Galleries

The National Gallery, to the north of the National Museum in Bangkok across the approach to the Phra Pinklao Bridge at 4 Chao Fa Road, tel: 281 2224, displays works by Thai artists and offers frequent film shows. Open daily from 9am–noon, 1–4pm except on Monday and Friday.

Exhibitions of paintings, sculpture, ceramics, photographs and weaving are varied and numerous. Check the Bangkok Post for details.

Silpakorn University, opposite the Grand Palace on Na Phralan Road, is the country's premier fine arts college. It frequently stages exhibitions of students' work. Other promoters of Thai art and photography are the British Council, Goethe Institute and Alliance Francaise, all of which sponsor exhibitions.

Art galleries seem more interested in selling mass market and "tourist" works than in promoting experimental art; but one, Visual Dhamma, takes an active role in ensuring that talented artists exhibit their works. As its name implies, it is interested primarily in a new school of Thai art which attempts to re-interpret Buddhist themes. It is located on Soi Asoke in a lane opposite the Singha Beer House.

Concerts

The Fine Arts Department periodically offers concerts of Thai music and dance/drama at the National Theatre. On Saturday afternoons at 2pm, programs of Thai classical dance are presented at the auditorium of the Public Relations Building on Ratchadamnern Klang Avenue opposite the Royal Hotel. Each Friday, Bangkok Bank offers traditional Thai music on the top floor of its Pan Fah branch (Ratchadamnern Avenue at the intersection with Prasumane Road) at 5pm.

Concerts of European music and dance are now regular events. The Bangkok Symphony Orchestra gives frequent concerts, as do groups from western countries.

Theaters

The National Theater presents Thai works and, occasionally, big name foreign ensembles like the New York Philharmonic. For more experimental works, Thai or foreign, look to the Thailand Cultural Center. The Center, which is a gift of the government of Japan, is located on Ratchadapisek Road north of Bangkok. Its three stages present everything from pianists to puppets. See the newspapers for announcements of forthcoming performances.

It is also possible to find Chinese opera performed as part of funeral entertainment or during the Vegetarian Festival each September in Chinatown. These performances are normally not announced, but are an unexpected surprise one stumbles across when wandering back alleys. It is hard to miss; the clash of cymbals and drums and the screech of violins identify it.

So, too, has likay bitten the dust. Likay, the village version of the great lakhon and khon dance/dramas of the palace, was once staple fare at temple fairs. Alas, most of the fairs have faded away in the city and are found only in rural areas. Even there, likay performances are often given second billing to popular movies shown in the open air on big screens. About the only place one can see truncated likay performances is at Lak Muang, where successful supplicants pay a troupe to perform for the gods of the heavens and the angels of the city.

Movies

Bangkok movie theaters present Thai, Chinese and subtitled Western films. The Western films are either megahits or are filled with violence – gore being substituted for dialogue. Thai films are either based on a set theme (good versus evil, with pathos, rowdy humor, ugly villains and plenty of fisticuffs) that appeal only to upcountry audiences (and indeed are made primarily with them in mind), or are silly comedies on the theme of young love. Only rarely does a film of social significance appear.

Libraries

For reading or reference, stop in at one of these libraries. All carry books in English on Thailand.

A.U.A., 179 Ratchadamri Road. Tel: 252 8953. Open from 8.30am–6pm on Monday–Friday; and from 8am–1pm on Saturday. The library is sponsored by the US Information Agency. In Chiang Mai, the library is on Ratchadamneon Road.

British Council, 428 Siam Square, Soi 2. Tel: 252 6136. Open from 10am–7pm on Tuesday–Friday; and from 10am–5pm on Saturday.

Neilson Hayes, 195 Suriwong Road. Tel: 233 1731. Open from 9.30am–4pm on Monday–Saturday; and from 9.30am–12.30pm on Sunday.

Siam Society, 131 Soi 21, Sukhumvit Road. Tel: 258 3491. Open from 9am–5pm on Tuesday–Saturday.

Bookstores

Bangkok has many good bookstores with a wide selection of books for information and for entertainment. If you want to read about something you have encountered in Bangkok or just want a good, light read for the beach, try one of these bookshops. Alternatively, your hotel bookstore may have something you want.

Asia Books, 221 Sukhumvit Road (between Soi 17 and 19) and 2nd floor, Peninsula Plaza, Landmark Hotel. Art books, coffee table books, travel books, bestsellers in English.

D.K. Books, bookstores at Siam Square and Sukhumvot Road (near Soi 12). The most complete bookstores in Bangkok with books in English on nearly every subject under the sun.

Central Department stores, all branches, have good book departments.

Nightlife

For years, Thailand has enjoyed a lusty reputation as a center for sex of every persuasion and interest. While the reputation was not altogether undeserved, times and clienteles have changed. The American GIs of the 1960s and the German and Arab sex tourists of the 1970s have been replaced by upmarket tourists, usually traveling as couples. Also common are Japanese men on packaged sex tours, sex included. Western pedophiles are a continuing problem.

While there has been no diminution in the number of massage parlors and bars, there has been an increase in other activities to meet the needs of the new breed of travelers, most of them in the 20–50 age range. Jazz clubs, videotheques, discos and open-air restaurants are the most popular form of entertainment in towns.

A sign of the drastic changes is that the queen of nighttime activities in Bangkok is shopping. Night markets have sprung up along Sukhumvit and Silom roads. Even that wrinkled old harlot of a street, Patpong, has not been immune to the breezes of change. Vendors' tables choke the street, drawing more patrons than the bars with a wealth of counterfeit Rolex watches, Benetton shirts and cassette tapes.

The change has rubbed off on the bars as well. Many of Patpong's bars have metamorphosed into discos, which begin to throb, so to speak, with life after 11pm.

Upcountry, the scene is essentially the same. Chiang Mai's Chang Klang night market attracts more tourists than the bars along Chaiyaphum Road. In Phuket, "barbeers" line the streets of Patong beaches' Soi Bangla and similar areas of Karon and Kata; but the hard sex of Bangkok's yesteryear has never established a foothold there.

Bars

There are three key areas in Bangkok where the types of entertainment for which the city has become famous can be found.

Patpong Road describes three streets: Patpong itself and Patpong 2, which is a welter of bars and bright lights, and Patpong 3, which is almost exclusively gay. Soi Cowboy is a somewhat downmarket version of Patpong. Here, the entertainment is more basic.

Midway between the two in geographic and entertainment terms, is the Nana Entertainment Plaza off Soi 4, Sukhumvit Road.

Massages

Massages fall into two categories: regular and irregular. Establishments billing themselves as "Traditional Thai Massage" and "Ancient Thai Massage" offer therapeutic services according to age-old traditions. In other words, a legitimate massage. The best place for this, however, is at Wat Po.

The second type of massage is sexual. You pick a woman, or sometimes a girl, from behind a one-way mirror and then spend the next hour getting a bath and whatever you arrange.

Discos

Patpong also offers discos, many of which continue to throb long after the bars have closed down. Here, there are no solicitations nor expectations.

Rachadapisek Road has developed into a new magnet for Bangkok's young sybarites. The discos appeal more to Thais than to foreigners, but there is room for both. The biggest and most frequented is Capital City.

Music Clubs

This is not the kind of jazz you will find in New York, London or Tokyo but it is very listenable and some of it is very innovative. Jazz clubs proliferate along Soi Sarasin, Lang Suan, and elsewhere. They differ from their murky, hostess-filled counterparts in being open – usually glass-fronted and with sidewalk tables – with the emphasis on good live music and good conversation.

These clubs appeal as much to professional Thais as they do to Westerners. Among the most popular with mixed nationality crowds is Brown Sugar (Soi Sarasin) and Round Midnight (Soi Lang Suan). Musicians at Saxophone at the Victory Monument (3/8 Phya Thai Road) play jazz standards. Open until 3am

If you like Dixieland jazz and a lively atmosphere, Bobby's Arms at 8.30

Sunday evenings is where you should head. The band comprises local residents who play for the fun of it. Bobby's offers good British cuisine and lots of beer in a convivial setting. Located on the first floor of the carpark behind Foodland on Patpong 2 Road.

Most of the more sophisticated nightclubs are found in first-class hotels. Classy and classic, the Oriental Hotel's famed Bamboo Bar nightclub is for dressier occasions. The scene is chic, normally with jazz singers from the United States playing long-term engagements. You can also find imported acts at the Dusit Thani Hotel's Tiara Lounge. Most hotels have lounge bars with good musical acts.

For other nighttime activities, check the daily newspapers for announcements of concerts, art shows, lectures and other offerings around the city.

Festivals and Fairs

Temple fairs upcountry are great fun to attend. They are usually held in the evenings during the cool season to raise money for repairs to temple buildings. There are carnival rides, freak shows, halls of horror, rumwong dances, food vendors and deafening noise – the one element without which a fair would not be a fair. If you see one in progress, stop, park and enjoy yourself.

The dates for these festivals and fairs change from year to year. Check the exact dates by calling the TAT in Bangkok.

January

New Year's Day is a day of relaxation after the festivities of the night before. It is a public holiday.

Phra Buddha Chinarat Fair is held in late January or early February. Enshrined in Phitsanulok's Wat Phra Si

Ratana Mahatat, Phra Buddha Chinarat is one of Thailand's most sacred and delicately-cast Buddha images of the Sukhothai style. The fair includes a display of giant birds made from straw, folk performances and various entertainment.

Don Chedi Memorial Fair in Suphanburi (late January) commemorates the decisive battle won by King Naresuan at Don Chedi. The fair features historical exhibitions, entertainment and local handicraft stalls.

Bo Sang Umbrella Fair, in Bo Sang near Chiang Mai, is held in the main street and celebrates the traditional skill of making gaily-painted umbrellas and other handicrafts.

February

Flower Festival is held in Chiang Mai during early February. This annual event features flower displays, floral floats, beauty contests and coincides with the period when the province's temperate and tropical flowers are in full bloom.

Dragon and Lion Parade is held annually between January and February in the central Thailand town of Nakhon Sawan, by people of Chinese ancestry. The Dragon and Lion procession is a traditional homage-paying rite to the golden dragon deity in gratitude for his benevolence to human beings. The lively parade comprises marching bands, golden dragon and lion dances, and a procession of deities.

Chinese New Year is not celebrated with the boisterousness of other Asian countries. The temples are a bit busier with wishes made for good fortune in the coming year, but otherwise there is nothing to mark the period. Shops close and behind the steel grills, private family celebrations go on for three or four days.

Magha Puja, a public holiday in Bangkok and a Buddhist holiday on the full moon night of February, marks the spontaneous gathering of 1,200 disciples to hear the Lord Buddha preach. In the evening, Thais gather at temples to hear a sermon by the chief monk of the wat. Then, when the moon is rising, they place their hands in a praying position before their faces and clasping candles, incense and flowers, follow the chanting monks around the bot of the wat three times before placing their candles and incense in trays at the front of the bot. It is a most solemn and moving ceremony.

March

Kite flying is not a festival but it would be difficult to convince kite enthusiasts otherwise. They gather on Sanam Luang, in Bangkok, in the afternoons as the brisk winds haul their large kites aloft, filling the sky with bright colors.

Barred Ground Dove Festival. Dove lovers from all over Asia come to Yala for this event. The highlight is a dovecooing contest involving over 1,400 competitors.

April

Chakri Day on 6th April celebrates the founding in 1782 of the dynasty that presently rules Thailand. It is celebrated in the palace but there are no public ceremonies. An official holiday, most Thais celebrate it as a day off from work.

The **Phra Chedi Klang Nam Fair** in April is one of the larger temple fairs. It is celebrated at the wat on the river's edge at Prapadaeng, 15 km (9 mi) south of Bangkok, on the Thonburi side of the river.

Songkran is a public holiday that, in the past, was the traditional Thai New Year – until royal decree shifted the date to January 1. It most closely resembles the Indian festival of Holi which occurs at the same time. Songkran is a time of wild revelry, a chance for the normally placid Thais to let off steam. The central event is the sprinkling of water on one's friends to bless them, but this usually turns into a boisterous throwing of buckets of water on passersby.

The celebration of Songkran in Bangkok is a little more subdued than in the north, and while it may be safe for a visitor to ride in an open-windowed bus down the street, he is advised to be prepared when walking in the street, riding a tuk-tuk or visiting the night life areas in Patpong, Nana Entertainment Plaza and Soi Cowboy.

To see Songkran at its most riotous, travel down the western bank of the Chao Phraya River to the town of Phrapadaeng. There, no one is safe, but in the April heat, who cares?

Songkran in the north of Thailand, particularly in Chiang Mai, is fervently celebrated over several days and attracts many visitors from Bangkok.

Turtle Releasing Fair. At Nai Yang beach in Phuket, young turtles are released for their journey to the sea. The festival begins early in the morning with alms offered to monks and is accompanied by music, dancing, sports and food.

May

Labor Day (May 1) is a public holiday. **Coronation Day** (May 5) is a private royal affair and a public holiday.

The **Rocket Festival** in Yasothon in the northeast of Thailand is held in early May. Well worth the trip to witness the launching of the locally-made missiles of all shapes and sizes, some as tall as a person.

The **Plowing Ceremony** is a colorful ancient tradition celebrated only in Bangkok. Held at Sanam Luang, it is presided over by King Bhumibol and marks the official start of the rice planting season. Crimson-clad attendants lead bullocks, drawing an old-fashioned plow, around a specially-prepared ground. The lord of ceremonies, usually the minister of agriculture, follows behind, scooping rice seed out of baskets held by pretty maidens and sowing it in the furrows left by the plow, all to the accompaniment of blaring conch shells and drums.

Visakha Puja is a public holiday on the full moon night of May that commemorates the birth, enlightenment and death of Buddha. The three things are all said to have happened on the same day. Visakha Puja is celebrated like Magha Puja, with a triple circumambulation around the temple as the moon is rising.

Fruit Fairs. Their are annual fairs in Chiang Mai, Rayong, Chantaburi, Trat and several other locations throughout Thailand to celebrate the harvest of lychees, durian, mangosteen, rambutan, jack fruit and zalacca. Besides stalls selling the produce of the surrounding orchards, there are beauty pageants, cultural shows and local entertainment.

June

Sunthorn Phu Day. This annual celebration in late June commemorates the birth of the Thai poet Sunthorn Phu. The festivities include dramatic performances and puppet shows depicting his literary works, poetry recitals and folk entertainment.

July

Asalaha Puja on the full-moon night of July is the third most-important Buddhist holiday and marks the occasion when Buddha preached to his first five disciples. It is celebrated on the full-moon night in similar manner to Magha Puja and Visakha Puja. It also marks the beginning of the three-month Lenten season. Tradition says that Buddha was approached by farmers who asked that he bar monks from going on their morning alms rounds for a period of three months, because they were trampling on the rice plants they had just planted. They offered instead to take food to the monks at the temple during this period, a practice which has been followed ever since.

Khao Phansa is celebrated immediately following Asalaha Bucha and marks the commencement of the annual three-month Rains Retreat.

Candle Festival takes place during Khao Phansa in the northeast town of Ubon. It celebrates the commencement of Phansa with a lovely spectacle where some beautifully-embellished beeswax candles are ceremoniously paraded before being presented to temples.

August

Queen Sirikit marks her birthday (August 12) by religious ceremonies and private celebrations. It is a public holiday.

September

On the first day of the eighth lunar month, Chinese celebrate the **Moon Festival**. They place small shrines laden with fruit, incense and candles in front of their houses to honor the moon goddess. It is a lovely festival, the highlight of which are the utterly scrumptious cakes shaped like a full moon. They are specially prepared, often by chefs flown in from Hong Kong, and found no other time of the year.

Phichit Boat Races. A regatta featuring long-boat races. Similar events are held in Phitsanulok and all over Thailand at this time of year. The low-slung, wooden boats are raced with great gusto.

October

The **Chinese Vegetarian Festival**, held in mid-October, is a subdued affair in Bangkok by comparison with the firewalkers of Phuket version. Enormous amounts of vegetarian food, Chinese operatic performances and elaborate offerings are made at various Chinese temples around the city. A superb photographic opportunity. Only those wearing all-white attire are allowed in the area of the altar, so dress appropriately.

Ok Pansa marks the end of the three-month Lenten season, and the beginning of the Kathin season when Buddhists visit wat to present monks with new robes and other necessities. Groups will rent boats or buses and travel long distances to spend a day making gifts to monks of a particular wat. If you are invited, by all means go, because it is a day of feasting and fun as well.

Chulalongkorn Day (October 23) honors King Rama V (1868–1910), who led Thailand into the 20th century. On this public holiday, students lay wreaths before his statue in the plaza at the old National Assembly building during an afternoon ceremony.

Lanna Boat Races. If you miss the Pichit Boat Races, this regatta is just as exciting.

The **Buffalo Races** held in late October in Chon Buri rival the excitement of the Kentucky Derby.

November

Golden Mount Fair held the first week of November in Bangkok is one of the noisiest of temple fairs. Carnival rides, food concessions, variety performances and product stalls are the main attractions. Buddhist temple fairs all over Thailand are held throughout the cool season to raise money for reparations.

The **Little Royal Barge Festival** at Wat Nang Chee in Phasi Charoen early in November is a smaller version of the grand Royal Barge procession, but it is marked by more gaiety in small towns.

Loy Krathong, one of the most beautiful festivals anywhere in Asia, is on the full-moon night of November. It is said to have been started in Sukhothai in the 13th century. A young queen, Nang Nopamat, is said to have floated a small boat laden with candles and incense downstream past the pavilion where her husband was talking with his friends. Whatever the origins, it has grown to be one of the country's most enchanting festivals, a night when Thais everywhere launch small candle-laden boats into the rivers and canals to ask blessings. The tiny dots of light and shimmering water are mesmerizing.

Long-boat races have become increasingly popular in the past few years and it is not unusual to open a newspaper during November and find that yet another race is being staged somewhere in Thailand. They are colorful and exciting and provide superb photo opportunities.

The **Elephant Round-Up** in Surin is held in mid-November and attracts visitors from all over Thailand.

The **Phra Pathom Chedi Fair** at the world's biggest chedi, in Nakhon Pathom, is another temple fair, and is regarded as one of the most exciting. Khon Kaen Silk Fair. Silk weaving demonstrations and a chance to buy lustrous silk in a major center of production.

River Kwai Bridge Week. A sound-and-light presentation recaptures this dark period of recent history when Asians and Europeans died in the thousands at the hands of the Japanese to build the infamous Death Railway during World War II.

Sunflower Fair. The photogenic sight of Mexican sunflowers in bloom is best seen in the hills of Doi Mae U-Khor, as Mae Hong Song holds a three-day festival of ox-carts decorated with the beautiful flowers. When the flowers fade, the seeds are used to make insecticides.

December

Trooping of the Colors (December 3). The royal regiments dressed in brilliantly-colored costumes pass in review before the king. Held on the plaza before the old National Assembly building, the Trooping of the Colors is the most impressive of martial ceremonies.

King Bhumibol celebrates his birthday (December 5) with a ceremony at Wat Phra Kaeo only for invited officials and guests and with a private party. It is a public holiday.

King's Cup Regatta. Long-distance yacht racing from Nai Harn Bay in Phuket with entries from around the world.

Constitution Day (December 10) is a public holiday in Thailand.

Christmas may soon be a Thai holiday if the merchants have any say in the matter. If endless repetitions of Christmas carols in department stores bludgeon everyone into acceptance, it may not be long before it becomes an official holiday.

But **New Year's Eve** on December 31 is indeed a public holiday.

Shopping

Whatever part of your budget you have allocated for shopping, double it or regret it. Keep a tight grip on your wallet or you will find yourself being seduced by the low prices and walking off with more than you can possibly carry home. If you cannot resist, see the "Export" section for an inexpensive way to get souvenirs home.

Over the years, there have been two major changes in the shopping picture. First, there have been subtle design alterations to make the items more appealing to foreign buyers. The purists may carp, but the changes and the wider range of products have found welcome reception by shoppers. At the same time, new products have been introduced which have found popular reception among visitors.

The other change is that while regional products were once found only in the towns that produced them, there has been a homogenization of distribution, so that it is now possible, for example, to buy Chiang Mai umbrellas in Phuket. The widest range of items are found in Chiang Mai and Bangkok, but if you never have a chance to leave Bangkok, do not despair; nearly everything you might want to buy in upcountry towns can be found in Bangkok.

Shopping Hours

Large department stores in Bangkok are open from 10am–9pm. Most ordinary shops are open from 9am–6pm.

Export

Shipping

Most shops will handle documentation and shipping for your purchases. Alternatively, the General Post Office on New Road, near the Oriental Hotel, offers boxes and a packing service for goods sent by sea mail. Packages can be shipped from most post offices. Post offices in most towns sell cardboard boxes specially created for shipping packages.

Thai International in Bangkok also offers a special service called thaipac that will air freight your purchases (regardless of the mode of transportation or the airline you are using) to the airline's destination closest to your home for 25 percent of the normal rate. Just take your goods to the airline's office at 485 Silom Road. They must fit into a special box and weigh no more than 33 kg (73 lbs) per box. Thai will also handle the documentation and customs clearance for a small charge.

Export Permits

The Fine Arts Department prohibits the export of all Thai Buddha images, images of other deities and fragments (hands or heads) of images dating from before the 18th century.

All antiques and art objects, regardless of type or age, must be registered with the Fine Arts Department. The shop will usually do this for you. If you decide to handle it yourself, take the piece to the Fine Arts Department on Na Prathat Road, across from Sanam Luang, together with two postcard-sized photos of it. The export fee ranges between 50 and 200 baht depending on the antiquity of the piece.

Fake antiques do not require export permits, but airport customs officials are not art experts and may mistake it for a genuine piece. If it looks authentic, clear it at the Fine Arts Department to avoid problems later.

Complaints

The customer is (nearly) always wrong might be the most candid way of putting it. Except for very large shops, expect that once you have paid for an item and left the store, or that unless the defect is very glaring and there is no possible way you could have caused it, the moment you walk out the door, that's it. You can report the shop to the Tourist Police, but they are not usually interested. Shop carefully. Caveat emptor.

Shopping Areas

If you cannot find it in Bangkok, you will not be able to find it anywhere else in the country. Aside from the traffic problems, Bangkok is the most comfortable place to shop. Shopping venues range from huge air-conditioned malls to tiny hole-in-the-wall shops, to crafts sections of large department stores.

Huge air-conditioned malls like **Amarin Plaza**, **Oriental Place (New Rd)**, **World Trade Center**, **Siam Center**, **Mahboonkrong**, **Gaysorn Plaza** and **Central Plaza** are filled with shops selling a variety of items. Some malls specialize in particular types of items; **River City**, for example, has dozens of shops selling superb antiques.

Queen Sirikit's Chitralada stores sell the rare crafts she and her organization, support, have worked so diligently to preserve by teaching the arts to village women. There are branches in the airport, Grand Palace, Oriental Plaza, Hilton Hotel and Pattaya. The Thai government's handicraft center, **Narayana Phand**, at 127 Ratchadamri Road, displays the full array of Thai handicrafts.

Most major department stores have special handicrafts departments carrying a wide selection of items. **New Road** between Silom and Suriwong, **Silom Road** in the vicinity of the Narai Hotel, upper sections of **Suriwongse** Road, and **Sukhumvit Road** are lined with crafts shops. Traditional shopping areas like **Sampeng Lane**, the **Thieves Market**, the Buddha amulet markets at **Tha Prajan** and **Wat Ratchanadda** have lost some of their allure over the years as new businesses have moved in, but one can still find the occasional bargain. By far the most challenging (and often most rewarding) is the huge weekend market at Chatuchak, which has special sections for porcelain, brassware and a number of old oddities that don't fit into any particular category.

Street Shopping

You will not find high-ticket items nor will the quality equal that found in finer stores, but for gift items, there are few better places to look. In Bangkok look in **Pratunam market** – now being redeveloped – and along both sides of **Ratchaprarop Road**. Try both sides of **Sukhumvit Road**, between Soi 3 and 11, where you will find Burmese puppets, handicrafts and perhaps most important, suitcases and bags to put it all in.

What to Buy

Real/Fake Antiques

Wood, bronze, terracotta and stone statues from all regions of Thailand and Burma can be found in Bangkok and Chiang Mai. There are religious figures and characters from classical literature, carved wooden angels, mythical animals, temple bargeboards and eave brackets. Note that most fake antiques passed off as real are crafted in Burmese backyard factories.

Although the Thai government has banned the export of Buddha images, there are numerous deities and disciples which can be sent abroad. Bronze deer, angels and characters from the *Ramakien* cast in bronze do not fall under the export ban. It is also possible to buy and export Burmese Buddha images.

Chiang Mai produces beautiful wooden replicas modeled on antique sculptures. Sold as reproductions, with no attempt to pass them off as genuine antiques, they make lovely home decor items. Animals, Buddha's disciples and dozens of items range in size from small to life-sized.

Chiang Mai also produces a wide

range of beautifully-crafted wooden furniture. Cabinets, tables, dining room sets, elephant howdah, bedroom sets or simple items like wooden trays are crafted from teak or other woods and carved with intricate designs.

Baskets

Thailand's abundant bamboo, wicker and grasses are transformed into lamps, storage boxes, tables, colorful mats, handbags, letter holders, tissue boxes and slippers. Wicker and bamboo are turned into storage lockers with brass fittings and furniture to fill the entire house. Shops can provide the cushions as well.

Yan lipao, a thin, sturdy grass, is woven into delicate patterns to create purses and bags for formal occasions. Although expensive, the bags are durable, retaining their beauty for years.

Ceramics

Best known among the distinctive Thai ceramics is the jade green celadon, which is distinguished by its finely crazed surface. Statues, lamps, ashtrays and other items are also produced in dark green, brown and cobalt blue hues.

Modeled on its Chinese cousin, blue-and-white porcelain includes pots, lamp bases, household items and figurines. Quality varies according to the skill of the artist, and of the firing and glazing.

Bencharong (five colors) describes a style of porcelain derived from 16th-century Chinese art. Normally reserved for bowls, containers and fine chinaware, its classic pattern features a small religious figure surrounded by intricate floral designs. The whole is rendered in five colors – usually green, blue, yellow, rose and black.

Earthenware includes a wide assortment of pots, planters and dinner sets in a rainbow of colors and designs. Also popular are the big, brown glazed Shanghai jars bearing yellow dragons, which the Thais use to hold bath water and which visitors use as planters. Antique stoneware includes the double-fish design plates and bowls originally produced at Sawankhaloke, the kilns established near Sukhothai in the 13th century.

Some of the best ceramics come from Ratchaburi, southwest of Bangkok. The wide variety makes a special trip there worthwhile.

Decorative Arts

Lacquerware comes in two styles: the gleaming gold-and-black variety normally seen on temple shutters, and the matte red type with black and/or green details, which originated in northern Thailand and Burma. The lacquerware repertoire includes ornate containers and trays, wooden figurines, woven bamboo baskets and Burmese-inspired Buddhist manuscripts. The pieces may also be bejeweled with tiny glass mosaics and gilded ornaments.

Black lacquer is also the base into which shaped bits of mother-of-pearl are pressed. Scenes from religious or classical literature are rendered on presentation trays, containers and plaques. Beware of craftsmen who take shortcuts by using black paint rather than the traditional seven layers of lacquer. On these items, the surface cracks, often while the item is still on the shelf.

Fabrics and Clothes

Thai silk is perhaps Thailand's best-known craft. Brought to world attention by American entrepreneur Jim Thompson, Thai silk has enjoyed enduring popularity. Sold in a wide variety of colors, its hallmark is the tiny nubs which, like embossings, rise from its surface. Unlike sheer Indian silks and shiny Chinese-patterned silks, Thai silk is a thick cloth that lends itself to clothes, curtains and upholstery.

It is more popular as blouses, ties and scarves. It is also used to cover purses, tissue boxes and picture frames. Lengths printed with elephant, bamboo, floral and dozens of other motifs are turned into decorative pillowcases to accent rooms.

Mudmee is a northeastern silk whose colors are somber and muted. A form of tie-dyed cloth, it is sold in lengths or as finished clothes.

Cotton is popular for shirts and dresses, since it breathes in Thailand's hot, humid air. Although available in lengths, it is generally sold already cut into frocks and shirts. The South is a batik center and offers ready-made clothes and batik paintings.

Burmese in origin and style, kalaga wall hangings depicting gods, kings and mythical animals have gained increasing popularity in the past few years. The figures are stuffed with kapok to make them stand out from the surface in bas relief.

Gems and Jewelry

Thailand is one of the world's exporters of cut rubies and sapphires. The rough stones are mostly imported from Cambodia and Burma, as local mines are not able to meet the demand. Customers should patronise only those shops that display trade's official emblem: a gold ring mounted with a ruby, which guarantees the dealer's integrity.

Thailand is now regarded as the world's leading cutter of gemstones, the "Bangkok cut" rapidly becoming one of the most popular. Thai artisans set the stones in gold and silver to create jewelry and bejeweled containers. Artisans also craft jewelry that satisfy an international clientele. Light-green Burmese jade (jadeite) is carved into jewelry and art objects. The island of Phuket produces international-standard natural, cultured, Mob (teardrop) and artificial pearls (made from pearl dust glued to form a globule). They are sold as individual items or are set into gold jewelry.

Costume jewelry is a major Thai business with numerous items available. A related craft which has grown rapidly in the past decade is that of gilding Thai orchids for use as brooches.

Hilltribe Crafts

Northern hilltribes produce brightly-colored needlepoint work in a wide variety of geometric and floral patterns. These are sold either as produced, or else incorporated into shirts, coats, bags, pillowcases and other items.

Hilltribe silver work is valued less for its silver content (which is low) than for the intricate work and imagination that goes into making it. The genre includes necklaces, headdresses, bracelets and rings the women wear on ceremonial occasions. Enhancing their value are the old British Indian rupee coins that decorate the women's elaborate headdresses.

Other hilltribe items include knives, baskets, pipes and gourd flutes that look and sound like bagpipes.

Metal Art Objects

Although Thai craftsmen have produced some of Asia's most beautiful Buddha images, modern bronze sculpture tends to be of less exalted subjects and execution. Minor deities, characters from classical literature, deer and abstract figures are cast up to 2 m (7 ft) tall and are normally clad with a brass skin to make them gleam. Bronze is also cast into handsome cutlery and coated in shiny brass.

Silver and gold are pounded into jewelry items, boxes and other decorative pieces; many are set with gems. To create nielloware boxes and receptacles, a design is incised in silver or gold. The background is cut away and filled with an amalgam of dark metals, leaving the figures to stand in high relief against the black background.

Tin, mined near Phuket, is the prime ingredient in pewterware, of which Thailand is a major producer. Items range from clocks and steins to egg cups and figurines.

Paintings

Modern Thai artists paint everything from realistic to abstract art, the latter often a weak imitation of Western art. Two areas at which they excel are depictions of everyday village life and of new interpretations of classical Buddhist themes. Artists can also work from live sittings or photographs to create superb charcoal or oil portraits. A family photograph from home can be transformed into a painting. The price depends on size: a 40cm x 60cm (16" x 24") charcoal portrait costs around 1,000 baht. There are several streetside studios in Bangkok, Phuket and Pattaya that specialize in this art.

Theater Art Objects

Papier-mâché *khon* masks, like those used in palace dance/drama, are painted and accented with lacquer decorations and gilded to create superb works of art.

Shadow puppets cut from the hides of water buffaloes and displayed against backlit screens in open air theaters tell the Ramakien story. Check to be sure the figure is actually cut from hide and not from a sheet of black plastic.

Bright-colored shadow puppets cut from buffalo hide make excellent wall decorations.

Inspired by the Ramakien, craftsmen have fashioned miniature models of chariots and warriors in gilded wood or glass sculpture. These two materials are also employed to create reproductions of the famous Royal Barges.

Umbrellas

Chiang Mai produces lovely umbrellas and fans made from silk or sa paper, a fine parchment often confused for rice paper but made from pounded tree bark.

Sports and Leisure

Thailand has developed its outdoor sports facilities to a considerable degree and air-conditioned the ones played indoors. Nearly every major hotel has a swimming pool and a fitness center; some have squash courts and jogging paths.

Participant Sports

Fitness Centers

In Bangkok, the Asia-wide Clark Hatch has a branch in the Thaniya Plaza, off Silom Road. Tel: 231 2250. Fitness International is located in the Dusit Thani Hotel. Part-time membership is available. All the top hotels in Bangkok have well-equipped fitness centers.

Fitness Parks

One corner of Bangkok's Lumpini Park boasts a fitness park. In Chiang Mai, there is a free fitness park on Nimmanhaemind Road that is open from 5am–10pm. In Phuket, the fitness park sits atop Rang Hill in the middle of Phuket town while in Pattaya, it is located on the slopes of Pattaya Hill.

Golf

Thais are great golfing buffs, going so far as to employ some of world golfing's stellar architects to design international-class courses. The best courses are in Bangkok, Phuket and

Pattaya, with other courses in Chiang Mai, Khao Yai and Hua Hin. Greens fees range from 500–1,000 baht per round on weekends and it is generally not difficult to reserve a time.

Among Bangkok's courses is the Navathanee Golf Course (22 M.1, Sukhapibal 2 Road. Tel: 376 1020) designed by Robert Trent Jones Jr. It is open from 6am–6pm. The Army Golf Course at 459 Ram Intra Road, tel: 521 1530, is open from 5am–9.30pm. The Railway Training Center Golf Course, on Paholyothin Road, tel: 271 0130, west of the Hyatt Central Plaza Hotel opens at 6am, closes at 8pm. The Krungthep Sports Golf Course, 522 Huamark Road, tel: 379 3732, opens at 5am, closes at 5pm.

In Pattaya, Siam Country Club Golf Course 10km (6 mi) east of town in rolling hills.

Jogging

Two jogging sites for those wise enough not to challenge Bangkok's traffic for right-of-way are in Lumpini Park and Chatuchak Park. The Siam-Intercontinental Hotel, Rama Gardens and the Hilton hotels have jogging paths.

Snooker

In recent years, Thailand has produced some excellent snooker players who are currently nipping at the heels of world champions in international competitions. As a result, parlors have sprung up everywhere in Thailand as budding aspirants focus their eyes on complex shots and potential riches. In Bangkok, there are numerous snooker parlors around the city. The "Rooks" chain is the most popular and dozens of its snooker parlors can be found.

Spectator Sports

Despite the hot climate, Thai men and women are avid sports enthusiasts, actively playing both their own sports and those adopted from the West according to international rules.

The king of foreign sports is soccer and is played by both sexes. Following a close second is badminton, with basketball, rugby, track and field, swimming, marksmanship, boxing, tennis and golf trailing only a short way behind. Check the English-language newspapers for schedules.

The principal sports venues in Bangkok are the National Stadium, on Rama I Road just west of Mahboonkrong Shopping Center; the Hua Mark Stadium, east of the city next to Ramkamhaeng University; and the Thai-Japanese Sports Center, at Din Daeng near the northern entrance to the expressway.

Thailand has also created a number of unique sports and these are well worth watching as much for the grace and agility displayed as for the element of fun that pervades every competition.

Kite Fighting

The heat of March and April is relieved somewhat by breezes that the Thais use to send kites aloft. Sanam Luang in Bangkok and open spaces everywhere across the country are filled with young and old boys clinging to kite strings.

The Thais have also turned it into a competitive sport, forming teams sponsored by major companies. Two teams vie for trophies. One flies a giant star-shaped male *chula* kite nearly 2 m (6.5 ft) high. The opposing teams (there may be more than one) fly the diminutive diamond-shaped female *pakpao* kites.

One team tries to snare the other's kite and drag it across a dividing line. Surprisingly, the odds are even and a tiny female *pakpao* stands a good chance of pulling down a big lumbering *chula* male. The teamwork and fast action make for exciting viewing. Competitions at Bangkok's Sanam Luang start at 2pm.

Takraw

With close relatives in the Philippines, Malaysia and Indonesia, takraw employs all the limbs except the hands to propel a woven rattan ball (or a more modern plastic ball) over a net or into a hoop. In the net version, two three-player teams face each other across a head-high net, like that used in badminton. As the match heats up, it is not unusual for a player to turn a complete somersault to spike a ball across the net.

In the second type, six players form a wide circle around a basket-like net suspended high in the air. Using heads, feet, knees and elbows to keep the ball airborne, they score points by putting it into the net. A team has a set time period in which to score as many points as it can, after which it is the opposing team's turn.

Tournaments are held at the Thai-Japanese Sports Center (Tel: 465 5325 for dates and times) four times a year; admission is free. Competitions are also held in the northwest corner of Bangkok's Sanam Luang during the March–April kite contests. Free admission. During the non-monsoon months, wander into a park or a temple courtyard anywhere in the country late in the afternoon.

Thai Boxing

One of the most exciting and popular Thai sports is Thai boxing. In Bangkok, Ratchadamnern Stadium on Ratchadamnern Nok Avenue, offers bouts on Monday, Wednesday, and Thursday at 6pm and on Sunday at 4.30 and 8.30pm. The Sunday matinee at 4.30pm is recommended, as it has the cheapest seats. Ticket prices run between 500 and 1,000 baht for ringside seats (depending on the quality of the card), running downwards to 100 baht.

Lumpini Boxing Stadium, on Rama 4 Road, stages bouts on Tuesday and Friday at 6.30pm and on Saturday at 1 and 6.30pm. Ticket prices are the same as at Ratchadamnern. As above, weekend afternoon matinees are the cheapest.

There are also televised bouts on Saturday and Sunday, and at 10.30pm on some weeknights. For many visitors this will be sufficient introduction to the sport. The Rose Garden and Phuket's Thai Village offer short demonstrations of Thai boxing, but these are played more for laughs than for authenticity.

Language

Origins and Intonation

For centuries, the Thai language, rather than tripping from foreigners' tongues, has been tripping them up. Its roots go back to the place Thais originated from, in the hills of southern Asia but overlaid by Indian influences. From the original settlers come the five tones which seem designed to frustrate visitors, one sound with five different tones to mean five different things.

When you mispronounce, you don't simply say a word incorrectly, you say another word entirely. It is not unusual to see a semi-fluent foreigner standing before a Thai running through the scale of tones until suddenly a light of recognition dawns on his companion's face. There are misinformed visitors who will tell you that tones are not important. These people do not communicate with Thais, they communicate at them in a one-side exchange that frustrates both parties.

Thai Names

From the languages of India have come polysyllabic names and words, the lexicon of literature. Thai names are among the longest in the world. Every Thai first and surname has a meaning. Thus by learning the meaning of the name of everyone you meet, you would acquire a formal, but quite extensive vocabulary.

There is no universal transliteration system from Thai into English, which is why names and street names can be spelled three different ways. For example, the surname Chumsai is written Chumsai, Jumsai and Xoomsai depending on the family. This confuses even the Thais. If you ask a Thai how you spell something, he may well reply "how do you want to spell it?" Likewise, Bangkok's thoroughfare of

Ratchadamnern is also spelled Rajdamnern. Ko Samui can be spelled Koh Samui. The spellings will differ from map to map, and book to book.

Phonology

The way Thai consonants are written in English often confuses foreigners. An "h" following a letter like "p", and "t" gives the letter a soft sound; without the "h" the sound is more explosive. Thus, "ph" is not pronounced "f" but as a soft "p". Without the "h", the "p" has the sound of a very hard "b", The word Thanon (street) is pronounced "tanon" in the same way as "Thailand" is not meant to sound like "Thighland." Similarly, final letters are often not pronounced as they look. A "j" on the end of a word is pronounced "t"; "l" is pronounced as an "n". To complicate matters further, many words end with "se" or "r" which are not pronounced.

Vowels are pronounced like this: i as in sip, ii as in seep, e as in bet, a as in pun, aa as in pal, u as in pool, o as in so, ai as in pie, ow as in cow, aw as in paw, iw as in you, oy as in toy.

In Thai, the pronoun "I" and "me" use the same word but it is different for males and females. Men use the word phom when referring to themselves; women say chan or diichan. Men use khrap at the end of a sentence when addressing either a male or a female i.e. pai (l) nai, khrap (h) (where are you going? sir). Women add the word kha to their statements as in pai (l) nai, kha (h).

To ask a question, add a high tone mai to the end of the phrase i.e. rao pai (we go) or rao pai mai (h) (shall we go?). To negate a statement, insert a falling tone mai between the subject and the verb i.e. rao pai (we go), rao mai pai (we don't go). "Very" or "much" are indicated by adding maak to the end of a phrase i.e. ron (hot), ron maak (very hot).

Listed below is a small vocabulary intended to get you on your way. The five tones have been indicated by appending letters after them viz. high (h), low (l), middle (m), rising (like asking a question) (r), and falling (like suddenly understanding something as in "ohh, I see") (f).

Numbers

1/Nung (m)
2/Song (r)
3/Sam (r)
4/Sii (m)
5/Haa (f)
6/Hok (m)
7/Jet (m)
8/Pat (m)
9/Kow (f)
10/Sip (m)
11/Sip Et (m, m)
12/Sip Song (m, r)
13/Sip Sam (m, r) and so on
20/Yii Sip (m, m)
30/Sam Sip (f, m) and so on
100/Nung Roi (m, m)
1,000/Nung Phan (m, m)

Days of the Week

Monday/Wan Jan
Tuesday/Wan Angkan
Wednesday/Wan Phoot
Thursday/Wan Pharuhat
Friday/Wan Sook
Saturday/Wan Sao
Sunday/Wan Athit
Today/Wan nii (h)
Yesterday/Mua wan nii (h)
Tomorrow/Prung nii (h)
When/Mua (f) rai

Greetings and Others

Hello, goodbye
Sawasdee (a man then says khrup, a woman says kha; thus sawasdee khrup)
How are you?/Khun sabai dii, mai (h)
Well, thank you/Sabai dii, Khapkhun
Thank you very much/Khapkhun Maak
May I take a photo?
Thai roop (f) noi, dai (f) mai (h)
Never mind/Mai (f) pen rai
I cannot speak Thai
Phuut Thai mai (f) dai (f)
I can speak a little Thai
Phuut Thai dai (f) nit (h) diew
Where do you live?
Khun yoo thii (f) nai (r)
What is this called in Thai?
An nii (h), kaw riak aray phasa Thai
How much?/Thao (f) rai

Directions and Travel

Go/Pai
Come/Maa
Where/Thii (f) nai (r)
Right/Khwaa (r)
Left/Sai (h)

Turn/Leo
Straight ahead/Trong pai
Please slow down/Cha cha noi
Stop here/Yood thii (f) nii (f)
Fast/Raew
Hotel/Rong raam
Street/Thanon
Lane/Soi
Bridge/Saphan
Police Station/Sathanii Dtam Ruat

Other Handy Phrases

Yes/Chai (f)
No/Mai (f) chai (f)
Do you have...?/Mii...mai (h)
Expensive/Phaeng
Do you have something cheaper?
Mii arai thii thook (l) kwa, mai (h)
Can you lower the price a bit?
Kaw lot noi dai (f) mai (h)
Do you have another color?
Mii sii uhn mai (h)
Too big/Yai kern pai
Too small/Lek kern pai
Do you have bigger?
Mii arai thii yai kwa mai (h)
Do you have smaller?
Mii arai thii lek kwa mai (h)
Hot (heat hot)/Ron (h)
Hot (spicy)/Phet
Cold/Yen
Sweet/Waan (r)
Sour/Prio (f)
Delicious/Aroy
I do not feel well/Mai (f) sabai

Further Reading

Cooper, Robert and Nanthapa. **Culture Shock: Thailand.** Singapore: Times Books, 1990. Very useful look at Thai customs and how to avoid faux pas. Written and illustrated in highly amusing manner.

Siam Society, Culture and Environment in Thailand. Siam Society: Bangkok, 1989.

Sternstein, Larry. **Thailand: The Environment of Modernisation.** Sydney: McGraw-Hill, 1976. Excellent geography text.

Stockmann, Hardy. **Thai Boxing.** Bangkok: D.K. Books, 1979. Excellent, well illustrated book on the basics of Thai boxing.

Warren, William. **The Legendary**

American. Boston: Houghton Mifflin. The intriguing story of American Thai silk king Jim Thompson.

History

Chakrabongse, Prince Chula. *Lords of Life*. London: Alvin Redman, 1960. A history of the Chakri kings.

Kasetsiri, Charnvit. *The Rise of Ayudhya*. London: East Asian Historical Monographs, 1976. A narration of the history of early Ayutthaya.

Coedes, George. *The Indianized States of Southeast Asia*. Trans. Susan Brown Cousing. Ed. Walter F. Vella. Honolulu: East-West Center Press, 1968. Well written scholarly work.

Hall, D.G.E. *A History of South-east Asia*. 3rd ed. London: Macmillan, 1968. The classic text.

Hutchinson, E.W. *1688: Revolution in Siam*. Hong Kong University Press. The events leading to the expulsion of the foreigners from Ayutthaya.

Moffat, Abbot Low. *Mongkut, the King of Siam*. Ithaca, New York: Cornell University Press, 1961. Superb history of one of Asia's most interesting 19th-century men.

Van Beek, Steve. *Bangkok Only Yesterday*. Hong Kong: Hong Kong Publishing, 1982. Anecdotal history of Bangkok illustrated with old photos.

Vella, Walter F. *Chaiyo!* Honolulu: University of Hawaii Press, 1979. The life and times of King Vajiravudh (1910–1925).

Wright, Joseph. *The Balancing Act: A History of Modern Thailand*. Oakland: Pacific Rim Press, 1991. Accessable and detailed history of modern Thailand.

Wyatt, David K. *Thailand: A Short History*. Bangkok/London: Thai Wattana Panich/Yale University Press, 1984. Concise and well-written.

People

Aylwen, Axel. *The Falcon of Siam*. London: Methuen, 1988. A fictionalized story of Constant Phaulkon, Greek adventurer in Siam in the late 1600s.

Campbell, Reginald. *Teak-Wallah*. Singapore: Oxford, 1986. Adventurers of a teak logger in northern Thailand in the 1920s.

Collis, Maurice. *Siamese White*. London: Faber, 1965. Fictionalized account of a contemporary of Constant Phaulkon in 1600s Siam.

Ekachai, Sanisuda. *Behind the Smile, Voices of Thailand*. Thailand. Thai Development Support Committee, 1990. Well-written and informative portraits of Thai life by local journalist.

Skinner, G. William. *Chinese Society in Thailand*. Ithaca, New York: Cornell University Press, 1957. Gives an insight into an important segment of Bangkok's history.

Religion

Bunnag, Jane. *Buddhist Monk, Buddhist Layman*. Cambridge: Cambridge University Press, 1973. Gives an insight into the monastic experience.

Nivat, Prince Dhani. *A History of Buddhism in Siam*. Bangkok: Siam Society, 1965. One of Thailand's most respected scholars.

Art and Culture

Diskul, M.C. Subhadradis. *Art in Thailand: A Brief History*. Bangkok: Silpakorn University, 1970. Dean of the Fine Arts University.

Klausner, William J. *Reflections on Thai Culture*. The Siam Society: Bangkok, 1987. Observations of a longtime resident anthropologist.

Rajadhon, Phya Anuman. *Essays on Thai Folklore*. Bangkok: D.K. Books. A description of Thai ceremonies, festivals and rites of passage.

Van Beek, Steve & Tettoni L.I. *The Arts of Thailand*. London, Thames & Hudson, 1991. Lavishly illustrated, includes the minor arts.

Warren, William. *The House on the Klong*. Tokyo: Weatherhill. The story of the Jim Thompson House.

Wray, Joe, Elizabeth Wray, Clare Rosenfeld and Dorothy Bailey. *Ten Lives of the Buddha; Siamese Temple Paintings and Jataka Tales*. Tokyo: Weatherhill, 1974. Well illustrated, valuable for understanding Thai painting and the Tosachat (Jataka Tales).

Thai Writers

Botan. *Letters from Thailand*. Bangkok: DK, 1977. A novel in letters, reflects a Chinese immigrants views of his new compatriots.

Khoamchai, Sila. *The Path of the Tiger*. Bangkok: Thai Modern Classics, 1994. Originally published in 1989. Jungle lore and philosophy by a former guerilla. This is among the first in a series of English translations of "the best 20 novels of Thailand".

Korpjitti, Chart. *The Judgment*. Bangkok: Thai Modern Classics, 1995. Originally published in 1981. Chart is the most popular living writer of quality fiction.

Pramoj, Kukrit. *Four Reigns*. Bangkok: DK, 1981. The nostalgia is sometimes cloying, but this is the work of a consummate Renaissance man.

Saipradit, Kularp (Seeb0orapha). *Behind the Painting (and Other Stories)*. Singapore: Oxford, 1990. Kularp was a crusading journalist and fiction writer who died in Chinese exile.

Surangkhanang, K. *The Prostitute*. London: Oxford, 1994. Originally published in 1937. Attitudes towards prostitutes haven't changed much.

Phongpaichit, Pasuk and Sungsidh, Priryarangsan. *Corruption and Democracy in Thailand*. Chulalongkorn University Political Economy Centre, Bangkok, 1994. Not for the faint-hearted. Especially good on the rise of provincial "godfathers".

Other Insight Guides

From the *Insight Guide* collection comes a range of travel guides, specially designed to help make your visit an unforgettable one.

Insight Guide: Thailand brings you to this exotic destination of ancient temples, majestic rivers, and friendly smiles.

Index

A

aesthetics 73
agriculture 55, 56
Aisawan Tippaya Asna 190
Amarin Vinichai Hall 143
Amporn Gardens 160
amulet market 158
amulets 68
Anand Panyacharun 50
Ananda (Rama VIII, king) 45, 56
Ancient City (outdoor museum) 185
Angkor Wat (model) 145
antiques 119
architecture 78
Arporn Phimok Prasad 144
Assumption Cathedral 167
Ayutthaya 30–32, 159, 186

B

baht 42
Ban Chiang (archeology) 27–28
bananas 96
Bang Pa-in 190
Bang Saen 210
Bang Thao 215
Bangkok Noi (khlong) 159
Bangkok Noi Railway Station 159
Bangkok Yai (khlong) 159
Bangrak market 88
Banharn Silpa-archa 50
beer 96
Benjamabophit (Marble Wat) 162
Bhumibol, King 47, 55
Big Buddha Beach 219
Bloody May 50
Borom Phiman Hall 142
Boroma Trailokanath (Trailok) 31
Boromakot (king) 34
bot (ordination hall) 78
Boworadet, Prince 45
Brahma (Hindu god) 173
Brahman priests 156
Brahmanism 29, 69, 146, 155
Bridge on the River Kwai 181
Buddhaisawan Chapel 147
Buddhism 28, 30, 38, 65–68
Burma 32, 179, 186
business 59, 84–86

C

canal (khlong) 159
cannon 31
Cathedral of St Joseph 187

cave
   Tham Lod 218
celadon 121
ceramics 121
ceramics (Sawankhalok) 203
Chakri (Rama I) 143
Chakri dynasty 36–42, 56, 142
Chakri Maha Prasad 37, 142
Chakri Throne Room 142
Chandrakasem Palace 187
chao lay (sea gypsy) 216
Chao Phraya River 27, 34, 141, 159
Chao Sam Phraya Museum 188
Charoen Krung (New Road) 39
Chart Thai 50
Chatuchak weekend market 88
chedi 78
Chiang Mai 204–207
Chiang Mai (history) 30–31
Chiang Mai University 206
Chiang Mai Zoo 206
Chiang Rai (history) 30
China 28, 49
Chinatown 164–167
Chinese 38, 45, 60, 85, 164
Chinese cuisine 95, 96
Chitralada Palace 56, 141, 162
Chon Buri 210
Christianity 67
Chuan Leekpai 50
Chulalongkorn (king) 39, 160, 161, 162, 159
Chulalongkorn University 41, 172
Chumbhot, Princess 174
coconuts 96
coffee 96
communists 47
constitution 57
construction 49
Coral Island (Ko Larn) 212
corruption 85
corvee labor 31
coup d'etat 42, 47, 49, 50
Cremation Ground, Royal (Phramane) 146
Crocodile Farm 184
crocodiles 165, 184
cuisine 92–97
curry 93

D

dance-drama 73–74
democracy 42, 45, 47, 50
Democracy Monument 48, 50, 157
development 86
Doi Pui (hilltribe village) 207
Doi Suthep 204, 207
Dusit 160
Dusit Maha Prasad 143
Dusit Palace 41
Dusit Zoo 161
Dutch 32

E – F

economy 84
education 86
Ekatat (king) 34

elephant kraal 190
elephants 187
elephants (white) 161
Emerald Buddha 34, 36, 57, 144, 206
England 38
Erawan (Elephant) Falls 183
Erawan Shrine 69, 173
ethnic Thai (origins) 27
exports 84
fascism, Europe 45
fish sauce (nam pla) 212
flag 41, 55
Flower Festival (Chiang Mai) 207
flower markets 88
food 92–97
France 33, 41, 46
fruits 94

G

gardens
   Siam Society 175
   Suan Pakkad Palace 174
   Thompson's house 171
garuda 79
gems 117
General Post Office 167
Giant Swing (Sao Ching Chaa) 155
gold 118
Golden Buddha 167
Golden Mount 158
Golden Mount (Ayutthaya) 189
government 58
Grand Palace 37, 141
Greek Favorite (Phaulkon) 33
green lanterns (khom khiew) 164

H – I

ham yon (sacred testicles) 175
hilltribes
Meo 207
Hinduism 28, 67
Hua Hin (history) 42
Hua Lamphong railway station 166
Inao (epic poem) 38
India (influence) 28
Indian influence 28–29, 76
instrument (music) 75
Intradit (king) 201
Isara Nuphap (lane, Chinatown) 166
Islam 67
ivory 122

J

jade 118
jai yen (cool heart) 55
jao pho 86
Japan 46
JEATH Museum 182
jewelry 117
Jim Thompson's house 171
Jomtien 211

K

Kamphaeng-hak (Broken Wall) Gate 201
Kamthieng House 175
Kanchanaburi 28, 181
Karon Beach 216
Kata Beach 216
kanom (sweets) 96
Khao Chamao National Park 213
Khao Khieo Open Zoo 210
Khao Phang Falls 183
Khao Yai National Park 192
khlong (canal) 159
Khlong Lawd 155
Khlong Saen Sap 159
Khlong San Sap 174
Khmer 31, 201
Khmer Rouge 49
khon (dance-drama) 73
Khunaraam 219
king 55
  Ananda (Rama VIII) 45, 47, 56
  Bhumibol (Rama IX) 47
  Boromakot 34
  Chakri (Rama I) 34, 36, 143, 144
  Chulalongkorn (Rama V) 39–41,
    160–162, 159
  Ekatat 34
  Intradit 201
  Li Thai 30
  Lo Thai 30, 201
  Mengrai 30, 206
  Mongkut (Rama IV) 38, 68
  Narai 33, 190
  Naresuen 32, 187
  Ngam Muang 30
  Phya U-Thong 30
  Prajadhipok (Rama VII) 42, 45
  Rama I 159
  Rama II 38
  Rama III 38
  Ramathibodi II 32
  Ramesuen 31
  Ramkamhaeng 29, 201, 203
  Taksin 34
  Trailok 31
  Vajiravudh (Rama VI) 41
kinnari 79
Ko Khao Ping Gun 218
Ko Larn 212
Ko Pannyi 218
Ko Pha Ngan 219
Ko Phi Phi 217
Ko Samet 213
Ko Samui 218
Ko Talu 218
kong tek ceremony 166
Korat Plateau 192
Krung Thep (Bangkok) 37

L

lacquer 80
lacquerware 120
Lak Muang 74, 141
lakhon (dance-drama) 73, 141
Lamai 219
Lanna Kingdom 204

Laos 34, 48
leather 117
Leonowens, Anna 39
Li Thai (king) 30
likay (dance-drama) 74
lingam 79
literature 75–77
Lo Thai (king) 30, 201
Loha Prasad 158
long-tailed boat (*rua hang yao*) 159
Lop Buri 190
Lop Buri Palace 190
Lumpini Park 174

M

mae chee 66
Mae Klong Railway 180
Mae Toranee 146
Mahidol, Prince 56
Mai Khao 215
mai sanuk 55
Man with the Golden Gun 218
Marble Wat (Benjamabophit) 162
markets 88
massage, traditional 149
Maugham, Somerset 171
medicine, traditional 149
mekhong (whiskey) 96
Memorial Bridge 45
Mengrai (king) 30, 206
merit-making 65
Merton, Thomas 157
middle class 84, 153
military 42, 45, 50, 57
monarchy 55–57
Mongkut (king) 38, 68
monk (Buddhist) 66
mother-of-pearl 80
mummified monk 219
museum
  JEATH 182
  National 146
  Royal Barge 159
music, traditional 74–75

N – O

naga 79
Nai Harn 216
Nai Yang 215
Nakhon Kasem (Thieves Market) 166
Nakhon Nayok 192
Nakhon Pathom 179
Nakorn Kasem (Thieves Market) 88
nam plaa (fish sauce) 92, 212
Nang Rong Falls 192
Narai (king) 33, 190
Narayana Phand 173
Naresuen (king) 32, 187
National Assembly (Parliament) 160
National Museum 146
national park
  Khao Chamao 213
  Khao Yai 192
nationalism 41, 45, 49
New Road 164
Ngam Muang (king) 30

nielloware 121
night markets 88
nirvana 65
Nong Khing Village 192, 212
noodles 95
October Revolution (1973) 48
Old Bangkok 155
Oriental Hotel 39, 110, 167

P

paintings 80
Pak Klong Talat market 88
Paknam 184
Parliament (National Assembly) 160
Pasteur Institute (Snake Farm) 172
Patong 215
Patpong 175
Pattaya 211
pearls 118
people (origin) 29
People's Party 42, 45
Petchburi 39
Phang Nga Bay 217
Phaulkon, Constantine 33
phi (spirits) 68, 141
Phitsanulok 203
Phnom Phot 186
Phra Pathom Chedi 179
Phramane Ground (Royal Cremation
    Ground) 146
Phuket Town 215
Pibul 45
Pibul Songram 42
Ping River 204
plagues 160
Plowing Ceremony 69, 146
politicians 58
pollution 152
Pongsawadan (Annals of Ayutthaya) 31
Portugal 32, 38
Prajadhipok (king) 42, 45
Prapas Charusathien 47
Prasat Phra Thep Bidom (or Royal
    Pantheon) 145
Pratunam market 88
Prem Tinsulanond, Gen. 58
Pridi 42, 45
prostitution 108
puppets 73, 74

R

Ra Wai 216
railway stn (Hua Lamphong) 166
Ramakien 38, 73, 75–76, 145
Ramathibodi II (king) 32
Ramayana 76
Ramesuen (king) 31
Ramkamhaeng (king) 29, 203
Ratchaprasong 174
Ratchaprasong intersection 173
Rattanakosin 36, 141–149
Rayong 212
rebellion (1933) 45
Reclining Buddha 149
Red Cross Snake Farm 172
reincarnation 65

Relax Bay 216
religion 65–69
rice 39, 69, 92, 146
River City Shopping Center 167
River Kwai 181
Rose Garden 179
Royal Bangkok Sports Club 172
Royal Barge Museum 159
Royal Barges 150
royal family (Ayutthaya) 32
royalty 55
rua hang yao (long-tailed boat) 159

S

sacred testicles (ham yon) 175
Sai Yok Falls 183
sakdi na 31
Salika Falls 192
Sampeng 36
Sampeng (Chinatown) 60, 164
Sampeng Lane 165
Samut Prakarn 185
Samut Sakhon 180
Samut Songkhram 180
Sanam Chand Palace 179
Sanam Luang 50, 143, 146
sanuk 55
Sarit Thanarat, Gen. 47
Sattahip 212
Sawankhalok ceramics 203
sculpture 79
sea gypsy (chao lay) 216
second/deputy king 146
sema 78
Seni Pramoj 46
Seni Thai 46
shopping center
    Bangkok Bazaar 174
    Mahboonkrong 171
    Pratunam 174
    Ratchadamri Arcade 173
    River City 167
    Siam Square 171
    World Trade Ctr 171, 173
Si Racha 210
Si Satchanalai 203
Siam Society 175
silk 116
Silom Road 175
Similan Islands National Marine
    Reserve 215
Sirikit, Queen 56
Sivamokha Biman Hall 147
Snake Farm (Pasteur Institute) 172
snakes 172
Songkran (festival) 205, 207
spirit house 69
spirits (phi) 68, 141
Sri Lanka (Ceylon) 30
student revolution 49
Suan Pakkad Palace 174
Suchinda Krapayoon, Gen. 50, 57
Sukhothai 29–30, 201
Sunthorn Phu (poet) 77, 213
Suphan Buri 30
surnames (origins) 41
swallow nests 217

sweets (khanom) 96
Swinging Ceremony 155

T

tailoring 117
takraw 179
Taksin (king) 34
Tamnak Daeng 147
tapioca 210
tattoos 69
temple (wat) 66
temple life 66
Temple of the Emerald Buddha (Wat
    Phra Kaeo) 144
textiles 117
Thailand, name 45
Tham Lod cave 218
Thammasart University 49, 159
Thanin Kraivichien 49
Thanom Kittikachorn 47
The King and I 38
theater, see dance-drama
Thewes market 88
Thieves Market (Nakhon Kasem) 88,
    166
Thompson, Jim 116, 171
Thonburi 34, 36
Three Pagodas Pass 181, 183
Throne Room, Chakri 142
tin mining 217
traditional medicine 149
traffic 50, 152–153
Traibhumikatha 30
Trailok (king) 31
Tribal Research Center 206
Tripitaka 145

U – V

U-Thong 30, 186
umbrellas 122
United States 46–47
Vajiravudh (Rama VI, king) 41
Vietnam War 47–48
viharn (assembly halls) 78
Viharn Phra Mongkol Bophit 188
Vimarn Mek 161

W – Y

Wang Luang 187
Wang Takrai Park 192
wat
    Arun 38, 150, 159
    Benjamabophit 40, 162
    Bowon Niwet 157
    Chakrawat 165
    Kanikaphon 166
    Monkhonkamalawat 166
    Pathum Wanaram 171
    Pathuma Kongkha 166
    Phra Kaeo 144–145
    Po 148–149
    Rakang 150
    Ratchabophit 155
    Ratchanadda 158
    Saket 160

Suthat 38, 156
Suwannaram 150
Traimit (Golden Buddha) 167
wat (Ayutthaya)
    Buddhaisawan 186
    Chai Wattanaram 187
    Konthi Thong 189
    Na Phra Meru 189
    Phanan Choeng 186
    Phra Mahathat 188
    Phra Ram 188
    Phra Sri Sanphet 187
    Phu Khao Thong (Golden Mt) 189
    Ratchaburana 188
    Suwan Dararam 189
    Yai Chai Mongkol 189
wat (Chiang Mai)
    Chedi Luang 205
    Chedovan 206
    Chiang Mun 205
    Doi Suthep 207
    Jet Yod 206
    Phra Singh 205
    Suan Dok 206
wat (other)
    Chom Long 180
    Phra Chedi Klang Nam 185
wat (South)
    Buddhabat Sam Yot 210
    Dhamma Nimitr 210
    Sumret 219
wat (Sukhothai)
    Chana Songkhram 202
    Chang Lom 203
    Chetupon 203
    Mahathat 201
    Phra Phai Luang 202
    Si Chum 202
    Sra Sri 201
    Sri Sawai 201
    Trakuan 202
wat (temple) 66
wat life 66, 78
white elephants 161–162
women 31, 59–60, 108
World Trade Center 171, 173
World War I 41
World War II 45–46, 181
Yaowarat Road 166

258

The Insight Approach

The book you are holding is part of the world's largest range of guidebooks. Its purpose is to help you have the most valuable travel experience possible, and we try to achieve this by providing not only information about countries, regions and cities but also genuine insight into their history, culture, institutions and people.

Since the first Insight Guide – to Bali – was published in 1970, the series has been dedicated to the proposition that, with insight into a country's people and culture, visitors can both enhance their own experience and be accepted more easily by their hosts. Now, in a world where ethnic hostilities and nationalist conflicts are all too common, such attempts to increase understanding between peoples are more important than ever.

Insight Guides:
Essentials for understanding

Because a nation's past holds the key to its present, each Insight Guide kicks off with lively history chapters. These are followed by magazine-style essays on culture and daily life. This essential background information gives readers the necessary context for using the main Places section, with its comprehensive run-down on things worth seeing and doing. Finally, a listings section contains all the information you'll need on travel, hotels, restaurants and opening times.

As far as possible, we rely on local writers and specialists to ensure that the information is authoritative. The pictures, for which Insight Guides have become so celebrated, are just as important. Our photojournalistic approach aims not only to illustrate a destination but also to communicate visually and directly to readers life as it is lived by the locals.

Compact Guides
The "great little guides"

As invaluable as such background information is, it isn't always fun to carry an Insight Guide through a crowded souk or up a church tower. Could we, readers asked, distil the key reference material into a slim volume for on-the-spot use?

Our response was to design Compact Guides as an entirely new series, with original text carefully cross-referenced to detailed maps and more than 200 photographs. In essence, they're miniature encyclopedias, concise and comprehensive, displaying reliable and up-to-date information in an accessible way.

Pocket Guides:
A local host in book form

However wide-ranging the information in a book, human beings still value the personal touch. Our editors are often asked the same questions. Where do *you* go to eat? What do *you* think is the best beach? What would you recommend if I have only three days? We invited our local correspondents to act as "substitute hosts" by revealing their preferred walks and trips, listing the restaurants they go to and structuring a visit into a series of timed itineraries.

The result is our Pocket Guides, complete with full-size fold-out maps. These 100-plus titles help readers plan a trip precisely, particularly if their time is short.

Exploring with Insight:
A valuable travel experience

In conjunction with co-publishers all over the world, we print in up to 10 languages, from German to Chinese, from Danish to Russian. But our aim remains simple: to enhance your travel experience by combining our expertise in guidebook publishing with the on-the-spot knowledge of our correspondents.